first comes

LOVE

first comes
LOVE

DOUGLAS E. BRINLEY, PH.D.
MARK D. OGLETREE, PH.D.

Covenant Communications, Inc.

Covenant.

Published by Covenant Communications, Inc.
American Fork, Utah

Printed in Canada
First Printing: February 2002

09 08 07 06 05 04 03 02   10 9 8 7 6 5 4 3 2 1

ISBN 1-57734-988-1

Library of Congress Cataloging-in-Publication Data

Ogletree, Mark, 1962-
    First comes love/Mark Ogletree, Douglas E. Brinley.
        p. cm.
Includes biographical references.
    ISBN 1-57734-988-1 (alk. paper)
    1. Mate selection. 2. Mate selection--Religious aspects--Church of Jesus Christ of Latter-day Saints.
    3. Marriage--Religious aspects--Church of Jesus Christ of Latter-day Saints. I. Brinley, Douglas E.
    II. Title.
        HQ801.O32 2002
        646.7'7--dc21
                            2002017514

We want to thank all who read the manuscript and made suggestions for its improvement. We also appreciate Angela Colvin and Katie Child at Covenant Communications for the effort it took to bring this to print, and the Covenant Design Department for the wonderful cover. But we are responsible for the final product and hope it will bless the lives of those contemplating the wonderful privilege of marriage and parenthood.

INTRODUCTION

The Doctrinal Framework

"No other success can compensate for failure in the home." [1]

Many years ago an Apostle of the Lord stated that "the most important single thing that any Latter-day Saint ever does in this world is to marry the right person in the right place by the right authority" (Bruce R. McConkie, *Choose an Eternal Companion*, Brigham Young University Speeches of the Year [3 May 1966], 2). This quote has been repeated in Church classes and manuals over the years because it succinctly points out the importance of marriage in the plan of salvation. Elder McConkie's statement is centered in the truth that mortality is the first time any of us can marry and become parents, because marriage and procreation were not open to us in our first estate. It is only now, in mortality, when your spirit body and your physical mortal body are united together, that marriage and procreation can finally take place (see D&C 49:16–17).

Because you are moving toward the ordinance of marriage, it is important that you understand the significance of what you are about to do. The prophets of our day have been clear about the importance of, and the consequences associated with, marriage. President Gordon B. Hinckley taught university graduates: "The most important step you have made or will make in your life is marriage. Its consequences are many, so important and so everlasting. No other decision will have such tremendous consequences for the future" ("Messages of Inspiration from the Prophet," *Church News*, 30 Sept. 1995, 2).

Can you see, therefore, that marriage and family life *are* what an LDS lifestyle is all about?[2] The highest of earthly opportunities and priorities should be centered in your home and family relations. So when a news reporter asked President Hinckley what his biggest concern was as the President of the Church, it was disappointing to hear him answer: "We have wonderful people, but we have too many whose *families are falling apart*. It is a matter of serious concern. I think it is *my most serious concern*" ("Pres. Hinckley notes his 85th birthday, reminisces about life," *Church News*, 24 June 1995, 6; emphasis added). When a prophet declares that the breakdown of the family is his most pressing concern, Latter-day Saints, especially those who are contemplating marriage, must pay attention. The following statement from President Spencer W. Kimball underscores the importance of the marriage decision. He declared, "In selecting a companion for life and for eternity, certainly the most careful planning and thinking and praying and fasting should be done to be sure that of all the decisions, this one must not be wrong" (*Marriage & Divorce*, [pamphlet, 1976], 144).

Our Worldly Environment

We do not wish to be overly negative about the conditions that surround us—we know how to make our families strong today.[3] However, you must be able to see that in these last days the family unit is under severe attack. Satan, the one who rejected the Father's plan in an earlier time and place, knows that he can never be a husband or father—*ever*. No wonder he seeks the dissolution of all marriages. He is using all his powerful weapons in an effort to prevent our enjoyment of what will never be his. And in a day of relative ease and prosperity, he is able to exact a heavy toll on the stability of marriage and family through popularizing polluted ideas and causes contrary to marriage between a husband and wife. We are beginning to understand that the psychological and emotional costs of divorce and broken families are a heavy burden for society to carry. Spouses reneging on their marital commitments are all too common in our land and in the Church, and the temporal and spiritual damage is staggering.

Imitating Marriage

While a temple marriage is designed to unite a couple together forever, in worldly circles it has become fashionable for people to live together before—or instead of—marriage. They wrongly conclude that the best way to prepare for marriage is to cohabit first.[4] The media are often the major purveyors of these themes—themes that at one time were considered offensive to most everyone's sensibilities. Now, talk-show hosts scurry to outdo each other in covering offbeat subjects about intimate conduct that would have caused studio heads to roll in the not-too-distant past. Producers of trash depicting immoral behavior seek ever greater numbers of viewers by portraying the most scandalous stories possible. In books and magazine articles that were formerly addressed only to married couples, writers now unashamedly describe intimate contact between "significant others," "lovers," or "partners." Intimacy, tragically, is no longer the exclusive domain of married persons, according to many publications of the day—surely an offense to God and people of integrity everywhere!

What Goes Wrong?

Most of us attend wedding receptions where we convey our best wishes to the new bride and groom. Usually we know little about how they met, how long they dated before committing to each other, and what dynamics brought them to the point of marriage. Nevertheless, we offer them our gifts and congratulations and assume they will "sail off into the sunset" as honeymooners to live "happily ever after." We assume that they will make their way in the world without any more assistance from us than the nicely wrapped, blown-glass candy dish we offered at the door. But sadly, we are finding that too many couples stumble during and after the honeymoon. Many newly formed family units are finding married life much more demanding and difficult than the carefree life of dating and courtship. We are compelled to ask ourselves if life is becoming more complicated and complex than it formerly was, or if individuals in our day are simply less prepared for the demands of marriage. We believe the answer may be both, and that the solution is to be found in better preparation.

Premarital Preparation

What can be done to prevent the failure of so many marriages and keep the marital union from tumbling down the mountain? Our solution is simple: *Let's put a fence up on the hillside rather than park ambulances down in the valley!* Surely we can do more to prepare individuals *before* marriage for the responsibilities that will come *after* marriage. The norm of our day is to look at damage control rather than prevention—our society tries to repair the damage *after* the devastating effects of divorce have already ravished homes and children. Instead of having to heal wounded and fractured marriages, would it not make more sense to prevent marital casualties in the first place? Fences are, after all, cheaper than those ambulances that never seem to find the right hospital.

As family life educators, we have learned that working with people to resolve problems *after* marriage has taken place is not only frustrating, difficult, time-consuming, and in many cases hopeless, but that there is a better way. We've often commented how much easier it would be if we could help couples realistically anticipate the complexities of marriage—before the ceremony—to ensure marital stability and maximize their chances of success. Sadly, divorce rates are embarrassingly high, even among Latter-day Saints. Surely by now you know that God's plan for us does not include divorce and the broken hearts that usually accompany it. He wants only the best for you, and that is to find your eternal companion the first time around, and then to build a great marriage together. It is our observation that when a couple break their covenants, the work of God is set back, for not only do they hurt themselves, but they negatively affect friends and acquaintances who supported their decision to marry. Divorce also does damage to those outside the Church whose only knowledge of our beliefs is that we put great emphasis on quality marriages and family living. More importantly is the sobering fact that when we break our marriage covenants, we disappoint our Heavenly Father, for it is His plan that we accepted in the premortal life.

Optimistically we declare to you that you *can* have a wonderful marriage if you are better prepared for this new adventure. Even if you or your sweetheart or fiancé came from what might be considered a dysfunctional background or family situation, there is great hope for your success. We see a number of young people who are scared to marry because of the poor marital examples in their lives. But with proper preparation, you can become more confident of your abilities to do well in marriage. Think of it from this perspective: If you have come from a difficult background (abuse, neglect, poor parental modeling, a broken home), membership in the Church brings you a new parent—Jesus Christ. You became one of His sons or daughters at the time of baptism (D&C 25:1). Because He was perfect, you may substitute His example and teachings for whatever in your life did not measure up to what you want to become. No one has to be a marriage casualty. Our Father in Heaven did not institute marriage for it to fail. That is not part of His plan. Marriage was designed to build character in those who enter its holy sanctuary. Union with another soul is designed ultimately to make gods out of those ordinary mortals who live the principles that lead to joy and happiness. You can grow together with your spouse in an unbelievably happy union of love, commitment, and mutual sacrifice if you will follow a few basic principles. As President Kimball reminded us, "While marriage is difficult, and discordant and frustrated marriages are common, yet real, lasting happiness is possible, and marriage can be more *an exultant ecstasy* than the human mind can conceive. This is within the reach of *every couple, every person*" (*Marriage & Divorce* [pamphlet, 1976], 146; emphasis added). That means you!

Our Goal

Our effort here is to help you and your fiancé (or a good friend with whom you are developing a serious relationship) plan, prepare, and realistically anticipate what marriage will require of you. As a single man or woman, it is important that you examine your motives for marrying and look carefully at your own marital readiness, as well as the readiness of the person you are considering as a spouse. We don't want you to "fall in love with love" just because your friends are marrying and you are feeling lonely or desperate. We do not want you to jump into marriage for the wrong reasons, only to face tragedy because you were unprepared. In what we might call at this point a "premarital innocence," you must keep both eyes wide open and your senses operating as you explore your relationship in more depth.[5] It is true, of course, that most of us are on our best behavior in dating situations. We often try to hide any negative traits. We can look pretty good out in the public arena. It is imperative that you don't get "faked" into marriage by someone who has a lot to hide. We want you to consider the strengths and weaknesses of your developing relationship. In other words, we want to help you prepare for the most important thing you will ever do in this life.

Of course, there are divorces that are justifiable and necessary. That is clear. But we agree with President Boyd K. Packer, who said, "One who destroys a marriage takes upon himself a very great responsibility indeed! Marriage is sacred! To willfully destroy a marriage, either your own or that of another couple, is to offend our God. Such a thing will not be lightly considered in the judgments of the Almighty and in the eternal scheme of things will not easily be forgiven" ("Marriage," *Ensign*, May, 1981, 14). By breaking our covenants we forfeit blessings we would have received. In divorcing, we prove to God that we are incapable of living in the highest degree of glory with other married couples, for the celestial kingdom's ultimate blessings are reserved for those who are married. Divorce prevents our reaching that highest of eternal opportunities.

The Lord Needs You to Do Well

The success of your marital odyssey requires that both partners be committed to each other and to the principles of the gospel of Jesus Christ. You will be teachers of these precepts of eternal life to your children by instruction and example. The Lord needs you to model gospel tenets so your children see the fruits of faithful observance of God's commandments. Remember they are His children too. The first principle of effective parenting is to build a strong marriage so your children can observe healthy interactions. Where do you think children learn to be emotionally healthy individuals? Stable parents tend to rear stable children who, as adults, can make their own stable marriages. We realize there are no perfect marriages, but when parents love each other and that love is extended to each child, the youngsters of that couple are more apt to adopt the values and behavioral standards of their parents.

We will pursue a number of themes here to prepare you for the great adventure of life: to meet, date, court, marry in the temple, and become parents of the faithful spirits our Father is sending to the earth in this final dispensation.

—*Mark Ogletree and Doug Brinley*

CHAPTER 1

A Lifetime of Preparation

"Considering the enormous importance of marriage, it is rather astonishing that we don't make better preparation for its success. Usually, young couples date for a few months or for a year or two, enjoying romance and getting acquainted. But once they are married, they soon learn that romance must blend with spiritual beliefs, in-law relationships, money issues, and serious discussions involving ethics, children, and the running of a home. Too many people are inadequately prepared for this lofty responsibility." [1]

One of my most memorable Christmases occurred when I (Mark) was in the second grade. On Christmas morning, much to my surprise, I learned that Santa had brought my brother and me a beautiful Shetland pony. I was absolutely thrilled. I had always wanted a horse for Christmas, but figured that there was no possible way Santa could fit one in his sleigh. Somehow, this Christmas, he had done it. Santa pulled off the miracle.

The next several days were the greatest days ever for a second-grade boy. Our Shetland pony, which we affectionately named Buttermilk, stayed in our backyard. Most of the time we used Buttermilk as a prop while we played cowboys and Indians. We also invited some of the neighborhood kids over for pony rides in our backyard. Buttermilk passed the time eating grain and an occasional apple while I sat on her back, daydreaming of riding her to school or to my practice, or pretending that I was John Wayne. It sure was great to have my own pony to ride!

Although it was exciting to have a real live animal in our back-yard, we all knew that the situation couldn't last much longer. After a week of eating our sod and flowers, it was time to take Buttermilk to her new home—a rented horse pasture where she could have more room and be with other horses. The only challenge would be getting her from our backyard to the pasture. Now, most people would probably have rented a horse trailer, but not my dad. He didn't think it was a wise use of his resources to rent a trailer just to transport a horse a few miles. Besides, we didn't have a trailer hitch anyway. Instead of being hauled in a trailer, Buttermilk would have to be ridden to the pasture. Since my brother's feet couldn't reach the stirrups, my dad's feet touched the ground, and my mom wouldn't even get near the animal because she thought it would bite her, I learned that I would be the "designated driver,"—you know, the guy who would drive the horse because no one else was physically able.

Finally, the day came for the big transfer. So, I climbed up into the saddle while my dad and the rest of the family jumped in our VW Bug. My dad was not big on teaching or giving instructions before any major activity took place. He always believed that anything worthwhile could be learned on the job. Therefore, his approach to teaching me how to ride a horse consisted of yelling at me out of the car window as he drove alongside me, with my brother and sister laughing hysterically inside the car. Meanwhile, I was at Buttermilk's mercy as I hung on for dear life as she trotted down the street. All too soon I learned why they called it "riding" horses instead of "driving" or "steering." Buttermilk simply went wherever she wanted to go, and I was just along for the ride. The next hour proved to be the most humiliating experience of my young life. Buttermilk trotted through neighbors' lawns and went into garages. She took me under trees with low branches or bashed me into fences as she tried to knock me off. I will not bore you with the details of what transpired when the neigh-borhood dogs chased us down the street. Suffice it to say that all I could do was hang on for dear life and occasionally scream. It was as if I were on an amusement park ride gone bad. She actually ran onto a busy street and hit a car. That was the low point.

In the meantime, my dad was still driving right next to me, barking directions from the car, telling me to "pull her to the right" or "pull her to the left." What my dad thought would take thirty minutes ultimately took most of the day. By the time we arrived at the horse pasture I really didn't care if I ever rode a horse again. In fact, I was just happy to be on the ground and in one piece. Eventually I did learn to ride Buttermilk, although she proved to be a pretty stubborn pony.

For the rest of my childhood, teenage years, and young adulthood, I scarcely thought about my experience with Buttermilk. It wasn't until after I had been married for a few years that I began to make comparisons between my first horse ride and preparation for marriage. Consider the following analogies:

1. Just as my father failed to prepare me for learning to ride a horse, many parents do not prepare their children for marriage—the single most important event of their lives. We rehearse for plays, we prepare for football games, we even do a fairly good job of getting our children ready for college. But, for some reason, parents often neglect preparing their children for marriage. My dad just threw me on the horse and said, "have a great ride," and many marriages begin the same way. As the bride and groom drive off into the sunset in a car decorated with Oreos, shaving cream, and tin cans, their parents wave and yell, "Good luck!" For some of us, all we can do is hang on the best we know how and enjoy the wild ride that often results.

2. I enjoyed playing "horse" with Buttermilk. I sat on her in the fenced backyard and pretended I was John Wayne. After the ride to the pasture, however, the pretending stage ended and it was time to face reality—sore body and bruises. Likewise, many couples who are dating or engaged like to play "house," imagining how great it will be to come home to each other every night, eat a gourmet meal together, and then spend a leisurely evening reading poetry to each other while lounging on the bearskin rug next to the fireplace. With Buttermilk, once I arrived at the final destination—the horse pasture—it wasn't really that big of a thrill. In fact, I often wondered what was so great about riding horses.

President Gordon B. Hinckley made the following observation about the danger of unrealistic expectations in a marriage:

> Some years ago I clipped from the *Deseret News* a column by Jenkins Lloyd Jones, who said in part: "There seems to be a superstition among many thousands of our young who hold hands . . . in the drive-ins that marriage is a cottage surrounded by perpetual hollyhocks, to which a perpetually young and handsome husband comes home to a perpetually young and ravishing wife. When the hollyhocks wither and boredom and bills appear, the divorce courts are jammed" (Gordon B. Hinckley, *Teachings of Gordon B. Hinckley* [1997], 324).

The joys of marriage should come *on the journey* to our destination of eternal life. In fact, working together to build a great marriage and family along life's path is the very process that will get us to our final goal. Of all the experiences we prepare for in life, whether it be playing musical instruments, mastering a variety of skills, participating in sports, or preparing for careers, perhaps marriage requires the most stringent and strategic preparation of anything we ever do. However, most people probably spend more time preparing to get their driver's license than they do preparing for their marriage license. Remember what it took? Hours of preparation and practice were required to learn to drive a car. You probably spent time in a driver's education course, reading textbooks and watching films. If you passed that experience successfully you were given a learner's permit. Then you spent hours in actual driving time— practicing left turns, staying on the right side of the road, and going the speed limit. Later you learned to parallel park. Finally, when you felt comfortable, you went down to the Driver License Division, paid the fee, and drove the officer around to obtain your license. However, in marriage preparation there is no "learner's permit"; there is no driving course; there is not even a written test. We must draw on a lifetime of experience, observation, and the counsel of others to make this decision.

Carlfred Broderick wrote about our success in this venture called marriage:

The most popular—and the roughest—contact sport in the country is not professional football; it is marriage. Consider the statistics: Over 90 percent of us try our hand at it, either ignoring the dangers or simply hoping for the best. A third of us, however, sustain so many injuries that we are willing to suffer the humiliation of divorce to get off the field. Yet the promise, the attractiveness, is so great that 80 percent of those divorced put themselves back into [the] marriage [game]—most of them within three years. Clearly, the problem is not how to make matrimony more popular; it's how to make it less hazardous (*Couples* [1979], 13).

A brief examination of current statistics confirms the point. Since 1960, divorces in our country have doubled; the percentage of single-parent homes has tripled; and 30 percent of all American births occur out of wedlock.[2] Recent data show that the divorce rate is actually closer to 60 percent, rather than 50.[3] In fact, 40 to 50 percent of all couples who marry this year will divorce sometime in their lives.[4] Even more alarming is the fact that, even in Utah, 54 percent of all divorces occur within the first five years of marriage, and 18 percent of all divorces occur within the first year (see Brent A. Barlow, *Just for Newlyweds* [1992], 7). It is understandable why Broderick argued that the key to doing well in marriage is not to make matrimony *more popular*, but *less hazardous*.

Why are marriages failing at such an alarming rate? We believe there are several explanations. First, as indicated earlier, we are engaged in a battle with Satan, whose full-time commitment is to destroy the family, and he has legions of associates who assist him in his work of destruction. Many years ago, Bishop Victor L. Brown warned: "I believe Satan's ultimate goal is to destroy the family, *because if he would destroy the family, he will not just have won the battle; he will have won the war*" ("Our Youth: Modern Sons of Helaman," *Ensign*, Jan. 1974, 108; emphasis added). Why would Satan be so obsessed with destroying the family? Elder J. Richard Clarke answered: "Because it stands for everything he wants and cannot have. He cannot be a husband, a father, or a grandfather. He cannot have posterity now or ever. Satan cannot even keep those he has led away from God" ("Our Kindred Family—Expression of Eternal Love," *Ensign*, May 1989, 60).

Another reason marriages are failing is because we have largely become a society of selfish individuals. It seems that so many people these days are more concerned with possessions and portfolios than they are with improving their family relationships. Dr. David Popenoe, a sociologist from Rutgers University, recently contended that during the last several years,

> [Families] have grown smaller in size, less stable, and shorter in life span. People have become less willing to invest time, money, and energy in family life, turning instead to investments in themselves.
>
> Moreover, there has been a weakening of child-centeredness in American society and culture. Familism as a cultural value has diminished. The past few decades have witnessed, for the first time in American history, the rise of adult-only communities, the massive voting down of local funds for education, and a growth in the attitude of "no children allowed."[5]

Long before Popenoe documented his conclusions about our selfish society, President Spencer W. Kimball had warned Latter-day Saints about this very issue. In a profoundly direct address entitled "The False Gods We Worship," he cautioned the Saints of the '70s to beware of pride and selfishness. In fact, he said that "we are, *on the whole*, an idolatrous people—a condition most repugnant to the Lord" (*Ensign*, June 1976, 6; emphasis added). How much more applicably would his diagnosis fit our current society?

Ultimately, the selfishness that comes from idolatry destroys civilizations, but it does not begin at that global level. Initially, selfishness originates in the individual heart, and then moves to attack relationships. Selfishness destroys families. Because of selfishness some spouses have affairs, some are wrapped up in their careers to the exclusion of home and hearth, and others simply seem unwilling to spend quality time with spouse and family. On another occasion, President Kimball declared that "every divorce is the result of selfishness on the part of one or the other or both parties to a marriage contract. Someone is thinking of self-comforts, conveniences, freedoms, luxuries, or ease" (Spencer W. Kimball, *The Teachings of Spencer W. Kimball,* ed. Edward L. Kimball [1982], 313).

Knowing that these two plagues—satanic influences and selfishness—often create the major obstacles we face in marriage and family life, we need to consider how these two influences destroy marriages as well as how to avoid them. To be free of Satan's influences, we must live righteously, be Christ-centered in our thoughts, and practice charitable behavior in our relationships. To overcome selfishness we must strip ourselves of pride and become like a child: meek, humble, submissive, patient, and full of love (see Mosiah 3:19). We can change our lives right now by purifying our hearts. Please don't wait until marriage. By then it is too late. The seeds of marital destruction through selfishness are planted long before marriage. Consider Elder Jeffrey R. Holland's promise:

> You can change anything you want to change, and you can do it very fast. Another satanic suckerpunch is that it takes years and years and eons of eternity to repent. That's just not true. It takes exactly as long to repent as it takes you to say, "I'll change"—and mean it. Of course there will be problems to work out and restitutions to make. You may well spend—indeed, you had better spend—the rest of your life proving your repentance by its permanence. But change, growth, renewal, and repentance can come for you as instantaneously as they did for Alma and the sons of Mosiah. . . . Only [Satan] would say, "You can't change. You won't change. Give up. Give in. Don't repent. You are just the way you are." That is a lie born of desperation. Don't fall for it (*However Long and Hard the Road* [1985], 6-7).

We have observed that many people "take no thought for the morrow" when it comes to preparing for marriage. It seems that most young couples spend more time planning their *wedding* than they do planning for *marriage*. Sometimes it is only a few weeks into the marriage when a husband or wife will say, "I had no idea my wife/husband was like that. He/she never did that before we were married." President David O. McKay once said that "during courtship we should keep our eyes wide open, but after marriage keep them half shut" (in Conference Report, Apr. 1956, 9). It appears that many couples are doing just the opposite: their eyes are half shut during the engagement period, as they consciously or unconsciously choose to ignore major warning signs and personality flaws in a prospective spouse or in themselves. Several years ago a newly married couple came to my office for a counseling visit. They had been married for about three months and their marriage was in serious disrepair. Sarah wanted to speak first. After about twenty minutes of sharing her concerns and venting her frustrations, it became clear to me that this young lady was more in a state of shock than anything else. Her entire life she had dreamed of marrying a returned missionary in the temple. She had no reason to believe that she and her husband would not live happily ever after. Sarah was asked to detail some of the specific things that she and her husband were struggling with.

First, she noticed that her husband was very possessive. David would get upset if she did not devote most of her time and energy toward him. If he saw her say "Hi" to another male, he would become extremely jealous. He seemed to want her exclusive attention. He didn't want her to have outside friends or serve in Church callings, but to be home waiting upon him. Second, David did not like Sarah's family. He treated them rather rudely. In fact, he was annoyed when she spent time with them, and he would often disappear when the family came over to their apartment. Third, when David came home from university classes, he would spend hours either watching television or surfing the Internet. He rarely spoke to Sarah despite her efforts to engage him in conversation. He seemed to want her home, but when she was, he ironically did not care to converse or spend time with her. Fourth, David did not pick up after himself. He would leave soiled clothing around the house and dirty dishes in the sink for days. His attitude was that his wife should handle such responsibilities, despite the fact that in their situation, Sarah was busier than he was.

After listing three or four more problems, Sarah put her head down in her hands and whispered, "I just don't know what to do." I decided to intervene at this point. "Sarah, did you notice any of these patterns or habits during your engagement?" She lifted her head and looked at me. "Yes," she said, "I noticed them all to some degree, but I didn't think they were that serious. Besides, I figured that once we got married, such problems *would disappear*."

As most married couples can attest, usually the opposite takes place. Most problems that seem so tiny before marriage become magnified after the ceremony. Marriage is not a magical cure-all for problems that surfaced earlier in the relationship. Too many betrothed couples are "suckered" into believing that once they marry, their new spouse's personality will change because of their great love for that person. However, after the excitement of the reception and honeymoon fades, they awaken to find that they are *still the same individuals they were before the marriage.* It was not surprising to hear that David and Sarah ended up divorcing several months later.

During the engagement period some individuals overlook the faults or bad habits of the person they are dating; others feel that as soon as they are married and can sleep together, any existing problems will evaporate. Isn't that the way it is portrayed in most movies? The point is that there are many topics that need your attention during this important transition from dating partners to more serious companions planning for marriage. A careful look at strengths *and* weaknesses is needed during this period.

A happy marriage is one of the most fulfilling and satisfying relationships in life, and it is the desire of your Heavenly Father that you succeed. When marital problems persist, when we don't find the happiness we expected to find, life can become frustrating. If we prepare ourselves properly before marriage, and continue to learn from each other after marriage, we can accomplish the purposes for which it was divinely instituted.

Questions to Consider

Consider the following questions as they apply to your situation. If you are dating someone, discuss the applicable questions between the two of you. If you are not currently in a relationship, decide where you stand on an issue or how you would like to improve before you start dating someone.

1. What areas of my life do I still need to evaluate to better prepare for marriage? (Refer to Elder David B. Haight's quotation at the beginning of this chapter for ideas.)

2. In what ways (specific to me) could Satan have an influence on me? What can I do to avoid any efforts on his part to prevent my success in marriage?

3. In what ways could selfishness tear down what I am trying to build with my friend or fiancé? What other influences might affect my personal happiness as a married person?

4. How well do we as a couple adjust now to differences between us? What strengths and weaknesses do we see in ourselves and each other that need our immediate attention?

5. How do our friends and families view us as a couple? Are both of our families supportive of our relationship and possible marriage?

6. Are we both realistic about our reasons to marry? Have we been on our best behavior only, or have we seen each other's "bad" sides? Have we been honest with each other? In what ways have we had our eyes open or shut?

CHAPTER 2

Keeping an Eternal Perspective

"Awareness of eternity affects our decisions. The more clearly we see eternity, the more obvious it becomes that the Lord's work in which we are engaged is one vast and grand work with striking similarities on each side of the veil. . . . If we live in such a way that the considerations of eternity press upon us, we will make better decisions." [1]

Several years ago on a beautiful Idaho summer morning, Devere Harris was sitting at his favorite spot on the Snake River, admiring the beauties of his surroundings. From his vantage point, a bend in the river, he could see for some distance. It was a magnificent view. Nearby were the headgates of the feeder canals that provided water for the farms in the valley below.

As Brother Harris was deep in thought, he observed a tiny object a great distance up the river. As the object came closer he was able to determine that it was a rubber raft. Soon, it became clear that there were several people aboard the raft. Apparent to Brother Harris, yet unknown to those in the raft, they were about to round the bend and head directly into the irrigation floodgates. The water was high and moving swiftly. Brother Harris reflected:

> To follow the main course of the river was safe, and it was traveled by hundreds of boaters every year. But I sensed the little party was having trouble in rounding the bend, and the raft was being sucked closer to the feeder gates. I felt that danger lay ahead for this company that appeared to be a family.

Brother Harris quickly made his way to the feeder canal, where to his horror, he helplessly watched the raft capsize. Although the adults in the raft were able to swim to safety, the two children, both young boys, were sucked into floodgates and drowned. Brother Harris explained:

> My mind was racing wildly. In a split second I had seen a happy family transformed into a family of panic, grief, sadness, and loneliness, just because they failed to negotiate a bend in the river, just because the turbulence had sucked them into the wrong channel and away from the right course. My heart ached for this young father and mother as I saw the look of grief and despair on their saddened faces ("The Message: The Promise," *New Era,* Nov. 1988, 4-5).

There is much we can learn from this tragic story. Aside from the literal meaning, this story can serve as a metaphor to teach the importance of perspective. Elder Harris's perspective allowed him to view the whole scene for several miles in both directions. He could see the currents; he could see the calm parts of the river and the safe course; he could also see the danger spots—the whirlpools and eddies. On the other hand, the family in the raft had a very limited view. All they could see was what immediately surrounded them. A bend in the river, a blind spot, prevented them from seeing the floodgates that would ultimately take the lives of their two children.

We all go through life with a limited perspective. Like the family in the story, often we neither see nor comprehend the entire picture. Most of our lives are spent dealing with the trivialities that loom directly in our paths; thus, each of us is unable to see the entire spectrum of what lies before us in eternity, or even what lies five or ten years ahead. We seem to focus, if you will, on the rocks and sticks on the trail and miss the beautiful mountains and forests that surround us. We should pay closer attention to eternity. Having an eternal perspective is critical if we want to successfully negotiate the bends in the river of life. An eternal perspective will particularly help us navigate our way safely through our courtship and engagement.

Many people approach courtship from a shortsighted perspective. They do not take into account the weightier matters of eternity. In fact, many individuals cannot see how their decisions now will impact their lives next month, much less what will take place four or five years down the road. Keeping an eternal perspective is critical when preparing for marriage. To borrow a phrase from Stephen R. Covey, you must "begin with the end in mind."[2] Like the family on the river, if you can only see several yards down the trail (or several years down the path, so to speak) and if you do not prepare thoroughly by charting the rapids on the river, the results of your adventure could be catastrophic. Therefore you must expand your vision and ask yourself, "How will my marrying this person impact my life?" It makes no sense to leap into a marriage without "counting the cost" (Luke 14:28), although that is exactly what many people do. The marriage decision will impact the course and destiny of your life, and the lives of future generations. It was President Kimball who declared:

> Marriage is perhaps the most vital of all the decisions and has the most far-reaching effects, for it has to do not only with immediate happiness, but also with eternal joys. It affects not only the two people involved, but their families and particularly their children and their children's children down through the many generations (Spencer W. Kimball, *Marriage and Divorce* [address delivered at Brigham Young University devotional, 7 Sept. 1976], 2).

Therefore, it is important that you keep an eternal perspective when you date, while you are engaged, and even during marriage. Let's take a closer look at each of these areas.

Keeping an Eternal Perspective When Dating

Having an eternal perspective should influence your dating experiences. If your focus is on marriage in not only this life, but eternal life, then you certainly would not date people who have lower standards than you. You would not date those who would be poor parents to your children, or those who have no interest in being faithful and committed members of the Church. A female college-age student wrote:

> An eternal perspective plays a vital role in successful dating. It allows us to look beyond today and look into tomorrow and

> forever. Eternal perspective gives the opportunity to think about what we want in the future. It relates to Stephen R. Covey's "Begin with the end in mind." We need to do just that. This perspective helps us keep priorities in line during our dating and engagement period. Now I find myself rearranging what's important in my life as far as school, work, money, friends, etc.

Moreover, if you have an eternal perspective while dating, you will not seek out individuals who bear *only* the traits of the world such as a gorgeous body, a beautiful face, a tan, wealth, and popularity. With this concept in mind, a young man of college-age said:

> Having an eternal perspective while dating is an important key when choosing an eternal companion. I think a lot about how Esau gave up his birthright for pottage. Dating can be a lot like that. Trivial things that aren't that important may make us lose focus on our goal and cause us to make mistakes. The greatest lesson I've learned about having an eternal perspective is to try to see the other person as God must see them, to see them for not only who they are right now, but who they can become. To see their potential and possibilities and then do all you can to help them reach their potential as they assist you to reach the same goal.

This young man seems to have his priorities in line. Unfortunately there are others who do not. It appears, for instance, that many young men are looking for Julia Roberts with a testimony. Although looks and physical characteristics may be important to some, they should not be the foundation stones on which long-term relationships are built. When stretch marks and wrinkles appear, when popularity fades, or when income is reduced, what strengths will be left? Cardinal traits such as kindness, consideration, empathy, commitment, spirituality, selflessness, and humility are paramount to marriage relationships, and they are portable—you can take them with you to the next life. In fact, from the inspired document *The Family: A Proclamation to the World*, we learn that successful marriages are built on principles of "faith, prayer, repentance, forgiveness, respect, love, compassion, work, and wholesome recreational activities" (September 1995). These traits are the foundation stones of healthy relationships. Notice there is no mention in the *Proclamation* about good looks, popularity, or wealth. Apparently, the Lord does not see a high correlation between such traits and successful marriages and families. That is not to say we shouldn't be interested in physical appearance. Of course it is important to us initially. But that criterion should not be the ultimate decision-maker for us. We need to find a spouse that fits into a range of attractiveness acceptable to us, and then as we build our relationship together, share our love, and develop deeper emotional and spiritual feelings, we become *more attractive* to each other. As President Hinckley stated, "I am satisfied that a happy marriage is not so much a matter of romance as it is an anxious concern for the comfort and well-being of one's companion" ("What God Hath Joined Together," *Ensign*, May 1991, 73). When compared to our youthful appearance, we all become physically unattractive as age eventually takes its toll. There had better be more to your marriage than physique when that happens. Spiritual and emotional strengths become even more important as we age together and find that our bodies, after all, are mortal.

The virtues acknowledged by the Lord and His prophets (faith, forgiveness, selflessness, etc.) should be present first in your own life. That is, you should be "anxiously engaged" in improving yourself in these areas rather than searching desperately for someone else you think possesses them. Brad Wilcox, while serving as bishop of a married-student ward at BYU, interviewed some of his ward members about what was most important to them in marriage preparation. One couple suggested that working on yourself is where marriage preparation begins. Bishop Wilcox explained:

> These young couples agreed that one of the best gifts to give your future spouse is your best self. Andrew and Jessica Child said, "Set goals and strive to reach those goals. We did, and now that we are married, we can see it not only helped us get to this point but it will continue to help us in the future."
>
> One of the first things that attracted Jessica to Andrew (besides his cute smile) was his willingness to learn. She recalls, "He was always interested in finding out new things. That made him interesting to be with." Similarly, Andrew was attracted to Jessica because she was actively pursuing positive goals in her

own life. Andrew says, "She was making herself into somebody and not just waiting around to become somebody's wife" ("Marriage Prep 101," *New Era,* Oct. 1999, 31).

You should also seek out members of the opposite sex who have healthy character traits, and who are working to improve them. Elder L. Aldin Porter shared an experience regarding this principle. He said that while he was serving as a full-time missionary, Elder Bruce R. McConkie, a new General Authority at the time, came to visit his mission. It was Elder Porter's opportunity, along with his companion, to drive Elder McConkie from Missoula to Butte, Montana. As they talked along the way, one of the missionaries asked Elder McConkie, "How can we know whom we should marry?" To their surprise, Elder McConkie's response was quick and certain. He asked the missionaries to turn to the Doctrine and Covenants section 88, and to read verse 40. Elder Porter and his companion turned to the reference and read:

> For intelligence cleaveth unto intelligence; wisdom receiveth wisdom; truth embraceth truth; virtue loveth virtue; light cleaveth unto light; mercy hath compassion on mercy and claimeth her own; justice continueth its course and claimeth its own; judgment goeth before the face of him who sitteth upon the throne and governeth and executeth all things.

Although the missionaries appreciated the verse that had been pointed out to them, they had no idea what it had to do with finding an eternal companion. Elder McConkie, sensing their bewilderment, then explained that if these two missionaries were men who loved the truth, they would be attracted to women who loved the truth; if they were men who loved virtue and believed in being pure and chaste, then they would be attracted to women who loved virtue and were morally clean; if they were men who loved light and justice and mercy, they would be attracted to women who loved these same attributes. Elder McConkie then said, "If you are men who love truth and virtue, go and find a young lady with these attributes, and then proceed to fall in love." Elder Porter later confessed that, at the time, Elder McConkie's counsel did not seem very romantic—seek out a woman with these traits, then *proceed* to fall in love—it almost sounded like a deer hunt. However, Elder Porter then added: "The principle . . . seems perfectly logical to me now. I have found that it even applies if you are already married, because when you continue to work to develop these characteristics, it will do much to build a marriage for eternity" ("Becoming Men and Women of Truth and Virtue," Satellite Broadcast, 13 September 1998, BYU-Idaho). The traits that are found in the *Proclamation* are lasting and enduring, and with time and seasoning, they will only increase in power and intensity.

If you have an eternal perspective when you date, you will be less inclined to break the law of chastity and more inclined to keep the commandments of God. Having an eternal perspective means that you understand that there are consequences for both your bad and good conduct. A female college student wrote:

> Knowing that I will only date those who have the highest standards and that they too are looking for someone with high values and morals, my dating experience will be more enjoyable and more successful. If I date the type of people I want to marry, then I will more likely marry that type of person. I will choose who I date carefully. Only young men worthy to hold the priesthood! Dating with a purpose (marriage) and only dating those who will be able to help me get to the highest kingdom are my priorities.

Consider Joseph Smith's situation. While he was involved in preparing for his future role in the Church, he was also engaged to Emma Smith. How interesting! For three years, each year (between 1824 and 1827), on 21 September, Joseph had a meeting with Moroni. Imagine having scheduled in your day planner or Palm Pilot for 22 September, "Visit with Moroni." We suspect you would use much discretion in who you dated. Who wouldn't be extra careful if they knew their actions would be directly reported to an angel? You do not, however, have to have a rendezvous with an angel to gain and maintain an eternal perspective. Each night, as you kneel in prayer and report your stewardship to a loving Heavenly Father, you can develop the same kind of maturity that was required of Joseph when he was engaged to Emma.

Like Joseph, you must keep your heart pure and clean. Then the Holy Ghost will be able to influence you and guide your life. This becomes particularly important when you are seeking a confirmation as to whom you should marry. A bishop of a student ward recently shared an interesting perspective. He said that it seemed ironic to him that many of his ward members who were seriously dating often spent hours with each other in "more-than-casual" kissing sessions. Then, the bishop related, when it came time to receive an answer from the Spirit about whether or not they should marry the particular individual, they had a difficult time getting a clear spiritual confirmation. The bishop explained, "They want an answer from the Spirit, but they do not even have the Spirit because of the way they are living their lives." It is critical that we have the Lord's Spirit with us. It is essential that we live a clean and pure life so that the Holy Ghost can be our constant companion. Elder Dallin H. Oaks taught this concept:

> The pure in heart have a distinctive way of looking at life. Their attitudes and desires cause them to view their experiences in terms of eternity. This eternal perspective affects their choices and priorities. As they draw farther from worldliness they feel closer to our Father in Heaven and more able to be guided by his Spirit (*Pure in Heart* [1988], 111).

Keeping an Eternal Perspective During Your Engagement

How does an eternal perspective influence your understanding of what engagement means? Not only will a long-range view influence your choice of a mate but it will also help you more effectively prepare for marriage. Having an eternal perspective will help you understand what you are going to *do* with your lives after you say *I do*. There is much more to marriage than merely planning a wedding. We know of an individual who made wedding planning her hobby. At her wedding, the flowers, the cake, the location, everything down to the groomsmen's socks, were the model of perfection. However, because the wedding day was the focal point of her attitude toward marriage, there was a major letdown when she and her husband came home from their honeymoon.

While you are engaged, an eternal perspective will assist you in seeing far beyond the wedding day and honeymoon, and will help you develop a deeper relationship with your fiancé. Instead of spending every waking hour romancing each other and making wedding plans, focus on areas that will help strengthen your present relationship. The engagement period is a good time to discuss mutual goals, dreams, and aspirations. You need to consider careers. You need to focus on serving and helping those around you so you do not become too absorbed with each other. Have you ever watched a newly engaged couple? Sometimes they do not even realize that there is a whole world going on around them. It is as if the entire universe is centered on them. A tornado could rip the roofs off the houses in the neighborhood, a fire could wipe out what remained of the homes, and a flood could really finish things off. It wouldn't matter. This couple would be oblivious to these events and just sit there and stare at each other, googly-eyed, talking to each other in their "secret code."

One wise father recommended that his daughter and future son-in-law go out and find some people to help. He was concerned that his daughter and her fiancé would become so busy concentrating on each other during their engagement that they would miss the events in the world. He cautioned them that they had only been around each other while on their best behavior (dressing their best, looking their best, and doing fun things together). How would they accept each other when more serious challenges surfaced? Would they understand each other? Would they be tolerant of each other's weaknesses?

The specific prescription the father recommended was this: that his daughter and her fiancé go and volunteer to babysit someone else's children. It was his feeling that babysitting small children would help reveal their true characters to each other. So, this couple went out and found a single mother that had two-year-old twin boys. The mother welcomed their invitation to watch her young sons each week for several months. This turned out to be a beneficial experience for all involved. The young couple related that they were able to see each other in a whole new light. The young lady laughed as she watched her future husband attempt to change a diaper and get squirted in the process. On the other hand, he was able to help her pull spaghetti out of her hair after one of the boys threw his bowl across the kitchen. Together, they played chase with those two boys, took them to the park, and wrestled with them.

When the boy's mom would come home, they felt relieved, but they also felt the satisfaction of knowing that they had helped someone else. For this particular couple, these babysitting dates proved to be much more beneficial than sitting on a couch, staring into each other's eyes, and discussing what color their napkins would be at the wedding reception. Furthermore, on the drive home from those visits, the couple would often discuss how they would raise their future children. They also shared their parenting beliefs and philosophies. Mainly, they enjoyed being together in a different setting. Incidently, several years after they were married, this couple had twins of their own. They testify that helping those twin boys not only prepared them to be better parents to their own set of twins, but to all of their children.

Engaged couples should work on developing strong character values and habits such as those listed in the *Proclamation*. Successful engagements are built upon the same principles that successful marriages are built upon. Therefore, focus on implementing those types of attributes into your own personal character and then strive to incorporate these principles into your relationship. Not only will these traits provide you with a more significant marriage in this life, but they will ultimately carry you into the highest degree of glory.

We have witnessed the scars borne by couples too absorbed with each other during courtships. We have often met with young couples who never discussed important character traits before they were married. During their engagement they spent most of their time in huggy-kissy sessions and planning how many harp players they would need at their wedding reception. Perhaps they thought that marriage would eliminate any character flaws. Now, after a year or so of marriage, they realize their relationship had little in the way of a sure foundation. Some of these couples end up going from one counselor to another. Your marriage is too important to be treated so trivially. Who you marry and how you decide to live after marriage are the most vital choices you will ever make.

Keeping an Eternal Perspective in Your Covenant Marriage

In Doctrine and Covenants 49:15-17, we learn that a significant purpose for the creation of the earth was for us to come and experience marriage and family life. That is the fundamental purpose of mortality. President Joseph F. Smith taught that "marriage is the preserver of the human race. Without it, the purposes of God would be frustrated; virtue would be destroyed to give place to vice and corruption, and the earth would be void and empty" (*Gospel Doctrine*, 8th edition [1949], 272). Similarly, President McKay declared "we must never lose sight of the fundamental fact that home is the basis of civilization and that members of the Church have the obligation to build ideal homes and to rear exemplary families" (*Man May Know for Himself: Teachings of President David O. McKay*, comp. Clare Middlemiss [1967], 228).

Marriage is not just a good idea; it is a critical doctrine and the most sacred obligation that we undertake. And once we undertake it, there's no looking back. It's rough out there, the waters are choppy, and too many people file for divorce when they get splashed by the first wave—but this is not how God intended for us to deal with trials.

James Dobson said, "Too many couples go into marriage with one eye on the exit door." In marriage, looking for the exit door or the escape hatch should never be an option. We are committed and bound to each other and to our Heavenly Father for all eternity. An eternal perspective assists couples in understanding that they *will* have problems, that there *will* be struggles, but that there is no need to pull the "ejection" lever. Elder Russell M. Nelson once declared that "with celestial sight, trials impossible to change become possible to endure" ("With God Nothing Shall Be Impossible," *Ensign*, May 1988, 40). With an eternal perspective, you can endure and overcome any challenge that comes your way. No matter how large or small your marriage and family problems might turn out to be, you can be successful. Elder Marlin K. Jensen related this event:

> Recently I visited with a widower as he stood bravely at the side of his wife's casket, surrounded by several handsome and stalwart sons. This man and his wife had been married for fifty-three years, during the last six of which she had been seriously ill with a terminal kidney disease. He had provided the 24-hour care she required until his own health was in jeopardy. I expressed my admiration for him and the great love and care he had given his wife. I felt compelled to ask, "How did you do it?"

> It was easy, he replied, when he remembered that fifty-three years earlier, he had knelt at an altar in the temple and made a covenant with the Lord and with his bride.
>
> "I wanted to keep it," he said. In an eternal marriage, the thought of ending what began with a covenant between God and each other simply has little place. When challenges come and our individual weaknesses are revealed, the remedy is to repent, improve, and apologize, not to separate to divorce. When we make covenants with the Lord and our eternal companion, we should do everything in our power to honor the terms ("A Union of Love and Understanding," *Ensign*, Oct. 1994, 51).

Having an eternal perspective in marriage means we are in this relationship for the long haul, for better or for worse, in sickness and in health. We keep our covenants—no matter what. We do not look for "easy outs" or "exits" when times get tough. Marriage is the most important thing a Latter-day Saint will ever do, and keeping our sacred promises and covenants that we make with God and our spouse is the most crucial aspect of our lives. Therefore, *being* the right person after the marriage ceremony is just as critical as *finding* the right person prior to the ceremony.

We know a man on the verge of losing his family through marital separation. He is concerned about his wife, and he is in deep despair over his children. Recently he asked, "Doesn't my wife understand the seriousness of divorce? Doesn't she realize that she made eternal covenants, not only with me, but God?" There are too many people today who do not understand the serious nature of covenants and commitments to God. Like those who live after the manner of the world, they go into marriage with one eye on the exit door. In the October 1996 general conference, Elder Bruce C. Hafen said:

> Many people today marry as hirelings. And when the wolf comes, they flee. This idea is wrong. It curses the earth, turning parents' hearts away from their children and from each other. . . . Covenant marriage requires a total leap of faith: they must keep their covenants without knowing what risks that may require of them. They must surrender unconditionally, obeying God and sacrificing for each other. Then they will discover what Alma called "incomprehensible joy" ("Covenant Marriage," *Ensign*, Nov. 1996, 26; emphasis added).

It Begins and Ends with Family

The central organization of God's plan for happiness is the family. We are born to a family, and when we die, we are often surrounded by family. In the celestial kingdom, we will be together forever—as families. When we marry in the temple, we are not merely uniting two people together to share a house, food, and a last name. We are creating eternal families.

To that union God will send His choice sons and daughters. The purpose of our existence can be summed up this way: We are here to bring our families back to the Father. Everything else must be done with that perspective in mind.

When it comes right down to it, our quest is to gain eternal life through living the gospel—the key element of that quest being marriage and family. Everything from family home evening, Scouting, Primary activity day, Young Men, Young Women, firesides, institute, and missions is to prepare each one of us to be well qualified for marriage. There are few people who on their deathbed say, "I wish I had spent more time at the office." Surely there are those who would admit that they should have spent more time with their sweethearts and their children. Some no doubt wish they had been nicer to their companions, or spent more time throwing a ball with a son, or telling stories to a daughter, rather than reading a newspaper or catching all eight versions of Sports Center.

Two of our colleagues have had close calls with death during the last several years. Though these men had different maladies, they had something in common. When they regained consciousness, all they wanted was to see their families; they wanted to touch them, hold them, and express their love to them. Both of these men came to the realization that family was the most important thing in their lives. When we are stripped of all that we have, the only important things to us will be our faith and our relationships with our loved ones. Accordingly, we should prepare to that end.

A friend of ours, Jack, was notified that one of his best friends from childhood was dying of leukemia. As soon as Jack found out about Gary's predicament, he went straight to the hospital to visit him. His goal was to cheer Gary up and provide him with some hope and optimism. However, Jack discovered that Gary had not only accepted his fate, but also had a lesson for Jack. Knowing that his friend had many opportunities to speak to the youth and married couples in the Church, Gary committed him to share this message as he traveled throughout the Church: "Tell the people from me . . . that what really matters in this life is God, family, friends, and home" (Jack R. Christianson, *Be Strong and of Good Courage* [1994], 122).

When all else is said and done, family turns out to be the really important thing in life. So as you prepare for marriage, don't neglect the eternal view. Begin with the end in mind. Marriage is not merely the joining of two individuals together for a beautiful wedding and a fantastic honeymoon. You are creating an eternal unit of the celestial kingdom. These are the things that matter.

Questions to Consider

Consider the following questions as they apply to your situation. If you are dating someone, discuss the applicable questions between the two of you. If you are not currently in a relationship, decide where you stand on an issue or how you would like to improve before you start dating someone.

1. How can an eternal perspective help us during our engagement period?

2. The *Proclamation* states that strong marriages are built on principles of faith, prayer, repentance, forgiveness, respect, love, compassion, work, and wholesome recreational activities. Discuss how each of these principles can contribute to a strong marriage and family life. See what you can learn about each other through a discussion of these principles, and decide on specific ways you can increase them in your life.

3. Read D&C 49:15–17. What do these verses teach us about the importance of marriage and the family?

4. Read the following quotes and discuss what you feel are the most important thoughts in each one:

Parley P. Pratt said:

It was Joseph Smith who taught me how to prize the endearing relationships of father and mother, husband and wife; of brother and sister, son and daughter. It was from him that I learned that the wife of my bosom might be secured to me for time and all eternity; and that the refined sympathies and affections which endeared us to each other emanated from the fountain of divine eternal love. It was from him that I learned that we might cultivate these affections, and grow and increase in the same to all eternity; while the result of our endless union would be an offspring as numerous as the stars of heaven, or the sands of the sea shore. It was from him that I learned the true dignity and destiny of a son of God, clothed with an eternal priesthood, as the patriarch and sovereign of his countless offspring. It was from him that I learned that the highest dignity of womanhood was, to stand as a queen and priestess to her husband, and to reign for ever and ever as the queen mother of her numerous and still increasing offspring. I had loved before, but I knew not why. But now I loved—with a pureness—an intensity of elevated, exalted feeling, which would lift my soul from the transitory things of this grovelling sphere and expand it as the ocean (*The Autobiography of Parley P. Pratt* [1979], 297–298).

George Q. Cannon said:

We believe that when a man and woman are united as husband and wife, and they love each other, their hearts and feelings are one, that that love is as enduring as eternity itself, and that when death overtakes them it will neither extinguish nor cool that love, but that it will brighten and kindle it to a purer flame, and that it will endure through eternity; and that if we have offspring they will be with us and our mutual associations will be one of the chief joys of the heaven to which we are hastening . . . God has restored the everlasting priesthood, by which ties can be formed, . . . which shall be as enduring as we ourselves are enduring, . . . and they and their children will dwell and associate together eternally, and this, as I have said, will constitute one of the chief joys of heaven; and we look forward to it with delightful anticipations (*Journal of Discourses* 14:320–321).

CHAPTER 3

Becoming the Right One

*"Success in marriage depends not so much on
finding the right person as on being the right person."* [1]

It seems that before marriage many of us compile some sort of list including all the qualifications we desire in a future spouse. For some of us the list is on a three-by-five card, or on a computer, or even on a yellow sheet of notebook paper. Some people keep their list in a private place, while others post it on their refrigerator. In our youth, perhaps the list included physical dimensions of a "fantasy" spouse: hair color, eye color, height, weight, physical measurements—whatever information is found on any driver's license. As time passes and individuals mature, the list changes. We begin to consider more important characteristics, such as spirituality, personality, gospel commitment, successful mission, hobbies, character, ability to manage money, etc. Many people hope to meet someone with all of their dream specifications. As often happens in life, we usually end up falling in love with someone who isn't anything like the person on our list.

Although compiling such a list may have some merit, the deficits probably outweigh the benefits for two basic reasons. First, a "wish list" is unrealistic. No one, except a goddess perhaps, would ever possess all of the attributes on the list. Thus, your list is as outdated as a BYU Student Ward Home Teaching Roster. Finally, perhaps most importantly, the "wish list" places all of the emphasis on the other person, leaving yourself out of the loop of responsibility. That is, you are basically making a list of all the ways someone else could make you happy, ignoring that you have a similar obligation to someone else. In selecting an eternal companion, you might be wise to focus on refining the attributes that *you* have to offer someone else, traits over which you have some direct control. Elder Neal A. Maxwell emphasized maintaining a focus on improving yourself when he declared: "If the choice is between reforming other church members (including fiancés, spouses, or children) or ourselves, is there really any question about where we should begin? The key is to have our eyes wide open to our own faults and partially closed to the faults of others—not the other way around!" ("A Brother Offended," *Ensign*, May 1982, 39).

President Boyd K. Packer told a story that illustrates this point. An elder who had served in his mission came to him for counsel. He was having a difficult time deciding if he should marry a particular young woman. He said to his former mission president, "President Packer, you tell me that it is all right to marry her and we'll schedule the marriage. You tell me that I shouldn't, and I won't. I've come for that counsel" (Boyd K. Packer, *Memorable Stories with a Message* [2000], 43–44). Once President Packer was assured by his former missionary that he would follow whatever counsel he was given, President Packer instructed him to go home and seek counsel from his *own* father. Somewhat apprehensive, the missionary approached his dad and asked for some advice on the matter. His father spoke boldly to him:

"David," said the father, "do you know what is wrong with this courtship? Every time you go out with this girl you go just as though you were going to buy a horse. You have a set of specifications, and you are testing and looking and seeing. You're measuring every particular to see whether she will measure up and be good enough and meet all of *your* specifications."

This wise father said, "David, the thing that is wrong with you is that you are selfish. If you would worry half as much about whether *you* were meeting *her* specifications as you worry about whether she met yours, you'd find your answer" (Boyd K. Packer, *Memorable Stories with a Message* [2000], 44; emphasis in original).

In short, this father's advice was that David should have worried whether *he* possessed any of the traits on his "wish list." David and his new companion were sealed in the temple shortly after this incident. We learn from this story that the only real value of compiling a list is so you will know what to look for in yourself!

Each of you possesses core values and standards that constitute your beliefs. Those beliefs affect your behavior; in fact, if they are positive, they can put you on the proper path to meet someone else with similar beliefs and values, a path that leads to the celestial kingdom. It is too late to get on the path once you are engaged, or even after you are married. You should get on the path when you are baptized, and stay the course through your childhood, teenage years, young adult years, engagement, and certainly your married years (see 2 Nephi 31:19–20).[2] During the dating period, you are merely seeking those who are on the same path and who are going the same direction as you are. Specifically, you are searching for a marriage partner who will help you stay on the Lord's path, and who is anxious to walk beside you. As you do your duty in the kingdom, and as your future spouse is doing his or her duty, you will notice each other on the path because you have both been about your Father's business. Together, you will continue your journey toward the celestial kingdom.

You will be required to pass through certain gates on the path. These gates represent the ordinances of the gospel. You have already passed through the gate of baptism, and when you and your spouse are sealed in the temple, you will pass through another gate. You will continue to walk together, side by side, leading your family into the kingdom of God.

Counsel from a Prophet

President Gordon B. Hinckley taught us how to stay on the path to marriage and eventually, to eternal life. In a classic message entitled, "Living Worthy of the Girl You Will Someday Marry," the prophet told the young men of the Church, "The girl you marry will take a terrible chance on you. She will give her all to the young man she marries. He will largely determine the remainder of her life. She will even surrender her name to his name" (*Ensign*, May 1998, 66). So, what did the prophet tell the young men about finding an eternal companion? Did he review "wish lists?" Did he reveal the institute of religion or college campus with the most desirable people to date? Not at all. Instead, he taught the principle that young women have certain *expectations* of the man they will ultimately marry. In fact, President Hinckley suggested that if a man wants to be worthy of the girl he marries, he should incorporate specific virtues (expectations of the young woman) in his life. Once again, the emphasis was on *preparing yourself*—not on seeking the one perfect person who will make you happy.

Here are the virtues he listed for a young man to measure himself against.

- *Be absolutely loyal.* As the old Church of England ceremony says, you will marry her "for richer or for poorer, in sickness and in health, for better or for worse." She will be yours and yours alone, regardless of the circumstances of your lives. You will be hers and hers alone. There can be eyes for none other. There must be absolute loyalty, undeviating loyalty one to another.

- *Be a young man of virtue.* The girl you marry can expect you to come to the marriage altar absolutely clean. She can expect you to be a young man of virtue in thought and word and deed.

   I plead with you boys tonight to keep yourselves free from the stains of the world. You must not indulge in sleazy talk at school. You must not tell sultry jokes. You must not fool around with the Internet to find pornographic material. You must not dial a long-distance telephone number to listen to filth. You must not rent videos with pornography of any kind. This salacious stuff simply is not for you. Stay away from pornography as you would avoid a serious disease. It is as destructive.

- *Live the Word of Wisdom.* Stay away from [alcohol]. It will do you no good. It could do you irreparable harm. . . . Likewise, stay away from illegal drugs. They can absolutely destroy you. . . . Would any girl in her right mind ever wish to marry a young man who has a drug habit, who is the slave of alcohol, who is addicted to pornography?

- *Avoid profanity.* [Profanity] is all around you in school. Young people seem to pride themselves on using filthy and obscene language as well as indulging in profanity, taking the name of our Lord in vain. It becomes a vicious habit which, if indulged in while you are young, will find expression throughout your life. Who would wish to be married to a man whose speech is laden with filth and profanity?

- *Learn now to control your temper.* There is another serious thing to which many young men become addicted. This is anger. With the least provocation they explode into tantrums of uncontrolled rage. It is pitiful to see someone so weak. But even worse, they are prone to lose all sense of reason and do things which bring later regret. . . . If you have a temper, now is the time to learn to control it. The more you do so while you are young, the more easily it will happen. Let no member of this Church ever lose control of himself in such an unnecessary and vicious manner. Let him bring to his marriage words of peace and composure.

- *Work for an education.* Get all the training that you can. The world will largely pay you what it thinks you are worth. . . . It is your primary obligation to provide for your family.

    Your wife will be fortunate indeed if she does not have to go out and compete in the marketplace. She will be twice blessed if she is able to remain at home while you become the breadwinner of the family. Education is the key to economic opportunity.

- *Be modest in your wants.* You do not need a big home with a big mortgage as you begin your lives together. You can and should avoid overwhelming debt. There is nothing that will cause greater tensions in marriage than grinding debt, which will make of you a slave to your creditors. You may have to borrow money to begin ownership of a home. But do not let it be so costly that it will preoccupy your thoughts day and night.

- *Encourage her to become her best.* She will wish to be married to someone who loves her, who trusts her, who walks beside her, who is her very best friend and companion. She will wish to be married to someone who encourages her in her Church activity and in community activities which will help her to develop her talents and make a greater contribution to society.

- *Go on a mission.* She will want to be married to someone who has a sense of service to others, who is disposed to contribute to the Church and to other good causes. She will wish to be married to someone who loves the Lord and seeks to do His will. It is well, therefore, that each of you young men plan to go on a mission, to give unselfishly to your Father in Heaven a tithe of your life, to go forth with a spirit of total unselfishness to preach the gospel of peace. . . . If you are a good missionary, you will return home with the desire to continue to serve the Lord, to keep His commandments, and to do His will. Such behavior will add immeasurably to the happiness of your marriage.

- *Be married in the temple.* You will wish to be married in one place and one place only. That is the house of the Lord. You cannot give to your companion a greater gift than that of marriage in God's holy house, under the protective wing of the sealing covenant of eternal marriage. There is no adequate substitute for it. There should be no other way for you.

- *Prepare to become a righteous father.* What greater thing in all this world can there be than to become the father of a precious child, a son or daughter of God. . . . How precious a thing is a baby. How wonderful a thing is a child. What a marvelous thing is a family. Live worthy of becoming a father of whom your wife and children will be proud ("Living Worthy of the Girl You Will Someday Marry," *Ensign*, May 1998, 49–51).

Each of these suggestions will help a young man think seriously about his own marriage preparation. You can control your destiny; you can make wise choices now; you can take charge of these areas of your life. Not one of these suggestions from the prophet is dependent on someone else! You have the ability to choose and internalize each of these cardinal principles. In so doing, your footing on the path will become more solid and true; then, as you walk upright on the path to eternal life, each of you young men President Hinckley addresses will be better prepared to attract a woman worthy of your companionship.

Although President Hinckley's talk was directed to the young men of the Church, these traits can apply equally to young women. Certainly single sisters in the Church should be loyal, virtuous, clean, pure, in control of appetites and emotions, educated, and worthy to serve in the Church and temple.

So, how can you best find your eternal sweetheart? Develop certain traits in yourself. When you possess them, you recognize these traits in others. As the old maxim says: "It takes one to know one!" The best suggestion we can give you is to begin with you. Examine your own life and determine the areas that need improvement and refinement. (At the end of this chapter is a page labeled "Preparing for Celestial Marriage" to walk you through points that may need work.)

Following the Model the Savior Has Set

We can learn a great deal regarding individual preparation for marriage from the Savior's life. Just as Jesus prepared for His public ministry, so you can prepare purposely and deliberately for your marriage. How did Jesus do it? In Luke 2:52, it states that "Jesus increased in wisdom and stature, and in favour with God and man." That is, Jesus prepared Himself for His public ministry in four key areas: intellect/education (wisdom); physical/mental health (stature);

spirituality (favor with God); and social abilities (favor with man). We suggest that you follow the example set by the Savior and seek to improve your life in these four important areas. Elder Joe J. Christensen recently reported:

> Consider the results of an informal survey taken of 150 young adults. They were asked to list three resolutions they felt would help them become more successful and happy. Almost everyone who was surveyed (98 percent) included a resolution to increase the level of his or her spirituality. Two out of three (68 percent) indicated that they would like to improve their social skills. Half (49 percent) indicated a desire to increase their level of physical fitness, and half (48 percent) wanted to grow intellectually. The group indicated a desire to improve in the same facets of life in which the Lord grew. After all, self-improvement is at the heart of why we are here in mortality (*One Step at a Time: Building a Better Marriage, Family, and You* [1996], 110).

There is another principle that comes from Luke 2:52. Jesus was proactive in improving His personal characteristics. Note that the verse teaches that Jesus *increased* in the four areas mentioned above. Some have supposed that the word *increased* is passive, meaning that during the course of Jesus' life, He improved in "wisdom and stature, and in favour with God and man" automatically, without any deliberate effort or attempts of His own. However, the Greek translation for the word *increased* is *prokopto*, which suggests "driving forward" or "advancing."[3] "Driving forward" implies an active, deliberate, and calculated course. It would not be surprising to learn that Jesus deliberately (with the help of parents and heavenly messengers) identified the areas He wanted to progress in, set goals, and then actively pursued His plan. Remember, although Jesus was perfect, His boyhood was a real boyhood and His progression and development were as necessary as yours is. Just as He did all that was possible in His own maturation process, we too should identify areas in our lives that need strengthening or shoring up (see Ether 12:27), and then actively do what we need to do in order to see that our goals come to fruition.

The four areas above are crucial to monitor in preparing for your marriage. It may be helpful to imagine for a moment that each one of these areas represents a leg on a chair. If a single leg becomes weakened, unbalanced, or broken, the chair will be unstable, if not entirely useless. So it is with us. If we neglect or choose to ignore our development in any of these key areas, we too can become unstable, or be perceived as less attractive. Let's review what we can do to steady our chair.

Intellect/Education

Education is an important aspect of personal development. In today's world, most individuals will need an education to make a contribution to society and in turn be compensated financially and enjoy what they do for a living. Of course, the level of education you attain will have a direct bearing on the type of job for which you can qualify. President Kimball gave this counsel:

> We . . . encourage our people to study and prepare to render service with their minds and with their hands.
>
> Some are inclined toward formal university training, and some are inclined more toward the practical vocational training. We feel that our people should receive that kind of training which is most consistent with their interests and talents. Whether it be in the professions, the arts, or the vocations; whether it be university or vocational training, we applaud and encourage it ("The Foundations of Righteousness," *Ensign*, Nov. 1977, 5).

At a fireside for youth and young single adults in the Church, President Hinckley admonished: "Sacrifice a car, sacrifice anything that is needed to be sacrificed to qualify yourselves to do the work of the world. That world will in large measure pay you what it thinks you are worth, and your worth will increase as you gain education and proficiency in your chosen field" ("President Hinckley Offers Counsel, Warmth," *Church News*, 18 November 2000, 3). Ask yourself: How am I doing in the area of intellectual growth? Is education important to me? What kind of grades do I typically make? Are they sufficiently high for me to obtain a good job or be admitted to graduate school? What about my study habits? Do I study on a regular and consistent basis, or are my study patterns erratic or nonexistent?

If education is *not* important to me, then I can't expect to marry someone who does value it.

Research shows that the more similar couples are when it comes to educational attainment, the more compatible they will be in marriage.[4] In fact, the risk of marital instability (divorce) is highest among couples who view education differently.[5]

Intellect and education, however, are not limited to a university setting. You can seek learning out of the best books (see D&C 88:118) and from life's experiences (see D&C 90:15). Just because we have graduated from high school or college does not mean that we should halt our learning processes. Here is a helpful suggestion:

> Ask a few respected people of high character—those you know read a lot—to share with you the titles of the five books (besides the scriptures) that they feel have had the most positive influence in shaping their lives for the better. You will soon accumulate a good list of titles to add to those you have already decided to read. This idea corresponds to a suggestion made by Emerson, "If we encountered a man of rare intellect we should ask him what books he read." Then I would add, if we follow the example of wise people who are readers, we will grow in wisdom. We will become more interested in life as well as more interesting to others (Joe J. Christensen, *One Step at a Time: Building a Better Marriage, Family, and You* [1996], 115).

How will you and a spouse further your educations? Will your home be filled with good books and magazines and literature, or will the TV be on most of the time? How would you rate yourself on a scale of 1–10 (ten being the highest) under the umbrella of intellect and educational interest and attainment right now? What do you expect from a future spouse in this regard? Do you want to marry someone who makes good use of his or her time, or someone who is up on all the shows on the tube, or who spends hours at the computer playing video games or surfing the Internet? These issues should be explored before the wedding day.

Physical/Mental Health

Physical and mental health are important aspects of marriage relationships. Weight and health issues are sensitive matters to many of us. We all are subject to mortal diseases and health factors beyond our control. Our love for each other should not be affected by things that happen to us naturally or accidentally. But there are many things that we do have influence over—and our eating and health habits are two of them.

President Ezra Taft Benson explained:

> Physical well-being is not only a priceless asset to one's self—it is a heritage to be passed on. With good health all the activities of life are greatly enhanced. A clean mind in a healthy body enables one to render far more effective service to others. It helps one provide more vigorous leadership. It gives our every experience in life more zest and more meaning. Robust health is a noble and worthwhile attainment (*The Teachings of Ezra Taft Benson* [1988], 479).

Physical health affects not only you, but also your posterity. Your children need a father and a mother with energy and ambition. You don't want to leave your spouse a widow or a widower because of poor health habits. What are you doing now to stay in shape? To keep physically fit? To remain that way? Are you interested in a spouse who will take care of his or her body and who is as concerned about his or her health and appearance as you are about yours? Physical health is a vital element in marriage. Of course people who have happy marriages suffer illnesses and health problems. That is not the point here. The point is that we can prevent some problems by starting to live healthy now. Today is the day to establish proper eating and nutritional habits, obtain sufficient rest, and exercise on a consistent basis. After marriage, stay healthy. Don't use marriage as an excuse to put on additional pounds or let healthy habits go. Nutritionists suggest that you not get above 10–15 pounds more than your high school weight the rest of your life (assuming that you are in a normal range at graduation). Even with general health as a goal, it is possible, however, to be extreme on nutrition and eating habits. The Lord doesn't ask us to be vegetarians or fanatical about white bread, drinks, etc., but to live a decent and healthy personal "word of wisdom."

Trying to get your spouse to be "just like you" in exercise or eating habits is often a source of marital contention. As with anything in marriage, empathy, patience, and loving concern are in order. Several years ago a couple came for help. They had been married about ten years and were having some "minor" problems. An interview with the wife revealed that they could use some help in strengthening their relationship. Then the husband was interviewed. He wanted his wife to lose enough weight so that she could fit into her old high school clothes. He laid down an ultimatum. If she couldn't lose the weight within the next two months, he wanted out of the marriage. It didn't seem to matter to him that his wife had had four pregnancies and deliveries in a six-year time frame. Nor was he concerned that it was difficult for her to lose weight. Incidentally, she wasn't just sitting around on the couch eating chocolate bars and watching soap operas. She worked full-time, served in the Church, and did her best to rear their four children. Moreover, he had wanted to be a father, and was happy when he learned of her pregnancies. It was made clear to him that he of all people should be the most understanding of her weight challenge. But he didn't want advice. In fact, he never returned for counseling. He eventually divorced his wife because he felt that if she really loved him, she would do whatever he wanted her to do. Ironically, he was quite overweight himself, with a pretty good-sized paunch hanging over his belt buckle!

How important is appearance to you? Will you, as a future husband, be prepared to love your wife after varicose veins and facial wrinkles show up—as they surely will? We are in marriage for better or worse, and that includes looks. Baldness is hereditary. Perhaps young women should decide now if they are prepared to love their husbands twenty years down the road, with potbellies and hair in their ears. The importance of physical appearance certainly goes both ways. Elder Joe J. Christensen advised:

> Occasionally, look in a full-length mirror. Certainly we should not become obsessed with how we look, but we should work to improve our physical appearance. . . . The Lord expects us to do the best we can with what He has given us. President McKay said, "Even a barn looks better when it's painted" (CES Fireside, 9 January 1994, Brigham Young University, Provo, Utah).

So, perhaps you should ask yourself: How do I like my appearance? When was the last time I looked in a full-length mirror? President Hinckley made this observation:

> How truly beautiful is a well-groomed young woman who is clean in body and mind. She is a daughter of God in whom her Eternal Father can take pride. How handsome is a young man who is well groomed. He is a son of God, deemed worthy of holding the holy priesthood of God ("Pres. Hinckley's Counsel," *Church News,* 18 November 2000, 12).

You also need to consider your own mental health and that of a prospective spouse. Do you both have stable personalities? What kind of demeanor and temperament do you possess? Do you keep commitments? Are you easily depressed or do you have a chemical imbalance that you're neglecting? Is temperament important to you? Could you live with someone who is sarcastic and of a critical nature, or someone who is unmotivated, or someone who is always stressed out? Of course none of us know ahead of time how we will react to a number of events in marriage, such as parenthood, work schedules, health, stress, Church callings, etc. We are simply saying here that temperament and critical natures do not change simply because we marry. "What you see" in dating and courtship, is most likely "what you get" in marriage.

Listen to this account of a young woman who thought she had found her spouse—only to find out that he wanted a maid rather than a wife:

> After being in school for about two months, I got into a relationship. The guy that I was dating was simply wonderful. Never before had I felt that someone treated me as well as he did. The first couple of months were indescribable. We did everything together, and believe it or not, I never felt like I was around him too much. Then things started to change. Some days we enjoyed a night out, and we took turns paying. I know that it must be hard for guys at times to always pay for girls, so I am more than willing to plan evenings out and "treat him" for a change.
>
> But it was the nights we did not go out that things went downhill. For example, he would call me after class and wonder

what I was going to make him for dinner that night. At first I went along with his every demand, but I began feeling very unappreciated. I mean we were both going to school and both had jobs, so it was not like I wasn't just as busy and sometimes even busier than he was. After dinner, he would always sit there and almost rush me to get things cleaned up because he was bored and wanted to do something else, but never once did he ever offer to do anything. I even began to do his laundry and clean his house at times. I do not know what I was thinking! I have never minded doing nice things for people and I will always go out of my way to do those things as long as I am appreciated, but simple acts of kindness become hard to do once you feel it is expected.

Well, this went on for some time before I was trying to think of some way to get rid of this "needy boy." It was almost as if he could not do anything for himself. To make a long story short, right about the time that I was ready to break the news to him that this would just never work, he began to break the news to me that he felt so deeply that I was the right one for him and that we should get married! It was CRAZY! I didn't know what to do. I was only eighteen and I was not really into the whole idea of dating for a couple of months and being married. I truly feel that he was a great guy, but definitely not for me. My advice to him was that he had better either change his ways, or I wish him the best of luck in one day finding a wife and maid in one!

A few years ago a young couple came for counseling. When the husband was asked what the problem was between the two of them, he indicated that he really didn't know. He felt everything was fine. After he left the room, his wife came in. She was asked the same question: "What's the trouble?" She tried not to cry, but it was obvious she was hurting. She explained that her biggest problem was that her husband was lazy—all he wanted to do was watch TV all day long, and all night too. Initially she thought she was marrying someone who was "going places." But shortly after their wedding day, the husband decided to drop out of school and start his own business. His idea of beginning a business was to stay home and watch *ESPN* all day with the hope that an idea or two would "pop" into his head during Sports Center. When no ideas came after a year and thousands of dollars of debt, she decided there was much more to marriage than living with a couch potato Sports Center expert. Perhaps it wasn't too surprising to see the end of this marriage.

Another aspect of emotional and mental health is an ability to handle stress or a crisis. You would not want to marry someone who hides in the closet or curls up in the fetal position every time something stressful occurs. You want to marry someone who faces life head-on, who can deal with the realities of life. A young father shared this story: Several years ago he and his wife of less than five years moved into a new area. The very week they moved in, their only car broke down, and they had no way to get around town while their car was being repaired. When Sunday came, and they still had no car, they knew that going to church would be a challenge. Since they had just moved into their home, they didn't know anyone to ask for a ride to church. They could have easily missed their Sunday meetings and no one would have known; however, they simply did not feel good about missing church. So they loaded their three children into their stroller and began to walk the one and one-half miles to the meeting-house. The incident occurred in Arizona during the month of June, so it was extremely warm. The husband related that not once did his wife complain or say, "This is ridiculous." That experience made him grateful that he had married someone who felt as strongly about the gospel and the Church as he did. You will want to marry someone who is unafraid of challenges or obstacles.

Spirituality

Spirituality is an important element in marriage and family life. Family scholars who study strong marriages and families (or characteristics of strong marriages and families) always report that *spirituality* is a critical component.[6] In fact, one study revealed that couples who attend church every week are 82 percent less likely to divorce than couples who do not attend any denomination at all.[7] President David O. McKay taught that, "the development of our spiritual nature should concern us most. Spirituality is the highest acquisition of the soul, the divine in man; 'the supreme, crowning gift that makes him king of all created things.' It is the consciousness of victory over self and of communion with the infinite. It is spirituality alone which really gives one the best in life" (in Conference Report, Oct. 1936, 103).

Elder Dean L. Larsen stated that "just as exercise, proper nourishment, and rest are essential to our physical well-being, so are such things as regular prayer, scripture study, Sabbath worship, partaking of the sacrament, and service to others necessary for our spiritual vigor" ("Winding up Our Spiritual Clocks," *Ensign*, Nov.1989, 62). How do you feel about your own spiritual progress? Are you progressing in your faith and personal testimony? Is your life in harmony with the teachings of the Savior and modern-day apostles and prophets? If your life is not where it should be spiritually now, can you make the necessary adjustments? Why is it important that you do? Because you yourself want to marry someone who loves the gospel and seeks to live its principles.

Do you study the scriptures on a regular basis? Do you routinely have your own individual prayer? Are your prayers rather superficial and mechanical in nature, or are you able to commune with your Heavenly Father? Of course, you will want to marry someone who reads the scriptures and prays regularly. Why? Because prayer and scripture study become an individual's armor, and when fully armored, the likelihood of sin and carelessness is greatly reduced, and you are more likely to enjoy the Spirit of the Lord in your life.

There are men and women in the world who seek to improve their intellect and physique before they marry, but there are not many who are working on the critical aspect of spirituality. Spirituality has nothing to do with your pioneer heritage or pedigree chart, academic degrees, social status, current Church calling, how many people you baptized on your mission, or how many verses you may have marked in 3 Nephi 11. Spirituality has to do with your interest in spiritual matters—doctrine, prayer, scripture and Church magazine study, taking institute courses, and listening to the impressions from the Holy Ghost. Spirituality springs from the desire to please your Heavenly Father and to follow the counsel of His servants. Being sensitive to matters of the Spirit does not make life boring. In fact, just the opposite will take place. President Hinckley declared, "We want you to have fun. We want you to enjoy life. We do not want you to be prudes. We want you to be robust and cheerful, to sing and dance, to laugh and be happy. But in so doing be humble and be prayerful, and the smiles of heaven will fall upon you" ("Pres. Hinckley's Counsel," *Church News*, 18 November 2000, 12).

Reading uplifting and inspiring books as individuals and as a couple should be normal and natural activities for both of you. If you were to read just two pages of the Book of Mormon a day (beginning January 1), you could finish the entire book by September. (see Joe J. Christensen, *One Step at a Time: Building a Better Marriage, Family, and You* [1996], 141). Reading scriptures daily helps us draw closer to the Lord. Personal prayer has a similar effect on us. These activities bring a large return for such a small investment.

Social Abilitites

Although there are several aspects to sociality, friendship is perhaps its most identifiable element. Having friends and being friends to others play a crucial role in our moral, emotional, intellectual, and spiritual development. One study of life satisfaction documented that friendship ranked third in importance as the most significant source of happiness.[8]

In Proverbs it states that "A friend loveth at all times" (Proverbs 17:17). The Savior Himself calls us friends when we simply do what He asks of us (see John 15:14). Joseph Smith once said, "If my life is of no value to my friends it is of none to myself" (B.H. Roberts, *A Comprehensive History of the Church*, 6:549). Both Jesus and Joseph were willing to live and die for their friends.

Being a good friend is vital to becoming a good spouse. There is a time-honored cliché that says, "marry your best friend." There aren't many people who are mean, nasty, and critical and then marry someone and live happily ever after. In fact, a good gauge to determine what kind of spouse you will be is to examine how well you treat your friends; for the way you treat your friends now is more than likely how you will treat your spouse.

Ralph Waldo Emerson said that the only way to have a friend is to be one. Elder Robert D. Hales taught the importance of friendship this way:

> Do you know how to recognize a true friend? A real friend loves us and protects us. In recognizing a true friend we must look for two important elements in that friendship: *A true friend makes it easier for us to live the gospel by being around him. Similarly, a true friend does not make us choose between his way and*

the Lord's way ("The Aaronic Priesthood: Return with Honor,"
Ensign, May 1990, 40; emphasis added).

What do real friends do? They love us, they protect us, they
encourage us, they build us up, and they are there for us when we
need a shoulder to lean on. As you prepare for marriage, focus on
being a good friend before you become a lover. Friendship will
become the foundation stone on which your marriage is built. A
marriage without friendship is merely a hollow relationship. Elder
Marion D. Hanks taught that "married people should be *best friends*;
no relationship on earth needs friendship as much as marriage"
("Eternal Marriage," *Ensign,* Nov. 1984, 36). How profound! You will
come to know that happiness for you will come from marrying your
best friend.

How would you rate yourself as a friend to others? Are you a loyal
friend? Are you tuned in to the needs of those around you? Are you a
giver as well as a receiver in your relationships with others?

The most frequently asked question we hear from college-age
students is this: "How can I know that this is the person I am
supposed to marry?" Aside from the obvious spiritual responses to
that question, such as praying and fasting, we in turn often ask this
question: "Is this person your best friend? Can you honestly say that
you would rather be with this person than anyone else?" If they
answer "yes" to this question, they are moving in the right direction.
When you marry your best friend, you are bound to someone who
will encourage you, lift you, and help you become a better person.
Because you are best friends, you will draw closer to your Heavenly
Father and be more likely to keep your covenants. That's what real
friends do for each other.

We suggest that you and your partner fill out the next three pages
individually (make a copy). Think about what you really want in a
future spouse, and then rate yourself in that area. If you are not
currently in a relationship, decide where you stand on an issue before
you start dating someone and how you would like to improve.

PREPARING FOR CELESTIAL MARRIAGE

	What I expect from my future spouse	What I offer
Intellect:		
College or equivalent training		
Plans for graduate studies		
Reading of uplifting material		
Study habits		
Grades attained		
Political views		
Language use/skills		
Continuing education		
Physical:		
Appearance		
Sleep habits		
Balanced meals		
Word of Wisdom observance		
Regular exercise		
Weight management		
Sports participation		
Emotional/Mental:		
Attitudes and Moods		
Emotional stability		
Self motivation		
Personality traits		

PREPARING FOR CELESTIAL MARRIAGE, Cont.

	What I expect from my future spouse	What I offer
Emotional/Mental:		
Dependability		
Sense of humor		
Task completion		
Honesty		
Sensitivity to feelings of others		
Depression/anxiety		
Feelings of self-worth		
Spirituality:		
Strength of testimony		
Patterns of prayer		
Scripture study		
Sabbath-day observance		
Payment of tithing		
Service for others		
Attendance at religious services		
Successful missionary service (male)		
Temple attendance		
Morality		
Obedience to civic and social laws		
Commitments to covenants and ordinances		

Preparing For Celestial Marriage, Cont.

	What I expect from my future spouse	What I offer
Spirituality:		
Magnification of callings		
Social Abilities:		
Friendliness/outgoing qualities		
People skills		
Kindness/Charity		
Television-viewing habits		
Appropriate music-listening habits		
Appropriate video-watching habits		
Manners		
Shared interests		
Leadership skills		
Desire to be an effective parent		
Money management		
Family background		
Current events awareness		
Care of possessions		
Attitude toward wealth/ possessions		

CHAPTER 4

Finding the Right Spouse

"The greatest single factor affecting what you are going to be tomorrow, your activity, your attitudes, your eventual destiny . . . is the one decision you make that moonlit night when you ask that individual to be your companion for life. That's the most important decision of your entire life! It isn't where you are going to school, or what lessons you are going to study, or what your major is, or how you are going to make your living. These, though important, are incidental and nothing compared with the important decision that you make when you ask someone to be your companion for eternity." [1]

Every couple has a unique story to tell about how they found each other. There are no ordinary circumstances, it seems, that lead a couple to decide to marry. The details about how couples meet, become engaged, and ultimately decide to marry always make for a fascinating tale. For instance, most of us have heard of couples who met in classes they took together, in family home evening groups, after dating each other's best friends, or on their missions. The most interesting stories, however, are those where the two actually detested each other at first, but somehow, through a series of unusual events, finally developed feelings of love for each other and made the decision to marry.

Janet Lee shared such an experience. She related that after her first date with Rex she wasn't sure if she would give him a "return appointment." The next day the phone rang, and it was Rex and his friend, serenading Janet over the phone. The lyrics of the song they sang, however, included these lines: "When I see you walk in the room, it makes my eyeballs smart. Why don't you go fall off your broom, and break your cold, cold heart." Of course, Janet wasn't impressed. To her, the lyrics of that song were cutting and hurtful. Rex had to explain that he only sang that song to the girls he really liked because it was one of the only songs he knew. For him, the lyrics had nothing to do with the song. Thankfully, Janet gave Rex another chance, and the rest, as they say, is history (See Rex and Janet Lee, "Keeping an Open Mind About things That Matter," in *Brigham Young University 1990–91 Devotional and Fireside Speeches* [1991], 9–11).

Some believe in love at first sight (if you see *Sleepless in Seattle* or *Saturday's Warrior,* you may get caught up in believing that too), while most of us believe it takes some time to "fall in love." Regardless of how it happens to you, deciding who and when to marry are the most exciting and thrilling decisions of your life. Your future children will be most interested in how you got together. It will be fun to share with them the details of the adventure that led you to make that important decision to marry in the temple.

On the other hand, the process of selecting an eternal companion is frustrating for many because of its difficulty and impact on the heartstrings. Because you want to be certain that the person you choose to marry is the best and most compatible individual for you, courtship can be a time of stress and anxiety. Listen to this young woman's thoughts:

> I think that we often get so caught up with finding the person the Lord wants us to marry that we forget that He wants US to make that decision. I was once dating a boy that I really could not see myself marrying. But when I came to campus I was very lonely and thought that maybe the Lord wanted me to marry this boy. When I knelt down to pray about it I couldn't even begin to ask. I knew that he was not what I was looking for and it dawned on me that the Lord would not want me to marry someone that I did not love and have a desire to be with forever. Marriage is hard enough as it is. A person should go into marriage knowing that they chose that person because they did not want to be with anyone else.

It comes down to this: Do you want someone to marry you because they are merely being obedient to the Lord? Or do you want to marry someone who knows you—good and bad points—yet loves you for all that you are and then asks the Lord's blessings in marrying you. I want someone to love me because they know me and not just because he feels that he has to marry me because he is getting older, or his parents or friends are pushing him on me. I want to marry someone whom I admire and respect and who I know will help me to become a better person, someone who loves me—warts and all! And I want to marry him because I know his weaknesses as well as his strengths and still love him with all my heart!

May we remind you that the Lord wants you to choose wisely. As the Apostle John taught, "There is no fear in love; [and] perfect love casteth out fear" (1 Jn 4:18). Put your trust in the Lord and move forward in faith. Marriage is the next step in your life if you are of the proper age, and it is the right thing to do. If you are mature in your personality and character, you will feel the gentle nudgings of the Spirit toward marriage, and feelings of peace will come to you as you seek the will of the Lord. Deciding who to marry is an adventure that generally can't be rushed. It can't be made after only one or two dates even if you do find yourselves compatible in music albums and yogurt flavors.

There are a number of issues that need your attention and consideration. Over the years many students have visited with us in our offices, wanting to know "how you know." In fact, "how do you know?" is the most frequently asked question among eligible men and women. So let's look at some issues that play a part in making this momentous decision. (At the end of this chapter we have summarized the key issues in a "final exam" to help you determine whether you are ready for marriage.)

Question #1: Why is marriage so important? There is an attitude among a few single adults that they should wait until they are older to be married. They simply do not have any urgency to marry. Occasionally, you hear some singles spout antimarriage, or antifamily messages. On one occasion, after a fireside speaker had addressed a group of young single adults on the need to be moving toward marriage, the individual who gave the closing prayer said, "Heavenly Father, we appreciate the message we heard tonight on marriage, but we are grateful that we are single!" Such individuals may not recognize that marriage, like baptism, is an essential ordinance of the gospel. When was the last time you heard nine- or ten-year-olds bragging that they hadn't yet been baptized? Baptism is the covenant of salvation and is necessary to enter the celestial kingdom, while marriage is the covenant of exaltation and a requirement for admittance into the highest degree in that kingdom (see D&C 131:1–4).

Do not misunderstand. We are not pleading here for returned missionaries to marry a week after they are home. How long you have been home from a mission is not the issue. The days of mission presidents advising (or even challenging) their departing missionaries to be married within six months after they arrive home are long gone. In fact, a few years ago, the First Presidency authorized this statement in a Church bulletin:

> It is entirely appropriate and desirable that priesthood leaders counsel returning missionaries on the importance of continuing to live standards that will lead to celestial marriage. *It is considered unwise, however, to recommend or imply that the missionary should be married within a specified time period following his release. . . . the returned missionary should not feel pressured by specific time constraints in approaching this very personal, sacred, and significant decision* ("General Announcement," *Bulletin*, 1993, no. 2, 2; emphasis added).

On the other hand, mature young adults should be "*anxiously engaged* in a good cause." Marriage is an obligation of every man who understands his duty and responsibility to initiate opportunities that lead to that ordinance. *The Family: A Proclamation to the World* states that "marriage between a man and a woman is ordained of God and that the family is central to the Creator's plan for the eternal destiny of His children"(September 1995). God wants us to marry, if we can, just like He wants us to be baptized.

Elder Bruce R. McConkie told of an experience where he and his wife were reviewing their blessings. His wife asked him: "What's the greatest blessing that has ever come into your life?" Without hesitation Elder McConkie said, "The greatest blessing that has ever come to me was [the day] when I was privileged to kneel in the Salt Lake Temple at the Lord's altar and receive you as an eternal companion." His wife congratulated him on his correct answer. Then the Apostle explained to the audience he was addressing that "the most important single thing that any Latter-day Saint does in this world is to marry the right person, in the right place, by the right authority" ("Agency or Inspiration," *New Era*, Jan. 1975, 38). A temple marriage is the crowning ordinance of the gospel. Joseph Fielding Smith, Jr., taught this simple concept: "No ordinance connected with the gospel of Jesus Christ is of greater importance, of more solemn and sacred nature, and more necessary to the eternal joy of man, than marriage" (*The Way To Perfection* [1984], 232).

In addition to marriage being an essential ordinance to qualify for exaltation, the attributes and traits that are necessary to live with others in the celestial kingdom are probably best learned in marriage and family life. The most effective way to learn selflessness is in a marriage. And who would not agree that humility accompanies parenthood? Thus, it is in our homes that we learn to be more Christlike; it is in the family that we learn to strip ourselves of pride; it is in marriage that we gain faith, virtue, knowledge, temperance, patience, brotherly kindness, godliness, charity, humility, and diligence (see D&C 4). No wonder marriage is ordained of God. Heavenly Father wants His children to become like Him, and marriage and family life are the best ways to prepare each of us to live with others in a celestial environment.

Question # 2: Dating can be frustrating. What attributes in another person are the most important to pay attention to? Finding a spouse involves dating and associating with people to learn which attributes they possess best fit your personality and makeup. Dating helps you "narrow the field." There are a number of filters used in the selection process.

The first filter is physical attractiveness. If we do not find a person attractive, generally there will be no first date. However, in many social environments, "hanging out" has replaced formal dating as a way of getting to know one another. This leads to initial friendships that may provide more opportunities for discovering "attractiveness." For beauty, we all understand, is in the eye of the beholder—and aren't we grateful for that? Otherwise everyone would be lined up to date only a few people. Physical attributes must not be the only criteria, for we will all lose that aspect of our attractiveness after a few years of mortality. President David O. McKay warned returned missionaries not to place physical attractiveness at the top of the scale for finding an eternal companion:

> Yes, men are attracted by beauty, and thousands are ensnared by it. There are thousands of men who look for nothing else and who desire nothing else but to have their senses pleased or their passions gratified. These outward adornments will satisfy and only outward adornment will retain. When beauty fades, the passion seeks for gratification elsewhere (*Gospel Ideals*, 450).

President Ezra Taft Benson counseled single sisters of the Church:

> Do not expect perfection in your choice of mate. Do not be so concerned about his physical appearance and his bank account that you overlook his more important qualities. Of course, he should be attractive to you, and he should be able to financially provide for you. But, does he have a strong testimony? Does he live the principles of the gospel and magnify his priesthood? Is he active in his ward and stake? Does he love home and family, and will he be a faithful husband and a good father? (Ezra Taft Benson, "To The Single Adult Sisters of the Church," *Ensign*, Nov. 1988, 96–97).

Of course, one of the most important components of attractiveness is a person's personality. It ought to be. Studies have confirmed that "people who are warm, kind, gregarious, intelligent, interesting, poised, confident, or humorous . . . are much more attractive than those who are rude, insecure, clumsy, unstable . . . irresponsible, or who manifest other negative traits."[2] Women, at least, contend that personality is much more important to them than physical makeup.

The second filter is similarity of world views and life experience. Individuals do best when they date those with similar values, beliefs, traits, education, religion, and cultural background. This is another sensitive area, of course. With the worldwide expansion of The Church of Jesus Christ of Latter-day Saints, we see more and more individuals of differing cultural backgrounds dating and marrying. Although such couples can certainly adapt to each other, our experience in marriage counseling shows that cultural differences can certainly complicate the issue of unification between husband and wife. We merely alert you here to the issue. If you are contemplating such a marriage, we suggest that you visit with a few married couples who come from different cultural backgrounds to become more aware of the added challenges and blessings such a union might produce. Our intent here is simply to make you aware that such differences can affect a marriage to varying degrees.

The long-standing principle has always been that the more similar two people are in their mental, emotional, and spiritual traits, the more likely they are to be compatible as marriage partners. Those factors can override other typical barriers. There are many wonderful people you might not be similar to, and that's okay. Their opinions may be too strong for you, or they don't match your energy level, or their self-centeredness is not to your liking. But there are many people who do have views and a background similar to yours and they are most likely the ones who will attract your attention. Research confirms that the more similar individuals are in areas of education, socioeconomic class, and age, the more likely it is that their marriage will succeed.[3] Look for a companion who has similar ideas, ideals, and standards to your own.

The third filter is similarity in religion and family background. We assume that if you are reading this book, you are a Latter-day Saint looking for a companion among those of your own religious persuasion. If not, make that your commitment now. The importance of the gospel in your life and that of your spouse is critical if you want to do well in marriage. Consider potential marriage partners from this viewpoint: How important is religion and the gospel to them? What are their attitudes on family home evening, following the prophets, seminary/institute attendance, individual and family prayer, scripture study, and personal honesty? If the individual is a returned missionary, you can tell something about their spirituality by how they regard their mission service and speak of their mission and its leaders. You will want to know something about each other's family background and family interests. You might want to observe if the person you are dating has stable parents, and if the parents have a stable marriage themselves. Even though understanding and applying gospel principles can help your spouse overcome difficulties in background, this issue needs your careful attention and evaluation.

The fourth filter is finding someone you get along well with—someone who complements your personality. You will want to find someone you enjoy being with and with whom you enjoy talking; one who is excited to see you—and you them—after a period of being apart. In our Church doctrine we talk of living with someone for eternity—far longer than a million years! Ask yourself: Do your interests mesh? Are your temperaments compatible? Are you prepared to be with a person who is high-strung and nervous? What about attitudes and values? Do you both have the desire and ability to meet each other's needs? Are you similar in expectations concerning gender roles? Personal habits? You will have a more fulfilling relationship if you are compatible in your expectations about the roles of men and women, and if you tolerate well each other's personal habits. We often joke about squeezing the toothpaste tube in the middle versus rolling it up from the bottom, or the direction the toilet paper hangs from the spool. In reality, if you are preoccupied with such trivial matters, you probably shouldn't be getting married in the first place. Marriage requires a high degree of maturity, flexibility and mutual tolerance of each other's idiosyncrasies.

President N. Eldon Tanner shared the following counsel:

> When young people come to me for advice about courtship and marriage I usually suggest that they ask themselves the following questions:
>
> What kind of mother or father do I want my children to have?
>
> What kind of parent am I prepared to be?
>
> Do I want to associate with someone because of his or her popularity only, or do I look deeper for spiritual and moral qualities?
>
> Am I analyzing our similarities and differences in background, culture, and intellect?

Am I prepared to adjust to these differences?

Do I realize that such adjustments need to be made before marriage?

These considerations will certainly help in making a proper choice for a companion with whom one is prepared to spend eternity. Then after the marriage there are many responsibilities that cannot be taken lightly; but with each contracting party assuming his or her full share of the responsibility, there is nothing in this life that will bring greater satisfaction and happiness ("Celestial Marriages and Eternal Families," *Ensign*, May 1980, 17).

What we so routinely label as "falling in love" turns out to be a process that occurs over a period of time and interaction. Time together and apart are important factors in building relationships. We all tend to be a little phony on the first few dates (despite our protests to the contrary). Personality deficiencies can be hidden when you're together only a few hours a day. Individuals can submerge bad temperament, selfishness, and arrogance during the short time on dates together. It is important that you see each other at times formal and informal; in private as well as in public. You must go into the dating and courting scene with your head and heart coordinated.

To review, key filters include attractiveness, a similarity of viewpoints and circumstances, similar backgrounds, and compatibility in feelings for one another. If a person to whom you are attracted makes it past these four filters, you know you have a more sound basis for continuing the relationship

Question #3: What counsel is there for a young woman trying to decide between a mission or marriage to a young man? When Dan came home from his mission he resumed a relationship with Sue, a young lady he had dated before his mission. As their relationship progressed, the young lady was torn. She really wanted to marry Dan, who was now home again, but she also wanted to serve a mission. After much prayer and fasting, Sue decided to go on a mission, although she was pretty smitten with Dan. Meanwhile, as Sue was preparing for her mission, Dan was hired as an instructor at the Missionary Training Center. As fate would have it, Sue ended up being with her cohort of missionaries in a classroom just a few doors down from the classroom where Dan taught. This was a challenging situation to say the least.

Due to the proximity of their classrooms, Dan and Sue ended up seeing each other more often than they felt comfortable with. It became an awkward situation. They both were having difficulty focusing upon their tasks. One day they decided to seek the counsel of the president of the Missionary Training Center. After explaining their feelings for each other to him, the president looked at her and said, "Whenever a young woman has a choice between marriage and a mission, we recommend that she marry. I can have you released in two minutes." Dan and Sue asked the mission president if they could have a few minutes to be alone. They prayed and contemplated the matter again. After their prayer, they eventually did get married—a year and a half later. They were married shortly after Sue returned from her mission to Belgium!

Perhaps above anything else, this story reminds all of us that the "mission or marriage" decision is personal—between those involved and the Lord. However, for those who struggle with this matter, consider prophetic counsel. Priesthood leaders are instructed that women should not be recommended for a mission if it would interfere with a suitable marriage proposal ("General Announcement," *Bulletin*, 1993, no. 2, 2). President Hinckley spoke directly on this sensitive matter:

> Now I wish to say something to bishops and stake presidents concerning missionary service. It is a sensitive matter. There seems to be growing in the Church an idea that all young women as well as all young men should go on missions. We need some young women. They perform a remarkable work. They can get in homes where the elders cannot.
>
> I confess that I have two granddaughters on missions. They are bright and beautiful young women. They are working hard and accomplishing much good. Speaking with their bishops and their parents, they made their own decisions to go. They did not tell me until they turned their papers in. I had nothing to do with their decision to go.
>
> Now, having made that confession, I wish to say that the First Presidency and the Council of the Twelve are united in

saying to our young sisters that they are not under obligation to go on missions. I hope I can say what I have to say in a way that will not be offensive to anyone. Young women should not feel that they have a duty comparable to that of young men. Some of them will very much wish to go. If so, they should counsel with their bishop as well as their parents. If the idea persists, the bishop will know what to do.

I say what has been said before, that missionary work is essentially a priesthood responsibility. As such, our young men must carry the major burden. This is their responsibility and their obligation.

We do not ask the young women to consider a mission as an essential part of their life's program. Over a period of many years, we have held the age level higher for them in an effort to keep the number going relatively small. Again to the sisters I say that you will be as highly respected, you will be considered as being as much in the line of duty, your efforts will be as acceptable to the Lord and to the Church whether you go on a mission or do not go on a mission.

We constantly receive letters from young women asking why the age for sister missionaries is not the same as it is for elders. We simply give them the reasons. We know that they are disappointed. We know that many have set their hearts on missions. We know that many of them wish this experience before they marry and go forward with their adult lives. I certainly do not wish to say or imply that their services are not wanted. I simply say that a mission is not necessary as a part of their lives ("Some Thoughts on Temples, Retention of Converts, and Missionary Service," *Ensign,* Nov. 1997, 52).

Do young women make fantastic missionaries? Yes. Should they serve missions? Perhaps. Nevertheless, if a young woman has a choice between serving a mission or being married to a faithful priesthood holder in the temple, she is advised to choose the latter.

Question #4: What about soul mates? Is there really just one person out there for me? There is not one particular person out there for you, though there will be only one that you eventually marry. Gratefully enough, your task is not to find the proverbial "needle in the haystack." Elder Joseph Fielding Smith wrote,

> We have no scriptural justification . . . for the belief that we had the privilege of choosing our . . . life companions in the spirit world. This belief has been advocated by some, and *it is possible that in some instances it is true,* but it would require too great a stretch of the imagination to believe it to be so in all, or even in the majority of cases (*The Way to Perfection* [1984], 44; emphasis added).

Of course, there can be exceptions, as President Smith indicated. We know of individuals who possess patriarchal blessings that seem to indicate some acquaintance and selection before this life. But the general counsel is that there is not one soul mate for you. To the question, "Is this the one person that I am supposed to marry?" we simply say, you're making the marriage decision much more difficult than it needs to be. Find a person that you feel a measure of compatibility with and you can *make* him or her your soul mate by the way you treat that person. Prophetic counsel is that *almost* any two people who love the Lord, who will follow His prophets, keep the commandments, and are humble, will do well in marriage. President Spencer W. Kimball clarified this point:

> "Soul mates" are fiction and an illusion; and while every young man and young woman will seek with all diligence and prayerfulness to find a mate with whom life can be most compatible and beautiful, yet it is certain that almost any good man and any good woman can have happiness and a successful marriage if both are willing to pay the price. (*The Teachings of Spencer W. Kimball,* ed. Edward L. Kimball [1982], 306).

Question #5: How do I know when I am in love? We aren't aware of a formula that answers this question exactly. But we can give you some general guidelines. First of all, when you are with your prospective mate, do you feel like you have "finally come home"? That is to say you no longer have to pretend or put up a false front in each other's presence; you can simply be yourselves together and your relationship feels normal and natural. As one mother commented, "I knew my daughter was in love because when she brought Steven home, she acted normal. I had never seen Lisa act that way with a young man before." Elder Bruce C. Hafen has written, "There is some kind of mysterious magnetism that draws us toward one another, like homing pigeons looking for home. And when we have paid the price of patient preparation, self-discipline, and an irrevocable commitment to another person's happiness, we can taste the sweet joy of authentic human love" (*The Belonging Heart* [1994], 8–9). Have you felt that magnetism with your prospective spouse?

Next, have you become best friends? When students ask how they can know if they are in love, we often ask them in return, "Can you honestly say that _____ is your best friend?" If the person you are courting has become your best friend, and you would rather be with them than with anyone else, including long-standing friends of the same or opposite gender, then you can be more assured that what you are feeling is approaching the definition of love. One young man grew up with three great Latter-day Saint friends. From the time they were deacons they planned to be college roommates. After their missions, their dream became a reality. Then, the young man began to date and fall in love with a special woman. He said, "I knew I was in love when I realized that I would rather be with Cindy than anyone else. I watched my roommates go and play intramural sports, snow ski, and hike, and I didn't even care. I just wanted to be with her." Indeed, happiness is marrying your best friend.

Elder Hafen counseled:

> Be friends first and sweethearts second. Relationships between young men and young women should be built like a pyramid. The base of the pyramid is friendship. And the ascending layers are built of things like time, understanding, respect, and restraint. Right at the top of the pyramid is a glittering little mystery called romance. . . . Now you don't have to be very smart to know that a pyramid won't stand up very long if you stand it on its point and expect the point to hold up everything else. In other words, be friends first and sweethearts later, not the other way around. Otherwise, people who think they are sweethearts may discover they can't be very good friends, and by then it may be too late ("The Gospel and Romantic Love," *Ensign*, Oct 1982, 67).

The test, then, is to look at the strength of your friendship without physical affection or romantic imagery clouding your mind and heart. If physical affection is the most important aspect of your present relationship, then you should be concerned about your reasons for being interested in the other person. If affection is your primary motivation for being in the relationship, there is a danger that your romance is built primarily on physical attraction, which is a rather sandy foundation. When reality hits in marriage, as it always does, there could be a major mud slide. You do not want to end up like the following couple that courted for five months, but ended up being married for only two months:

> During four of these courtship months they were engaged, yet they passed through this period being simply entertained, with almost no interaction other than sharing physical expressions of affection hour after degenerating hour. Following the honeymoon, they awakened to find that neither had married the type of person [they] thought [they] were married to. They both thought each had married an apple. But it turned out that one partner was a peach and the other was an orange. They are now paying the price of trying to figure out whether they can become compatible and fulfilled in their relationship. It's tragic to think that they didn't pay the price of determining their compatibility prior to marriage (Yorgason, Baker, & Burr, *From Two to One* [1981], 32).

Another important component: Does your prospective mate inspire you to be your best self? Does being together foster within you a desire to do better, to be a more complete person? President David O. McKay shared an experience he had while a college student. He was walking from the campus with his friend, George Q. Morris. As they were walking they began to talk about girls and how they would know when they were in love. "Brother George answered this on the subject, 'I don't know, but my mother once told us boys we should choose the girl who inspires us to do our best, in whose presence we feel a desire to achieve and to make the most of ourselves'" (David O. McKay, *My Young Friends: President McKay Speaks to Youth*, ed. L.R. McKay [1976], 48). Does the person you are dating inspire you to nobler heights? Do you want to live more righteously because of your association with that person?

The way we use the term *love* in our culture is vague at best. We say that we *love* steak, that we *love* skiing, and that we *love* our families. The Greeks didn't have the same problem we have in modern English; they had several different words for *love*. In Greek, *philia* is brotherly love, or love for mankind, the kind of love we express to friends, ward members, and family members. *Eros* is romantic, affectionate love; it is the love that has physical overtones, that attracts people of the opposite sex to each other. *Poimaino* is nurturing love. It is the type of love that inspires us to care for others. Another type of love is *agape*. Simply put, this is godlike love, unlimited, allowing us the capacity to forgive. It is selflessness, kindness, and charity all wrapped up in one word. It is loving someone else more than you love yourself. Elder Marvin J. Ashton taught that "True love and happiness in courtship and marriage are based upon honesty, self-respect, sacrifice, consideration, courtesy, kindness, and placing 'we' ahead of 'me'" ("We Serve That Which We Love," *Ensign*, May 1981, 23). We believe that to be prepared for marriage, each of these dimensions of love must be present in your relationship.

President Spencer W. Kimball declared that "if two people love the Lord more than their own lives and then love each other more than their own lives, working together in total harmony with the gospel program as their basic structure, they are sure to have . . . great happiness" (Spencer W. Kimball, *The Teachings of Spencer W. Kimball*, ed. Edward L. Kimball [1982], 309). So, here is the question to consider: Do you love your prospective partner as much or more than you do yourself? Are you willing to sacrifice (if you were married to each other) your interests for the good of this individual? We believe in the adage that says "when you sacrifice for a cause, you will come to love that cause." How do you learn to love another person? By sacrificing your own interests in their behalf. You become anxious to have the other person see and feel the blessings of life.

Another question to consider is whether you would love the person you are dating or engaged to if something tragic happened to their now-perfect body? If they incurred a mental or physical illness, would you still be kind and charitable to them? President Kimball gave this example:

For many years, I saw a strong man carry his tiny, emaciated, arthritic wife to meetings and wherever she could go. There could be no sexual expression. Here was selfless indication of affection. I think that is pure love. I saw a kindly woman wait on her husband for many years as he deteriorated with muscular dystrophy. She waited on him hand and foot, night and day, when all he could do was blink his eyes in thanks. I believe that was love. If anyone feels that petting or other deviations are demonstrations of love, let him ask himself: "If this beautiful body that I have misused suddenly became deformed, or paralyzed, would my reactions be the same? If this lovely face were scarred by flames, or this body I have used were to suddenly become rigid, would there still be love?" Answers to these questions might test one to see if he really is in love or if it is only physical attraction that has encouraged the improper physical contacts (Spencer W. Kimball, *Faith Precedes the Miracle* [1972], 158).

You must learn to distinguish between love, lust, and infatuation. Some people think they are feeling love when in reality their feelings are more of infatuation, or worse, lustful in nature. President Spencer W. Kimball explained the difference this way:

The young man who protects his sweetheart against all use or abuse, against insult and infamy from himself or others, could be expressing true love. But the young man who uses his companion as a biological toy to give himself temporary satisfaction—that is lust.

A young woman who conducts herself to be attractive spiritually, mentally, and physically but will not by word or dress or act stir or stimulate to physical reactions the companion beside her could be expressing true love. That young woman who must touch and stir and fondle and tempt and use exhibits lust and exploitation (Spencer W. Kimball, *Faith Precedes the Miracle* [1972], 158–159).

He also described true love this way:

One might become immediately attracted to another individual, but love is far more than physical attraction. It is deep, inclusive, and comprehensive. Physical attraction is only one of the many elements; there must be faith and confidence and understanding and partnership. There must be common ideals and standards. There must be great devotion and companionship. Love is cleanliness and progress and sacrifice and selflessness. This kind of love never tires or wanes, but lives through sickness and sorrow, poverty and privation, accomplishment and disappointment, time and eternity. For the love to continue, there must be an increase constantly of confidence and understanding, of frequent and sincere expression of appreciation and affection. There must be a forgetting of self and a constant concern for the other. Interests, hopes, objectives must be constantly focused into a single channel (Spencer W. Kimball, *Faith Precedes the Miracle* [1972], 157–158).

Consider the following chart that compares love, infatuation, and lust.

LOVE * (I Corinthians 13)	INFATUATION	LUST•
Suffers long; is long lasting; endures difficulty	Is always in a rush; doesn't do well with problems	Bails out on the first "bump" or problem.
Does not envy; is not jealous	Is jealous and suspicious	Is based on envy and covetousness
Is not puffed up, boastful, or arrogant	Is more worried about what others think instead of what God thinks	Is boastful, proud, and arrogant
Does not behave unseemingly, or indecently	Much of the relationship is private, behind closed doors	Is indecent, lewd, and inappropriate
Seeketh not her own; is not selfish	Is self-gratifying	Craves itself; pure selfishness
Is not easily provoked; secure	Is insecure and suspicious	Is easily provoked to arguments, anger
Thinketh no evil	Relationship is based on physical contact	Bathes itself in evil; leads to fornication
Rejoices not in sin, but in truth; wants to be good; wants to improve self	Is willing to compromise or rationalize truth for sin	Enjoys sin more than truth
Beareth all things	Will worry about consequences later	Believes there are no consequences

* Adapted from R.W. Jeppson, *Turn Yourselves and Live: Is Anything Too Hard for the Lord?* [1998], 10. Adapted from Todd Parker, *Serving with Strength* [1994], 190.
• Adapted from Spencer W. Kimball, *Faith Precedes the Miracle* [1972], 151–158.

Question #6: What are some red flags that we should be sensitive to as we approach the decision to marry? When we visit with troubled married couples, we ask if any of the behavior that is now so distressing or disturbing to them was present during their courtship. Surprisingly, many will say, "Yes, I noticed it, but I thought once we were married it would go away." Others say, "I tried not to notice it." Our counsel to you: Please don't ignore the clues, hints, and cues you pick up in dating. If your fiancé tells you to only call at night between the hours of 11:30 and 11:45 P.M., and requests that you do not ask for them by name, but just give the code "A6758," you might want to reconsider the relationship! If you believe they have nuclear weapons in a storage facility, or a bionic limb, you have not dated one another long enough! Count the red flags in this young woman's narrative:

> Throughout my childhood I always planned on getting married in the temple. However, I never really gave it much thought because I had no idea how hard Satan was going to try and take that away from me. For the first time in my life, I am coming to realize that it (a temple marriage) may not happen unless I change a lot of things in my life. Therefore, I am taking this class, hoping to regain my eternal perspective.
>
> The number one thing that I have to change is who I date. I have not made very wise decisions on who I spend my time with. I am currently dating a man who is divorced. The more I attend class and read the material, the more I realize that that is a serious red flag. I knew that divorce was bad, but I can see its effects on him. Unfortunately, I have fallen in love with him, and I don't know if I can leave him. He is not good for me. Everything I have learned tells me that loud and clear, but I am scared of being alone. However, I am learning that if I stay with him, I will be alone (in eternity). When I am reading the text and manual I sometimes think it says, "Betty, get out now." But I don't. And every day, I grow even closer to someone who cannot give me what I want and think I deserve.
>
> Sometimes I feel it is too late for someone like me. I feel I lost my chance a long time ago. But I catch myself thinking these things and I know that it is Satan. His biggest tool against me is my sense of self-worth. I am fighting like crazy against him. I am finally understanding why he tries so hard to ruin a celestial

marriage. I always knew that it was because we cannot be exalted without a temple marriage. But I never realized what is motivating Satan even more. He will never have the opportunity to be a spouse or a parent. Since I am fighting to be those things, he is working even harder to take it away so I can be miserable like him.

The scariest thing that I've learned so far is that if I continue on the path I am on, I will be single for eternity. That frightens me. I want all the things that you talk about in class. I want to be married in the temple and sealed to a dozen children forever. I want a companion. I can't imagine what it would be like to have someone in my life that wants to talk all night with me about our relationship. My boyfriend now hates to talk, and it seems that I have to talk about everything, right down to why he blinked twice when he said he loved me last night. The combination does not make for a pleasant conversation.

We fight every day and I know it is because we do not have the Spirit with us. He left his wife and children for petty reasons as far as I am concerned. I know that I am not the one to judge if the divorce was justified, but if it wasn't, then perhaps the same problems will develop in our relationship. The main reason I know that he is wrong for me is that I am not happy. I am simply not happy.

There are a number of red flags that you should be on the lookout for. As you consider a possible spouse, ask yourself the following questions:

Does this person:

- Have extreme views on politics, gospel topics, religion, family, or world affairs?
- Encourage me to develop my own talents and skills, or do they want to keep me hidden in a closet away from the rest of the world?
- Allow me private time? Are they possessive in wanting to be with me all day, all the time, or do they encourage me to have my own interests, and my own life too?
- Allow me to spend time with my friends and family members, or are they jealous of that time? Do they like my friends? Are they threatened by my spending time with others?

- Compare me to past boyfriends or girlfriends?
- Take an interest in other people? Is he or she selfish? Does the world seem to revolve around them? (Be alert to severe personality faults that may represent deep insecurities, excessive jealousy, uncontrolled temper, and inflexibility.) Am I prepared to deal with someone who is never wrong, who came from the "true family"? (Look for humility and meekness, yet someone who possesses personal confidence too.)
- Find fault with Church policies, leaders, or programs? Are they often critical or negative about the requirements of the gospel way of life? Is obedience to gospel principles an important priority in their life?
- Complain about spending time with my family? When they are with my family, do they enjoy that time building relationships with my family members, or do they hide in the corner watching television or continually look at their watch? How do they relate to their own family members? Is there a "good spirit" in their home? Is everyone friendly with each other? (People who come from dysfunctional families may have difficulties in their own families later on.)
- Enjoy work, or do they complain about colleagues and supervisors? What about such character traits as honesty, morality, humility, or meekness?
- Critical of my appearance? Do they tell me that I need to lift weights, go jogging, or join a health club to lose some extra pounds? Do they make light of my weight or other bodily characteristics?
- Verbally, physically, or emotionally abuse me? Do they tear me down, and then try to recover a few days later as "Mr. (or Ms.) Nice Guy," promising me that their outburst will never happen again? (Please don't fall for this line. In our counseling experience we have seen too many tragedies that have been perpetrated by this insincere attempt to manipulate others.)
- Need to make major spiritual or emotional changes? Do they promise that these changes will occur *after* I marry them? (If you believe this story, we have a 1971 Datsun for sale.)

- Have a stable history of work, jobs, school, and missions? Are they responsible for their actions or is someone else always to blame?
- Have the same goals, dreams, and aspirations as I do?
- Have a sports addiction and I don't? Can they survive life and important events without viewing Sports Center every night? Do they spend an excessive amount of time on the computer or the Internet? Could pornography be a factor in their life?[4]

We have listed these warning signs, or red flags, in the hope that you will look carefully at the individual you are dating, and at the dynamics of your relationship. Perhaps you can adjust to one or two of those traits we listed above, and, of course, change and repentance is always a possibility for all of us, but we compiled the list from working with people and their marital problems. If there are several of the problems listed above in your present relationship, you might want to look elsewhere, or perhaps rethink a decision to move toward a marriage for unwise reasons that could backfire later.

Question #7: Will the Lord help me know that this is the right person for me to marry? This is an important question. Let's review: So far the relationship feels right. You feel strong feelings of love and affection for each other. You want to marry in the temple. You enjoy being together and spending quality time talking and playing. It seems as if everything is falling into place. You have studied it out in your mind and heart and it just feels right. If all of these characteristics of the relationship are present, it is time to ask the Lord for His sanction of the marriage.

There are a few things to be aware of when you approach the Lord with this question. LDS author Gerald Lund shared a story about his experiences in teaching institute classes in southern California. There wasn't a semester that went by, he recalled, that he didn't have an experience wherein a female student would approach him and tell him that the young man she had been dating had received a revelation that they were to marry. He went on to say that it was interesting how many of his female students not only felt intimidated by such a declaration, but also obligated. LDS family therapist and scholar Carlfred Broderick has labeled these revelations "hormonal revelations" (*Brigham Young University 1997–98 Speeches* [1998], 81–82).

Let's analyze this issue a little more carefully. Is a young woman bound by her boyfriend's "revelations"? She may wonder if this is a priesthood issue with which she is unfamiliar. The answer is *no*. There is a principle of stewardship involved in obtaining revelation. A young man cannot receive a revelation for a young woman any more than he can receive a revelation for the stake president where he lives. The presiding officer of the stake receives revelation for the stake, the bishop for his ward, and parents for their children, especially when the children are still immature. It would not pertain to whom their child is to marry, though a young man or woman would be wise to listen to their parents. Young single adults don't receive revelation for other young single adults. Elder Dallin H. Oaks explained this idea further:

> If a revelation is outside the limits of stewardship, you know it is not from the Lord, and you are not bound by it. I have heard of cases where a young man told a young woman she should marry him because he had received a revelation that she was to be his eternal companion. If this is a true revelation, it will be confirmed directly to the woman if she needs to know. In the meantime, she is under no obligation to heed it. She should seek her own guidance and make up her own mind. The man can receive revelation to guide his own actions, but he cannot properly receive revelation to direct hers. She is outside his stewardship (*Speeches of the Year* [1981], 25).

Of course you will want the Lord's approval of your choice of an eternal companion. Here is some counsel from an Apostle to help you make such an important decision:

> It is not, never has been, and never will be the design and purpose of the Lord— however much we seek Him in prayer— to answer all our problems and concerns without struggle and effort on our part. This mortality is a probationary estate. In it we have our agency. We are being tested to see how we will respond in various situations; how we will decide issues; what course we will pursue while we are here walking, not by sight, but by faith. Hence, we are to solve our own problems and then to counsel with the Lord in prayer and receive a spiritual confir-

mation that our decisions are correct (Bruce R. McConkie, "Why the Lord Ordained Prayer," *Ensign,* January 1976, 11).

Elder McConkie spoke to those who feel they need the Lord to tell them *who* they should marry. He explained the following:

> Maybe it will be a little shock to you, but never in my life did I ever ask the Lord whom I ought to marry. It never occurred to me to ask Him. I went and found the girl I wanted; she suited me; I evaluated and weighed the proposition, and it just seemed a hundred percent to me as though this ought to be. Now, if I'd done things perfectly, I'd have done some counseling with the Lord, which I didn't do; but all I did was pray to the Lord and ask for some guidance and direction in connection with the decision that I'd reached ("Agency or Inspiration," *New Era,* Jan. 1975, 40).

Of course, the perfect way would be to seek the Lord's inspiration along the way as you are getting acquainted and you see the relationship flowering and developing between you. In prayer, plead and ask your Heavenly Father to guide you so that you will not be deceived. If you are eligible to go to the temple, that would be a good place to discuss the matter with your Heavenly Father. Fasting and prayer are appropriate ways to seek confirmation and inspiration. Take your decision to the Lord and ask Him to confirm your feelings that marriage with this particular person is the right decision. You've done your best thinking and now you need His help. If it is right, you should feel peace and joy, happiness, and confidence about your decision. If it is not right, you will feel doubtful, anxious, depressed, and confused.

Now, a few warnings. Don't think that you will have an angel visit you on top of Mount Olympus (complete with trumpets, harps, and sealed books) to confirm your choice. Many people feel that because this is the most important decision of their lives, the heavens will surely open up to them. After all, you are not simply asking the Lord to help you find a set of lost keys. However, the Spirit of the Lord generally works with us in quiet, calm, gentle, and peaceful ways. Prepare yourself, therefore, for quiet, sure answers. Prepare yourself for answers that are logical. Often, a confirmation will come as you begin to reflect on the way you met and the feelings that have grown inside of you. What caused your hearts to skip a beat each time you were together? Perhaps it was the Spirit of the Lord that influenced your dreams and aspirations to come together, that allowed you to feel right all along. Remember the words of Paul: "All things work together for good to them that love God, to them who are the called according to his purpose" (Rom. 8:28).

There is another point to consider. In the past we have asked couples who are contemplating divorce, "Did you two feel inspired to marry each other in the first place?" Somewhat surprisingly, they will say, "Yes, there was no question that we were to marry each other." When asked why then they are planning a divorce, the spouse will usually say, "He (she) has changed since we got married. This is not the same person I married." Consider the possibility that as you approach Him with this question of marriage, the Lord may say to you, "Yes, you two can have a terrific marriage if you will apply the principles of the gospel to your marriage relationship." This answer presupposes this point: If you do not keep the principles of the gospel and your covenants at the forefront of your marriage, you could end up in difficulty. It is difficult to believe that the Lord would confirm for a couple the decision to marry only to have the couple later divorce. It was not the Lord who changed, but one or both of the individuals. A confirmation on marriage, like all blessings in the gospel, is conditioned upon the worthiness of the two parties and the way they live the gospel in their marriage. We often talk about marriage as a growth mechanism, but we have learned it can also destroy Christlike traits we formerly possessed if we fail to keep our covenants and obligations to the Lord.

Also, you must be ready for Satan's attacks. As you prepare to marry in the temple, he knows he is about to lose another battle, and he is a sore loser. Not only will he increase his efforts to make you unworthy to marry in the house of the Lord, but he will place doubts about marriage in your mind. He is the "master doubt creator"! We have seen many couples make it to the week or even the day before the wedding, only to have cold feet and doubts assail them. Then is the time to remember the peace you felt when you made your decision about marriage and felt a spiritual confirmation. Go forward with faith. Hear these comforting words from Elder Jeffrey R. Holland:

This opposition turns up almost any place something good has happened. It can happen when you are trying to get an education. It can hit you after your first month in your new mission field. It certainly happens in matters of love and marriage. . . . I would like to have a dollar for every person in a courtship who knew he or she had felt the guidance of the Lord in that relationship, had prayed about the experience enough to know it was the will of the Lord, knew they loved each other and enjoyed each other's company, and saw a lifetime of wonderful compatibility ahead—only to panic, to get a brain cramp, to have total catatonic fear sweep over them. They "draw back," as Paul said, if not into perdition at least into marital paralysis.

I am not saying you shouldn't be careful about something as significant and serious as marriage. And I certainly am not saying that a young man can get a revelation that he is to marry a certain person without that young woman getting the same confirmation. I have seen a lot of those one-way revelations in young people's lives. Yes, there are cautions and considerations to make, but once there has been genuine illumination, beware the temptation to retreat from a good thing. If it was right when you prayed about it and trusted it and lived for it, it is right now. Don't give up when the pressure mounts. You can find an apartment. You can win over your mother-in-law. You can sell your harmonica and therein fund one more meal. It's been done before. Don't give in. Certainly don't give in to that being who is bent on the destruction of your happiness. He wants everyone like unto himself. Face your doubts. Master your fears. "Cast not away therefore your confidence." Stay the course and see the beauty of life unfold for you (Jeffrey R. Holland, *Brigham Young University 1998–99 Speeches* [1999], 157–158; emphasis in original).

Questions to Consider

Consider the following questions as they apply to your situation. If you are dating someone, discuss the applicable questions between the two of you. If you are not currently in a relationship, decide where you stand on an issue before you start dating someone and how you would like to improve.

1. Are we better people when we are with each other? Do we bring out the best in each other? In what ways? How do we want to be better for each other?

2. Do either of us want to date anyone else? (If you answer yes to this question, then you are likely not ready for marriage.) In what ways are we committed to each other?

3. In what ways do we enjoy being with each other? Are our motivations healthy and nonphysical in nature? What types of activities do we enjoy doing together?

4. In what ways are my partner's needs as important as my own?

5. Are we both free to be ourselves, or as a couple are we guarded with our conversation, sense of humor, behavior, etc.?

6. Am I prepared to marry the family of my prospective mate? (Although you may think you are only marrying one person, you are indeed marrying the entire family. The parents of your partner will become the grandparents of your children.)

7. How do I presently treat my own parents and family members? What about my prospective spouse? (How you treat family now is a good indicator of how you will treat your future spouse and children.)

8. How do we feel about each of us being the parent of our children? Will we both be the kind of mother or father that children will respect and follow?

9. Does each of us accept the basic assumptions of the patriarchal order? (Is he the type of priesthood holder you can trust? Will she counsel with you in righteousness? Will he love you as Christ loved the Church and gave Himself for it? (see Eph. 5:25) Can we make decisions together?

10. What will our destiny be as a couple? Will we set goals together and plan for the future? Do any of our goals clash? Can we see ourselves as companions twenty years down the road with a number of children? (How about a million years?)

11. Do we feel that the Lord has confirmed our decision to marry? In what ways?

12. How have we prepared ourselves to receive an answer from the Spirit?

(Questions for this chapter adapted from Burton C. Kelly, "A True and Sufficient Love," *Ensign*, Feb. 1979, 47–49.)

Special Note: If you and the one you're dating would like more information on your compatibility and potential as a couple, we strongly recommend that you complete the *RELATE* assessment, which you can do online, or you can order it by telephone or through the mail. *RELATE* is an instrument that measures the compatibility of couples who are preparing for marriage. It measures your feelings and attitudes on a number of issues that are important in a marriage relationship. You can e-mail for more information at RELATE@BYU.EDU, or write to: RELATE, P.O. Box 24391, Provo, UT, 84601-5391.

CHAPTER 5

Why Marry in the Temple?

*"The foundation for a happy and successful marriage is a marriage
solemnized in the temple. . . . Participating in these
sacred ordinances should be your most important objective for
achieving a successful marriage."* [1]

As members of The Church of Jesus Christ of Latter-day Saints,
we stand alone in our belief that marriage and family relations can be
eternal. Because you are approaching the ordinance of marriage, we
feel it is important that you understand the need to marry in the
Lord's house. Some members of the Church do not really understand
the full implications of marriage in the temple; many like that it is
less expensive than other places, or they want to marry in the temple
because of tradition—grandparents, parents, aunts, uncles, and
cousins all married there, so they don't want to disappoint anyone.
But the real reason to marry in the temple is far more profound than
any of these.

Marriage is the highest and holiest ordinance of the gospel of
Jesus Christ. This is not only because it is a saving ordinance for
ourselves, but because it is a responsibility we have to move the
kingdom of God forward. This doctrine was lost to the world during
the Apostasy, and was restored in our day as a part of the "restoration
of all things" (see D&C 27:6; 86:10). This chapter will acquaint you
with the proper reasons to marry where the Lord would like you to
marry—in His house.

Abraham and Isaac

An account in the Old Testament teaches well the importance of a covenant marriage. In Genesis 24 we learn that Abraham was "well stricken in age" (v. 1) and that before his death, he deeply desired that his son, Isaac, would marry in the covenant. At the time, they lived in Canaan, so finding a daughter of the covenant would be difficult. Therefore, Abraham made an oath with his servant to go to his (Abraham's) country (v. 4) and find Isaac a wife he could marry in the covenant.

The servant departed for the land of Abraham's forefathers. He prayed that the Lord would assist him in this challenge—to roam the countryside to find the *right one* for Isaac to marry. Talk about trying to find a needle in a haystack. The servant must have had great faith because he went and simply prayed that the Lord would bring her *to him*. He even had the scenario planned out and believed the Lord would honor his request. He suggested that the following events take place: while he is sitting by a well, a beautiful, covenant young lady will walk up to him, offer him a drink, and then subsequently water all of his camels!

Remarkably, the servant's prayer was answered precisely as he had asked. The beautiful young lady was named Rebekah. After the servant explained to her that she was the answer to his prayer, they decided to visit her home, where the entire story was recounted to the family. Rebekah's family recognized that this chance meeting had to be of God (v. 50). However, it must have been difficult for her to leave with a total stranger. The family asked Rebekah what she wanted to do (v. 57). Specifically she was asked, "Wilt thou go with this man?" (v. 58). Rebekah responded with three simple yet profound words: "I will go" (v. 58). Like Nephi, Rebekah was willing to go and do whatever the Lord commanded.

Great blessings usually accompany such manifestations of faith. It appears that Rebekah was given a blessing before she left and was promised that she would become "the mother of thousands of millions" (v. 60); so she did. After a long ride back to Abraham's residence, she and Isaac met for the first time and were subsequently married in the covenant.

Isaac could have married anyone locally. Surely it would have been much simpler to go and find a wife in a neighboring village. However, that was not Abraham's commitment, nor was it the Lord's plan. Abraham knew that the most important thing any disciple of Christ ever does is to marry the right person, in the right place, by the right authority.

As our prophets have testified, marriage is the most vital of all decisions and has an eternal impact on ourselves and our posterity. As you recall, the marriage of Isaac and Rebekah was the cornerstone for the rest of the Old and New Testament, the twelve tribes of Israel, and ultimately the birth of the Son of God.

Orders of the Priesthood

Marriage in the temple is a Melchizedek Priesthood ordinance.[2] Joseph Smith explained that "all priesthood is Melchizedek, but there are different portions or degrees" which he referred to as "grand orders" (Joseph Smith, *Teachings of the Prophet Joseph Smith*, comp. Joseph Fielding Smith, Jr. [1979], 180). The first grand order is the **Aaronic Order**, consisting of four ordained offices: deacon, teacher, priest, and bishop. A bishop is also ordained a high priest, and he presides over this appendage to the Melchizedek Priesthood in the ward (see D&C 107:14–15).

Another "grand order" of the priesthood is the **Melchizedek Order**. This order consists of five ordained offices: elder, high priest, patriarch, Seventy, and Apostle. The offices of Seventy and Apostle are reserved for General Authorities.

The **Patriarchal Order** is yet another "grand order." It is also called the "order of marriage," or the "new and everlasting covenant of marriage" (D&C 131:2).[3] Elder Bruce R. McConkie said of this order: "[A couple] can enter an order of the priesthood named the new and everlasting covenant of marriage (see D&C 131:2), named also the patriarchal order, because of which order we can create for ourselves eternal family units of our own, patterned after the family of God our Heavenly Father" ("The Doctrine of the Priesthood," *Ensign*, May 1982, 34).

Elder McConkie used his own marriage to explain the principle:

> I went to the temple, and I took my wife [to be] with me, and we kneeled at the altar. There on that occasion *we entered, the two of us, into an 'order of the priesthood.'* When we did it, we had sealed upon us, on a conditional basis, every blessing that God promised Father Abraham—the blessings of exaltation and eternal increase. The name of that order of priesthood, which is patriarchal in nature, because Abraham was a natural patriarch to his posterity, is the New and Everlasting Covenant of marriage ("The Eternal Family Concept," Devotional address at the Second Annual Priesthood Genealogical Research Seminar, Brigham Young University, 23 June 1967).

You and your sweetheart will enter this order of priesthood the day you marry in the temple. The first callings the two of you will hold are those of husband and wife. This order of priesthood is not one of "laying on of hands" but at marriage, the two of you will be commanded to use your procreative powers to provide physical bodies for the spirit children of our heavenly parents. Together, you will assist in the great work of bringing to pass the immortality and eternal life of God's children (Moses 1:39). When you are sealed in the temple, the offices of husband and wife are activated for you, and they will be eternal callings if you are faithful marriage partners.[4]

President Boyd K. Packer explained how a man and woman are together in a temple sealing:

> No man receives the fulness of the priesthood without a woman at his side. For no man, the Prophet said, can obtain the fulness of the priesthood outside the temple of the Lord. And she is there beside him in that sacred place. *She shares in all that he receives.* The man and the woman individually receive the ordinances encompassed in the endowment. But the *man cannot ascend to the highest ordinances*—the sealing ordinances—*without her at his side.*
>
> No man achieves the supernal exalting status of worthy fatherhood except as a gift from his wife. In the home and in the Church, sisters should be esteemed for their very nature ("The Relief Society," *Ensign,* May 1998, 73; emphasis added).

It is noteworthy that these callings—husband and father, wife and mother—are the most important "offices" you will ever hold in mortal life or in eternity. Of all the titles by which our Heavenly Father could be addressed, He prefers the title "Father." Elder H. Burke Peterson made this point: "In this life a father is never released from his responsibility. We call bishops, and they serve for a time and are released. Stake presidents likewise are called, serve, and are released. But a father's calling is an eternal calling if he lives worthily" ("The Father's Duty to Foster the Welfare of His Family," *Ensign,* Nov. 1977, 87). Of course, the same principle holds true for wives and mothers. These are eternal callings.

"Those who endure in perfect faith, who receive the Melchizedek Priesthood, and who gain the blessings of the temple (including celestial marriage) are eventually ordained kings and priests. These are offices given faithful holders of the Melchizedek Priesthood, and in them they will bear rule as exalted beings during the millennium and in eternity" (Bruce R. McConkie, *Mormon Doctrine,* 2nd ed. [1966], 599).[5] Men who attain exaltation are spoken of as "they who are priests and kings, who have received of his fulness, and of his glory" (D&C 76:56). Wives have promises similar to their husbands. Elder McConkie explained:

> If righteous men have power through the gospel and its crowning ordinance of celestial marriage to become kings and priests to rule in exaltation forever, it follows that the women by their side (without whom they cannot attain exaltation) will be queens and priestesses (Rev. 1:6; 5:10). Exaltation grows out of the eternal union of a man and his wife. Of those whose marriage endures in eternity, the Lord says, "Then shall *they* be gods" (D&C 132:20); that is, each of them, the man and the woman, will be a god. As such they will rule over their dominions forever (Bruce R. McConkie, *Mormon Doctrine,* 2nd ed. [1966], 613; emphasis added).

In your marriage ceremony you will be organized into a kingdom. At first there will be only two of you. Expanding your kingdom will require some "subjects"—the children who are born (or adopted and sealed) to you in the new and everlasting covenant of marriage. As rulers in your earthly kingdom, you will need to teach your subjects how to live and function in your home and in the world. These new members come to you initially about 19–20 inches long, rather helpless, and they don't appear too threatening. They are your students and you are their teachers. They are your brothers and sisters from the premortal life, and you have been asked by Heavenly Father to assist them back to Him. You have come before them, and must pass your knowledge of the lessons of mortal life on to them. The curriculum in your home will include such themes as learning who they are, where they came from and where they are going. You must teach them how to care for themselves, respect property, relate well with other human beings, and understand the rules of conduct in family and in society—those things essential to maintain order in your kingdom as well as beyond the front door.

As a married couple you will oversee the physical, social, emotional, intellectual, and spiritual growth of your offspring. Even as Jesus "increased in wisdom and stature, and in favour with God and man" (Luke 2:52), so you too will have the responsibility to assist your children to develop their potential in areas of personality and character development.

The blessings of a temple marriage are conditional at the time of the ceremony. Even though that sacred ordinance contains blessings, pronouncements, and promises that pertain to eternity, it is not a guarantee at that time that you will be exalted. The blessing of being "sure" comes only as the two of you faithfully observe the laws and covenants associated with your temple sealing.[6] If you are faithful, the order of marriage—the patriarchal order—allows you to continue in eternity that kingdom which you begin in this life (see D&C 131:1–4; 132:30).

Restoration of the Priesthood

"The Melchizedek Priesthood is the highest and holiest order ever given to men on earth," said Elder Bruce R. McConkie. "It is the power and authority to do all that is necessary to save and exalt the children of men. It is the very priesthood held by the Lord Jesus Christ Himself and by virtue of which He was able to gain eternal life in the kingdom of His Father" ("The Doctrine of the Priesthood," *Ensign,* May 1982, 33).

These two priesthoods, or more accurately, two divisions of the Melchizedek Priesthood (D&C 107:5), were restored in 1829. Seven years later, in 1836, Moses, Elias, and Elijah appeared to Joseph Smith and Oliver Cowdery in the Kirtland Temple and restored further keys of the Melchizedek Priesthood. Moses restored specific keys of missionary work that empower missionaries to search the earth for the house of Israel and to lead them (including the lost tribes) to Zion. (See D&C 110:11.)

Power of Elias

"After [Moses' visit], Elias appeared, and committed the dispensation of the gospel of Abraham, saying that in us and our seed all generations after us should be blessed" (D&C 110:12). The blessings of Abraham's dispensation include the right to receive the gospel and the priesthood in the flesh and to administer those same blessings to those in all nations of the earth. Abraham's seed is charged to take the gospel to the world community (Abr. 2:9–11). These blessings include the right to enter the "order of marriage" (see D&C 131:1–4). Children born in the covenant (children whose parents marry in the temple) are heirs to all the blessings of their parents and those of the ancient patriarch. These children are eligible to receive certain blessings that include the fullness of the gospel, the opportunity to minister in priesthood service, opportunities for full-time missionary service, marriage in the temple, and the right to the fullness of the Restoration blessings to qualify for eternal life. These blessings will be automatically passed to your posterity (see D&C 132:29–32) because you married in the temple. (However, being eligible means that your children will receive the *opportunity* to obtain priesthood blessings. One may be eligible by birthright, yet unworthy to receive blessings.) Your children can receive all of these blessings if they are faithful, blessings that come to them because you married properly and they are "born in the covenant," meaning the covenant of Abraham.

Foreordained Spirit Children

Couples who marry in the temple (or who have their children sealed to them at a later time) are given a promise that the spirits assigned to them as their mortal offspring were among the most faithful and valiant of the Father's spirit children in the premortal world. Elder Bruce R. McConkie explained, "Alma taught the great truth that every person who holds the Melchizedek Priesthood was foreordained to receive that high and holy order in the premortal councils of eternity" (Bruce R. McConkie, *Mormon Doctrine*, 2nd ed. [1966], 290). That promise is part of what Elias restored.[7] Elder McConkie explained:

> Now what was the gospel of Abraham [restored by Elias]? Obviously it was the commission, the mission, the endowment and power, the message of salvation, given to Abraham. . . . It was a divine promise that both in the world and out of the world his seed should continue "as innumerable as the stars; or, if ye were to count the sand upon the seashore ye could not number them. . . ." Thus the gospel of Abraham was one of celestial marriage; . . . *it was a gospel or commission to provide a lineage for the elect portion of the preexistent spirits.* . . . This power and commission is what Elias restored (Bruce R. McConkie, *Mormon Doctrine,* 2nd ed. [1966], 219; emphasis added).

The commission to "provide a lineage" refers to the authority given you as a married couple to begin a lineage by creating physical bodies for the Father's spirit children. Because you married in the right place, Heavenly Father will honor you with valiant spirits as your children.[8] This opportunity to bring foreordained spirits to the earth is a sober reminder that we must be conscientious and responsible parents.

The temple is the only place on earth where the promises of Abraham are *sealed* upon a couple. That is why you simply *must* marry in the temple, for it is there that you will receive the authority to continue in the resurrection with the power to procreate. The priesthood keys for that authority are not available *outside* the house of the Lord. That is one reason President Gordon B. Hinckley has been so vigorous in extending the privileges of the temple worldwide. The Lord explained:

> In the celestial glory there are three heavens or degrees; And in order to obtain the highest [degree], a man *must* enter into this *order of the priesthood* [meaning the new and everlasting covenant of marriage]; And if he does not [enter that order of marriage], he cannot obtain it [meaning the highest degree of exaltation]. He may enter into the other, but that is the end of his kingdom; he cannot have an increase [posterity] (D&C 131:1–4; emphasis added).

Power of Elijah

Elijah restored the sealing power and authority that allows you to be married eternally. The keys to direct the sealing power are the right of the President of the Church. Only certain General Authorities, members of temple presidencies, and those called to be "sealers" hold this sacred sealing power. These men assist the prophet (and thereby the Lord) in performing the ordinance work of sealing couples and families together. Unless you marry in the temple where this sealing power is available, you cannot benefit from what Elijah restored. Without this ordinance, no one could be eligible for exaltation.[9]

Elijah's restoration of the sealing power assured that all essential priesthood keys to prepare the Saints for eternal life were now back on the earth. "Therefore, the keys of this dispensation are committed into your hands," he said to the prophet Joseph Smith, "and by this ye may know that the great and dreadful day of the Lord is near, even at the doors" (D&C 110:16).

The most important reason, therefore, for you to marry in the temple, is to receive the blessings restored by a complement of angels who came to the Prophet Joseph Smith as a part of the restoration of the gospel and priesthood. The Lord said of those who fail to obtain these blessings: "For these angels did not abide my law (of marriage); therefore, they cannot be enlarged, but remain separately and singly, without exaltation . . . to all eternity; and from henceforth are not gods, but are angels of God forever and ever"(D&C 132:17).

You would not want to begin your marriage with that limitation. Why would you want to marry someone whom you love for this life only? Can you imagine not continuing the associations of marriage and family life beyond this brief mortal period? Can you fathom the implications of not having posterity in the next life or maybe not even having access to those who have been your mortal family because you failed to marry properly? If you do not marry in the temple, it indicates that you do not understand the importance of the restoration of the gospel and the priesthood from God.

Family history work and temple worship allow us the opportunity to return again and again to remind ourselves of the great blessings that God has restored in our day. No wonder Elder A. Theodore Tuttle could say:

> No man can receive a fulness of the priesthood without the temples, without the sealing power. No man can gain eternal life, no woman can gain eternal life, without the temples. Temple building is not optional in this church. . . . May I be bold enough to suggest that one of the reasons some Latter-day Saints are not blessed and do not prosper is because they are not attending regularly to their responsibilities in the great work of the temples (A. Theodore Tuttle, "The Key to Our Redemption," *1980 Devotional Speeches of the Year* [1980], 111).

President Ezra Taft Benson reminded us:

> When you attend the temple and perform the ordinances that pertain to the house of the Lord, certain blessings will come to you: You will receive the spirit of Elijah, which will turn your hearts to your spouse, to your children, and to your forebears. You will love your family with a deeper love than you have loved before . . . You will be endowed with power from on high as the Lord has promised. You will receive the key of the knowledge of God. (See D&C 84:19) You will learn how you can be like Him. Even the power of godliness will be manifest to you. You will be doing a great service to those who have passed to the other side of the veil in order that they might be "judged according to men in the flesh, but live according to God in the spirit." (D&C 138:34) Such are the blessings of the temple and the blessings of frequently attending the temple ("What I Hope You Will Teach Your Children about the Temple," *Ensign,* Aug. 1985, 10).

Keeping Your Focus on the Temple

Now that we have discussed why you should marry in the temple, let's consider how this information should help you prepare for such a sacred ordinance.

- *In Dating:* Now you can understand why the counsel over the years was that you not date until you reached a certain level of maturity. Marriage is certainly not for children. Marriage is the most important decision of your life, and it requires the very best you have to make it work well. For this reason you were asked to refrain from dating until you were sixteen years of age. You needed to be old enough to have a mature perspective on the experiences you would have in dating, and to give you more of an opportunity to understand and respect the sacred nature of intimate relations.

- *In Morality:* Because the Lord grants the privilege of sexual intimacy only to married couples, we know that it is a sacred rite, to be used only in the right setting—with the right stewardship—and with a mature understanding of its significance. Now it should be clear as to why so much emphasis was given to chastity during your formative years. True love is founded squarely on the foundation of a chaste life.

- *In Marriage:* Without stable marriages, our social fabric disintegrates. Signs of social decay are all about us and they are reaching ominous levels. The citizens of the world are losing the ideal of a God-ordained marriage. You will be expected to show those around you a better way. You will continue your courtship after marriage, of course, and closely monitor your marriage commitment and partnership.

- *In Bearing Children:* As Latter-day Saints, we are profamily, prochildren, and anti-abortion because the Lord is sending spirits to the earth who have been reserved and foreordained to carry out His great latter-day work. It will be your privilege to bear and rear these sons and daughters of God so they understand their destiny, and are willing to accept their obligations to build Zion and keep themselves on the path to eternal life. "Our young people are among the most blessed and favored of our Father's children," said President Joseph Fielding Smith. "They are the nobility of heaven, a choice and chosen generation who have a divine destiny. Their spirits have been reserved to come forth in this day when the gospel is on the earth, and when the Lord needs valiant servants to carry on His great latter-day work" (in Conference Report, Apr. 1970, 6).

What better way could Satan thwart the work of God? Listen to the thoughts of the people of the world: There is no need to bear many children; they are too expensive; they intrude into a couple's happiness. One or two children are enough for any couple because of limited resources and the need for a decent standard of living. Women need careers to be fulfilled, as motherhood alone is simply insufficient. Mothering should be secondary to a career. Smaller family size allows women the best of both worlds. Adequate day care is now available to allow women to achieve goals that their mothers couldn't. To postpone or prevent the birth of children is a mark of sophistication and culture. With so much divorce going on today, few or no children makes it easier for the parents to make the break without so much guilt.

In contrast to this thinking, Latter-day Saints understand the privilege of becoming parents to some of the finest spirits to come to this earth.

> To carry forward his own purposes among men and nations, the Lord foreordained chosen spirit children in preexistence and assigned them to come to earth at particular times and places. . . . These preexistence appointments. . . simply designated certain individuals to perform missions which the Lord in his wisdom knew they had the talents and capacities to do.
>
> The mightiest and greatest spirits were foreordained to stand as prophets and spiritual leaders. . . . In all this there is not the slightest hint of compulsion; persons foreordained to fill special missions in mortality

are as abundantly endowed with free agency as are any other persons. By their foreordination the Lord merely gives them the opportunity to serve Him and His purposes if they will choose to measure up to the standard He knows they are capable of attaining (Bruce R. McConkie, *Mormon Doctrine,* 2nd edition [1966], 290).

• *In Effective Parenting Practices:* Your sons and daughters will be born in a day of great challenges to the standards of decency the gospel teaches. Though your children were foreordained to participate in the spreading of the gospel worldwide, President Harold B. Lee warned of what happens when we allow our children free reign:

> There is a warning: Despite that calling which is spoken of in the scriptures as "foreordination," we have another inspired declaration: "Behold, there are many called, but few are chosen. . . . " (D&C 121:34).
>
> This suggests that even though we have our free agency here, there are many who were foreordained before the world was, to a greater state than they have prepared themselves for here. Even though they might have been among the noble and great, from among whom the Father declared He would make His chosen leaders, they may fail of that calling here in mortality. Then the Lord poses this question: ". . . and why are they not chosen?" (D&C 121:34)
>
> Two answers were given—First, "Because their hearts are set so much upon the things of this world. . . ." And second, they ". . . aspire to the honors of men" (D&C 121:35) ("Understanding Who We Are Brings Self-Respect," *Ensign,* Jan. 1974, 5).

In the years ahead, you will need to do your best as a parent to see that your children are valiant and will be positive contributors to the latter-day work of God. That is why it will be important for you to marry someone committed to having family home evening, family prayer, and scripture and gospel study in your home. The Lord is expecting you to prepare well the spirits He will send you. In a day of great wickedness, when even some of the "elect according to the covenant" will falter (JST, Matt. 1:22), you and your spouse must teach your children well. How will your children understand the importance and value of serving a mission or marrying in the temple if you don't provide them with good reasons and a strong, healthy example to follow? (This is an important reason for a young woman to marry a returned missionary. Ideally, you want to marry someone who can teach your children, and the best preparation for that assignment is to have served a mission as a young man.) In this final dispensation, the Lord needs you to provide a home environment where the gospel will be taught with clarity and power so that your posterity will be prepared to move the cause of Zion forward.

Wilford Woodruff taught this idea:

> There never was a dispensation on the earth when prophets and apostles, the inspiration, revelation and power of God, the holy priesthood and the keys of the kingdom were needed more than they are in this generation. There never has been a dispensation when the friends of God and righteousness among the children of men needed more faith in the promises and prophecies than they do to-day; and there certainly never has been a generation of people on the earth that has had a greater work to perform than the inhabitants of the earth in the later days (*Journal of Discourses,* 15:8).

Your preparation to enter the House of the Lord should begin now. Countless blessings await those who diligently serve Him there. The following thoughts on the temple are from a college-age student:

> Ever since I received my endowments I have attended the temple regularly and cannot count the many blessings I've received from doing so. I sincerely believe this habit of attending the temple has helped increase my power of godliness and perspective. I have been able to build a wonderful relationship with my Father in Heaven, which in turn has prepared me to meet and build a successful relationship with my . . . fiancée. . . .

I feel . . . my upcoming marriage will have a better chance of success and happiness. I have reaped the blessings of the spirit far more than I could ever imagine and have a firm testimony. Our marriage will be greatly blessed if we hold up our covenants.

Summary

The Lord is counting on you to move His work forward. The temple is the place where you and your spouse will organize a unit of the celestial kingdom. As a newly married couple, you will be authorized to add to your family through procreation (or adoption). In your marriage ceremony, God will confer upon you priesthood blessings that will qualify you for an eternal relationship.

You marry in the temple not because it would disappoint your parents or grandparents if you didn't, but because marriage is an *essential ordinance* of the gospel; it is necessary to attain eternal life. The restoration of this ordinance required angels from God's presence. The temple experience will help you to be a better companion. "I am satisfied that if our people would attend the temple more, there would be less of selfishness in their lives," said President Gordon B. Hinckley. "There would be less of absence of love in their relationships. There would be more of fidelity on the part of husbands and wives. There would be more of love and peace and happiness in the homes of our people" (address delivered at regional representatives' seminar, 6 April 1984).

You and your spouse will need the power that comes from this heavenly source. Elder Royden Derrick explained:

> In the temple we are taught by the Holy Spirit. When we come to the temple properly prepared—that is, with our minds devoid of carnal thoughts and well fed with spiritual food—the Light of Christ comes into focus to enable us to better understand the things of God. The knowledge we gain is not of much value unless it influences our life for good. In the temple, through the power of the Holy Spirit, knowledge is transformed into virtues. A person who attends the temple more regularly grows more patient, more long-suffering, and more charitable.

He becomes more diligent, more committed, and more dedicated. He develops a greater capacity to love his wife and children and to respect the good qualities and the rights of others. He develops a greater sense of values, becoming more honorable and upright in his dealings and less critical of others (*Temples in the Last Days* [1987], 53).

Questions to Consider

Consider the following questions as they apply to your situation. If you are dating someone, discuss the applicable questions between the two of you. If you are not currently in a relationship, decide where you stand on an issue before you start dating someone and how you would like to improve.

1. Read Doctrine & Covenants 97:15–17. What does the Lord say about being worthy to enter His house?

2. How can I specifically prepare now to be worthy to marry in the Lord's house?

3. What are some of the promises from our Church leaders regarding marriage and family life to those who regularly attend the temple?

4. What can I do right now to better prepare for the holiest ordinance of temple marriage?

CHAPTER 6

Chastity and Moral Purity Before Marriage

"Ask yourself this question: When I get married, am I going to be faithful to my husband/wife? It seems incomprehensible to you that you would cheat on your spouse, right? Now ask yourself another question: Should I be faithful to my future husband or wife even before I know who he or she is? I'm sure each one of you hopes your future spouse is being true to you now, and is saving those things reserved for marriage for you." [1]

Several years ago Dr. Brent Barlow, a professor at Brigham Young University and a bishop at the time, received a late-night phone call from one of his students. After the caller indicated that she wanted to remain anonymous, she explained that she and her returned-missionary fiancé had become sexually involved, even though they planned to be married in the temple in just a few months. The young woman was concerned that they would not be worthy to be married in the temple. Dr. Barlow confirmed that her distress was legitimate. The story continues:

> But then she said her fiancé had instructed her that she must not tell their bishop what they had done. In fact, he told her that she must lie in their forthcoming temple recommend interview.
>
> That concerned me greatly. I've been around many single Latter-day Saints for the past two decades, and I'm well aware that some young couples step past the boundaries of propriety in their premarital relationships. But I was particularly disturbed

that their transgression didn't seem to trouble her future husband.

My anonymous student on the phone continued: "My fiancé asked me a straightforward, simple question: 'Why wait? We'll be married in only a few weeks. What difference does it make if we start to be intimate now?' And he argued that many other young couples are doing the same thing." She hesitated and then continued. "He also said it was not necessary to confess to the bishop or the stake president. We'll work it out ourselves with the Lord after we're married."

Since I was serving as an LDS bishop at the time of the phone call, I told the student that the temple recommend interview asked plainly if the applicant was honest. How, I asked, could both she and her fiancé lie to their bishop during the interview process? I suggested she go back to her fiancé and encourage him to reconsider his suggestion . . .

My student thanked me for taking time to talk to her and hung up. I went right to bed, but I didn't go to sleep for a long time. I kept replaying the conversation in my mind—along with similar conversations I'd recently had with a few other young Latter-day Saints. They all asked me the same question: "Why wait?" Some felt that (1) sexual behavior prior to marriage no longer mattered, or mattered less than in "less enlightened times;" (2) it was no longer necessary to "confess" one's sins to either a bishop or stake president; (3) that sexual impropriety before marriage was now quite common and "many others are doing it;" and (4) (and perhaps most disturbing) that "we'll work it out ourselves. It is just a matter between us and the Lord"(Brent A. Barlow, *Worth Waiting For* [1995], 1–3).

Dr. Barlow's four concerns are warranted. It certainly seems that in our day sexual immorality is much too common, particularly among those who are courting or engaged. In student wards, bishops spend a great deal of their time helping students deal with their sexual transgressions. Your goal should be to make it through your engagement period unscathed by immorality so that you can approach the temple altar clean before God and angels. Too many couples have adopted the twin notions that "everyone else is doing it" before marriage and "you can repent later." Both of these ideas are satanic in origin, and the father of all lies would have you believe them. The truth is that there are no successful sinners. Transgressions do not make you a well-rounded person; you do not need to experience the bad and the wicked to appreciate the good and the righteous. President Kimball explained, "That man who resists temptation and lives without sin is far better off than the man who has fallen, no matter how repentant the latter may be. . . . *How much better it is never to have committed sin!*" (*The Miracle of Forgiveness* [1969], 357; emphasis added). He added, "Your focus should be on preventing sin rather than being faced with the much more difficult task of curing it" (*The Miracle of Forgiveness* [1969] 216–217).[2]

Sexual Immorality: The Plaguing Sin of this Generation

As we have entered a new millennium, we find that we are deluged with more and more immoral messages from the media. Images, plots, and dialogues that were once thought to be scandalous now fill prime time television, the Internet, and magazines. Movies that were rated R in the '70s and '80s are rated PG today. We see a definite correlation between media presentations and a low threshold of moral behavior. *Time* magazine reported the sad tale: "By the time they are 20, three-quarters of young Americans have had sex."[3] Moreover, a 1988 study found that "25 percent of females have had sexual relationships by age 15 and 80 percent by age 19. A 1988 National Survey of Young Men found that by age 15, 33 percent of males have had sexual relationships and by age 19 the number had risen to 86 percent."[4] According to the *Janus* report (a comprehensive study on sexuality in recent times) religion does not seem to greatly deter early sexual behavior; 71 percent of the very religious had sexual relations before marriage, compared to 93 percent of those who were not religious.[5]

Our latter-day prophets have warned us of the consequences of this permissive attitude. President Joseph F. Smith, at the turn of the century, forewarned the saints that sexual immorality would become the plaguing sin of this generation and that it would challenge the elders more than any other vice (see *Journal of Discourses* 8:55). That prophecy is being fulfilled in our time. President Ezra Taft Benson in more recent years taught that "sexual immorality is a viper that is striking not only in the world, but in the Church today. Not to admit it is to be dangerously complacent or is like putting one's head in the sand" (Ezra Taft Benson, *God, Family, Country* [1975], 239).

Unfortunately, as President Benson said, Latter-day Saints are not immune to sexual involvement and deviance; it is the plaguing sin among our own young people. Engaged couples can be lulled into complacency as Satan persuades ever so slyly, whispering half-truths into their ears until they are caught in inextricable chains. Consequently, many couples must postpone or cancel their temple weddings because they yielded to sexual temptations. Frankly, there is too much sexual transgression among the college-aged youth of the Church. "*Any* is too much, and we have *much* too much" (Jeffrey R. Holland, "The Inconvenient Messiah," *Brigham Young University 1981–1982 Devotional and Fireside Speeches* [1982], 79; emphasis in original). Here are some ideas as to why so many are succumbing to a sin next only to murder (see Alma 39:5).

The Influence of Satan

On one occasion, President Marion G. Romney declared, "I know that God lives. Through my own experiences I have come to know of his spirit and his power. I know also that Satan lives. I have detected his spirit and felt of his power" ("Satan—The Great Deceiver," *Ensign*, June 1971, 36). We are not used to hearing people "bear testimony" of Satan in a Latter-day Saint context. Nevertheless, there is a devil and he seeks to destroy our lives. He can keep you from accomplishing your earthly mission if he can trap you in the snare of immorality. Satan will do everything in his power to cause you to stumble, fall, and ultimately fail during your engagement if you are not on guard. Immorality is one of his prime tools. He does not want you to be worthy to attend the temple, much less have a temple marriage, for therein is power and protection to you. Once you are behind the walls of the holy house of the Lord, it will be more difficult for Satan to influence you. He knows that the dating and engagement period will be one of the *best* times to destroy you because you are already focusing on feelings of affection and love. You and your fiancé may become an easy target—like deer in the headlights—on the opening day of hunting season!

When you consider the three most serious sins, it is certain that you will probably not be a son or daughter of perdition, and it is unlikely that you would be tempted to actually kill anyone (until you have your own teenagers). Thus, your most vulnerable spot for commission of serious sin lies in the third-gravest sin—sexual immorality. Satan knows that his window of opportunity—the time when you are most vulnerable—is during your engagement. President Boyd K. Packer explained, "[Satan] knows that if he can entice you to use this power prematurely, to use it too soon, or to misuse it in any way, you may well lose your opportunities for eternal progression"(in Conference Report, Denmark, Finland, Norway, and Sweden Area Conference 1974, 83–84). And, if you don't plan ahead, he may ruin your life.

The reason Satan is the master of "Life Destruction 101" is because he knows you well; he knows exactly where to tempt you, where the weak spots are in your armor. President Spencer W. Kimball explained:

> If one's weakness is sex, Satan in his erudition [learning] and experience and brilliance knows a thousand reasons why sex may be liberated to run rampant and express itself and satisfy itself. Lucifer is real. He is subtle. He is convincing. He is powerful. . . . The devil knows where to tempt, where to put in his telling blows. He finds the vulnerable spot. . . . The adversary is subtle; he is cunning, he knows that he cannot induce good men and women immediately to do major evils so he moves slyly, whispering half-truths until he has his intended victims following him, and finally he clamps his chains upon them and fetters them tight, and then he laughs at their discomfiture and their misery" (Spencer W. Kimball, *The Teachings of Spencer W. Kimball*, ed. Edward L. Kimball [1982], 151).

Many engaged couples are unaware of Satan's intentions. Perhaps they feel that he can have no influence over them. Maybe they even know other couples who have fallen, and yet they think they are immune to sexual transgression. They may feel that immorality is a temptation that *others* must contend with, but not themselves. However, immorality is no respecter of persons; infidelity is an equal-opportunity employer. No one, without the armor of the Lord, is exempt from such temptations and possible errors. It doesn't matter who you are, what your position in the Church is, your grade point average, or whether or not you teach at the Missionary Training Center. All of us are susceptible to fall if we become careless. Think of engagement as Satan's prime battleground. During this period of time, you are frequently together with the person you are most attracted to, the very person you have strong love feelings for, who also happens to be the one Satan tries to tempt you to take advantage of. The danger may be likened to trying to quit smoking while carrying a pack of cigarettes in your pocket. President Spencer W. Kimball explained that even "the very elect would be deceived by Lucifer if it were possible. He will use his logic to confuse and his rationalizations to destroy. He will shade meanings, open doors an inch at a time, and lead from purest white through all the shades of gray to the darkest black" ("President Kimball Speaks Out on Morality," *Ensign*, Nov. 1980, 94).

Some have used the story of David and Bathsheba's sexual transgression, (see 2 Sam. 11) as an example of two people simply being in the wrong place at the wrong time. "If David had been out on the battlefield instead of home at the palace," they argue, "he would never have sinned with Bathsheba." Although the logic here is indisputable, there is another point to emphasize: *even the very best, the most righteous, can stumble if they are not careful.*

"David" means *beloved,* or *beloved son.* He was the King of Israel who began as a humble shepherd and rose to become king of the Israelites. He was a true friend to the Lord in his early days. His early life was exemplary, and he was a "type" of Christ.

Bathsheba was a chosen daughter of Israel. In fact, her name means *daughter of the covenant* (see 2 Sam. 11, footnote 3a, 439). Here were two strong, stable individuals. Surely neither one would have suspected that he or she would ever yield to such a serious transgression. But we learn from this account that even the very best individuals can fall if they put themselves in a compromising situation. President Kimball counseled:

> The devil knows how to destroy our young girls and boys. He may not be able to tempt a person to murder or to commit adultery immediately, but he knows that if he can get a boy and a girl to sit in the car late enough after the dance, or to park long enough in the dark at the end of the lane, the best boy and the best girl will finally succumb and fall. He knows that all have a limit to their resistance (Spencer W. Kimball, *The Miracle of Forgiveness* [1969], 66).

All of us have the responsibility to avoid sexual temptations.[6] None of us, whether single or married, can put ourselves in situations that will compromise our standards without risking serious transgression. A friend—a noted Church leader and person of influence in his community—once exemplified this point. When his daughters were teenagers and wanted to stay out late, or go out with individuals he didn't know well, he would say, "I'm sorry, but not tonight." Usually the daughters would ask, "Why Dad, don't you trust us?" This friend said he would often respond, "I don't even trust myself," an idea echoed even by the prophet Brigham Young.[7] We need to stay as far away from the edge of the cliff as we possibly can. The lesson is clear: even the most righteous can fall if they are careless.

Why We Must Be Clean

In Alma 39:5–6 we learn that sexual sin ranks next to the sins of murder and denial of the Holy Ghost. Why is premarital (or extramarital) sex so serious? Robert L. Millet, a former dean of the College of Religious Education at Brigham Young University, gave this explanation: "Sexual immorality ranks third in order of serious offenses before God, because it, like murder, deals with life. One who tampers with virtue prematurely or inappropriately—outside of marriage— tampers with the powers of life" (Robert L. Millett, *The Power of the Word* [1994], 156). Meddling with the powers of procreation outside of a covenant marriage can be tragic.

Perhaps no one has addressed the "why" of purity and chastity more candidly or effectively than Elder Jeffrey R. Holland. He cited three reasons why personal purity is so important.

His first reason to remain chaste is that our bodies are not ours—they belong to the Savior who bought them with His atoning blood. Our body is an intricate part of our individual soul. We have no right to tamper with our own soul or with the soul of another individual, for our souls do not belong to us; therefore, we have no right to "do with them as we please." It is that simple.

Second, Elder Holland taught that physical intimacy between a man and wife is a symbol of total union and oneness in marriage. To give yourselves to each other outside of that bond creates a *moral schizophrenia,* which Elder Holland defines as having a *sexual relationship* (the welding of two lives) without a personal relationship (the weld itself). For example, "not to eat or live or cry or laugh together, not to do the laundry and the dishes and the homework, not to manage a budget and pay the bills and tend the children and plan together for the future" and yet be sexually intimate does not work without serious emotional consequences. (*On Earth As It Is In Heaven,* "Of Souls, Symbols, and Sacraments" [1989], 190). Victor L. Brown, Jr. called the resulting problem "sexual fragmentation" (*Human Intimacy: Illusion & Reality* [1981], 6).

Third, sexual intimacy is a type of sacrament where we unite our will with God's will and take upon ourselves part of His divinity in the life-creating process (*On Earth As It Is In Heaven,* "Of Souls, Symbols, and Sacraments," [1989], 194). We literally become partners with God in the divine plan of salvation.

Personal purity during engagement is critical. Violating the laws of God can only bring suffering and severe spiritual consequences. One college-age student wrote his thoughts and understanding on the importance of chastity as follows:

> Chastity is the most important aspect of dating and preparing for marriage because the restored doctrine tells us that our bodies are the Lord's and by that we need to remain clean. He gave His clean and pure body to us and we need to give Him the same respect. It is essential to the plan of happiness because by staying clean and worthy, we will receive the great blessings the Lord has planned and be worthy to make and keep sacred covenants in the temple. By being chaste, the Lord will protect us and guide us by His Holy Spirit.

Consequences of Sexual Sin

Staying clean and pure during courtship and engagement is a sign of maturity; it signifies an ability to function as an adult, that a person is responsible in their sexual stewardship. President McKay taught that "he who is unchaste in young manhood is untrue to a trust given to him by the parents of the girl, and she who is unchaste in maidenhood is untrue to her future husband and lays the foundation of unhappiness in the home, suspicion, and discord" (*Stepping Stones to an Abundant Life* [1971],11). It is unwise, as well as sinful, to engage in immoral behavior because of the consequences that accompany it: 1) a loss of the Spirit of the Lord; 2) a loss of personal peace and happiness; 3) a loss of confidence and trust in present and future relationships (immorality prior to marriage is related to infidelity after marriage); 4) a loss in mental, emotional, and perhaps physical health[8]; 5) a possible pregnancy out of wedlock[9]; 6) an increase in sexual activity and possible addiction[10]; 7) a greater tendency to excuse involvement in extramarital affairs[11]; and 8) a great disappointment to friends and family, and an embarrassment to the Church and kingdom of God. (Taken from Randal A. Wright, *A Case for Chastity* [1993], 5-14).

Just as there are many tragic consequences for immoral behavior, there are also many blessings for remaining chaste: enjoying peace of mind, spiritual happiness, trust of self and another, freedom of conscience, wholeness, purity, and strength of character. Chastity before marriage serves as the basis for any healthy marriage.

Common-Sense Guidelines

As an engaged couple, set common-sense guidelines to ensure that wisdom prevails in being together. A good rule to follow, for example, is that the two of you never go into a bedroom alone or lie down on a bed or couch together. Be careful about sitting in hot tubs or jacuzzis. A wise mother we know teaches her children that it is smart never to be alone as a couple late at night. Instead of sitting in the car and talking, or visiting in a bedroom or in a quiet area, it makes more sense to be in public places where you would feel awkward acting inappropriately. Talk together in a quiet restaurant, in a crowded building on campus, or in a lighted park area. Good counsel! Also, be sure to discuss and set time limits as to when you will be home at night. Eleven or eleven-thirty is a good time to be back in your own place.

We would suggest that you date for a sufficient period of time before you become engaged in the first place. An engagement is a serious step toward marriage and strong feelings of obligation develop once there is a ring on your finger. That is both good and bad. It's good because it forces you to look carefully at the quality of the relationship that is progressing, and ensures that you don't bail out at the least provocation. On the other hand, it's bad because it is tough to break off an engagement. We don't hesitate to say that a broken engagement (though often painful and embarrassing at the moment) is a successful engagement! Think of it this way. An engagement is a public declaration that you intend to marry. You notify everyone of your decision by placing an announcement in the newspaper. That notifies everybody that you are both off limits to further outside dating. However, if during that time of magnifying your personality and character traits with each other, you see negative things that were hidden in the heady days of dating and earlier courtship, please have the courage to break off the relationship. (Temperament that borders on, or is, abusive; money management practices that include major amounts of frivolous debt; and spiritual or mental weaknesses including a shallow testimony, hypocrisy, or unwillingness to have children, take a job, obtain an education etc., could be examples of major shocks that surface only after you become engaged.) In such cases, it is wiser to break off the engagement before marriage than to believe you can change your partner after the wedding. Many who are now divorced deluded themselves on this last point.

Another point: be wise in the length of your engagement. Our counsel is to avoid a long engagement—no more than six months. That is not because it is impossible for you to restrain yourselves from intimate contact for longer than that, but because of what an engagement is. It is not the time to decide if you want to marry—you should not be engaged until you have already decided to marry and you both feel your decision is right. Six months is plenty of time to do what needs to be done in the engagement period—tell the public you intend to marry, zero in on each other, and plan the wedding. Therefore, six months should be the maximum period of time to be engaged unless there are extraneous variables. Normally you can plan your wedding and honeymoon in two to three months.

Putting on the Armor of God

There is help to prevent immoral behavior, and there is hope for those who have made mistakes. Our Heavenly Father has not left us without hope or a way to make corrections. In Ephesians 6:11–18, Paul admonishes the Saints to put on the armor of God. The key to remaining chaste during your engagement period is to keep the armor of God tightly in place, or if you have not already put it on, to put it on now! The armor described by Paul is spiritual armor designed to protect you from temptations (see v. 12). Specifically, armor protects you from the wiles or tricks of the devil, and also from his fiery darts of suggestion. His methods can include rationalization (like telling yourselves you are not kissing, you're just talking with your lips touching), staying out late at night and being alone too often, watching videos on the couch or on the floor, or studying together only to find yourself involved in physical passion instead. Satan's efforts can lead you to the commission of serious sins. Other temptations include involvement in inappropriate kissing, intimate physical touching, or watching movies with suggestive and provocative content.

President Harold B. Lee commented that the armor Paul describes protects the four most vulnerable parts of the body: 1) the loins, typifying virtue and chastity, 2) the heart, typifying conduct, 3) the feet, representing movement towards the positive goals and objectives in your lives, and 4) your head, which is where your thoughts are generated (see *The Teachings of Harold B. Lee*, ed. C.J. Williams [1996], 168–170). These four areas of your body will be most important as you prepare for marriage. Your *loins*, or reproductive parts of your bodies, will be used to express affection and mutual love for each other within the context of marriage and bringing children into the world. Your *heart* will guide your feelings and mutual devotion and conduct throughout life, particularly during your engagement as you stay close to the inspiration of the Holy Ghost. Your *feet* will help you move toward the mutual goals and dreams you have set as a couple. Your *head* allows you to think clearly of the consequences of wrong choices, as well as acknowledge the joy that comes in marriage from knowing you have kept the commandments of God.

There are two helpful weapons that Paul mentions in chapter 6 of Ephesians. The first is faith. God lives, He exists, and He would be most disappointed should you err so grievously after all His blessings to you. Faith implies active conviction and testimony. Your faith in gospel principles and your testimony of the reality of this latter-day work should empower both of you to be strong and stable. How you feel about the Savior and the truths of the gospel will determine to a great extent your behavior. Another weapon you possess is the sword of the Spirit, which President Lee defined as "the word of God" (*The Teachings of Harold B. Lee*, ed C.J. Williams [1996], 168). The principles of the gospel as found in the scriptures will keep you on the path of safety, because as you read from them, power will come into your lives to faithfully execute the counsel of prophets past and present. Such power will assist you in making wise decisions.

Here are some specific suggestions that will help you to forge and hammer out the armor of God and put it in place to protect your very souls.

- *Study the teachings of Jesus Christ.* Elder William R. Bradford taught us to "resist temptation by building a strong relationship with Jesus Christ. No other relationship will give you greater joy and happiness" ("Are We Following Christ's Pattern?" *Ensign*, May 1976, 98).

- *Have personal prayer.* Pray so that you have the strength to turn from temptation. In Doctrine & Covenants 10:5, we learn that consistent, fervent prayer helps us overcome and overpower Satan's efforts to destroy us. President Ezra Taft Benson promised that "[i]f you will earnestly seek guidance from your Heavenly Father, morning and evening, you will be given the strength to shun any temptation" ("A Message to the Rising Generation," *Ensign*, Nov. 1977, 32). Similarly, President Heber J. Grant said that he had no fear for the young man or young woman who would pray twice a day because they would have the Spirit to help them resist any temptation that came their way (see *Gospel Standards, Selections from the Sermons and Writings of Heber J. Grant*, comp. G. Homer Durham [1969], 26).

- *Read scriptures daily.* In Matthew 4, Jesus refuted each one of Satan's darts by quoting a scripture from the book of Deuteronomy. Scriptures are a source of power that can strengthen our resolve to do what is right. President Packer taught that "The study of the doctrines of the gospel will improve behavior quicker than a study of behavior will improve behavior. Preoccupation with unworthy behavior can lead to unworthy behavior. That is why we stress so forcefully the study of the doctrines of the gospel" ("Little Children," *Ensign*, Nov. 1986, 19). In 1 Nephi 15:24 we learn that by immersing ourselves in the scriptures, the fiery darts of Satan will have no power over us. In a recent study done among Church members, two LDS scholars concluded:

> [Those] in our study who exercised faith in the Lord by consistently and conscientiously communing with their Heavenly Father in personal prayer showed greater strength to resist many of the peer pressures and temptations of the world. Similarly, those teens who also personally studied the scriptures on a regular, if not daily, basis evidenced significantly lower levels of unworthy behavior (Brent L. Top & Bruce A. Chadwick, *Rearing Righteous Youth of Zion* [1998], 87).

- *Keep affection within proper bounds.* Avoid passionate kissing sessions. Such intimate behavior can only lead to more serious involvement. Exercise self-control that will keep you away from danger. (Be aware that each is waiting for the other to hold up the stop sign.) Kissing can be the "spark" for more serious deviations. President Kimball declared: "Kissing has been prostituted and has degenerated to develop and express lust instead of affection, honor, and admiration. . . . What is miscalled the "soul kiss" [French kiss] is an abomination and stirs passions to the eventual loss of virtue. Even if timely courtship justifies [a] kiss, it should be a clean, decent, sexless one" (Spencer W. Kimball, *The Teachings of Spencer W. Kimball,* ed. Edward L. Kimball [1982], 281).

- *Avoid inappropriate touching.* Once couples become too familiar with each other, it is difficult to turn back. "Among the most common sexual sins our young people commit are necking and petting" (Spencer W. Kimball, *The Miracle of Forgiveness* [1969], 65). *Necking* is contact between unmarried partners from the neck up, and it includes kissing or stroking the other person's hair. *Petting* is unmarried couples touching each other anywhere that would be covered by modest clothing. President Kimball warned of engaging in such activities when he said the following:

> Immorality does not begin in adultery and perversion. It begins with little indiscretions like sex thoughts, sex discussions, passionate kissing, petting and such, growing with every exercise. The small indiscretion seems powerless compared to the sturdy body, the strong mind, the sweet spirit of youth who give way to the first temptation. But soon the strong has become weak, the master the slave, spiritual growth curtailed" ("President Kimball Speaks Out on Morality," *Ensign,* Nov. 1980, 94–95).

One couple shared the following story:

> The simple kisses we had often exchanged gradually developed into petting. . . . We loved each other so much that we convinced ourselves that it was not so wrong merely to pet since we sort of belonged to one another anyway. *Where we ended one night became the starting point for the next night,* and we continued on and on, until finally it happened—almost as though we could not control ourselves—we had intercourse. We had even talked about it and agreed that whatever else we did, we would not go that far. And then when it was late—so late—so

everlastingly late—we woke up to the meaning of what we had done (Spencer W. Kimball, "President Kimball Speaks Out on Morality," *Ensign,* Nov. 1980, 94–95; emphasis added).

- *Avoid pornography like the plague.* We are astounded by the number of men we have met, often returned missionaries, who struggle with this problem. Pornography is easily accessed these days. No longer do individuals need to leave home to find trouble; they can find it right in the privacy of their own rooms through the Internet. President Kimball declared: "That person who entertains . . . pornographic pictures and literature records them in his marvelous human computer, the brain, which can't forget this filth. Once recorded, it will always remain there, subject to recall" ("Be Ye Therefore Perfect," *Speeches of the Year, 1974–1975* [1975], 241). Elder Joseph B. Wirthlin taught, "Pornography in all its forms . . . constitutes a spiritual poison that is addictive and destructive. Every ounce of pornography and immoral entertainment will cause you to lose a pound of spirituality. And it will only take a few ounces of immorality to cause you to lose all of your spiritual strength, for the Lord's Spirit will not dwell in an unclean temple" ("The Message: Little Things Count," *New Era,* May 1988, 7).

- *Stay away from self-stimulation (masturbation).* This sinful behavior can become a difficult habit to break. Some have supposed that once they marry and become sexually active with their spouse, this habit will dissipate, only to find that they continue to have trouble ("Talking with Your Children about Moral Purity," *Ensign,* Dec. 1986, 58). President Kimball said of this self-abuse: "[This practice] is not approved of the Lord nor of his church, regardless of what may have been said by others whose "norms" are lower. Latter-day Saints are urged to avoid this practice. Anyone fettered by this weakness should abandon the habit before he goes on a mission, or receives the holy priesthood, or goes in the temple for his blessings" ("President Kimball Speaks Out on Morality," *Ensign,* Nov. 1980, 97).

The Joy of Marital Intimacy

Now, in our efforts to warn you of the consequences of sexual involvement outside of marriage, we need to say here that marital intimacy will be a wonderful blessing for the two of you if you keep it within marriage. It is true that on your wedding night, after years of abstinence, you will be authorized to participate in something that has been heretofore forbidden. But, if you come to the marriage bed clean and pure, the two of you can rejoice together in your innocence, both heart and soul. Then, as married companions, you can afford to be patient with your sexual progress because you have a long time after marriage to be involved in this wonderful experience. If your honeymoon does not turn out to meet your expectations, for example, you can be assured that in time you will be able to more fully enjoy this expression of physical intimacy. Because intimacy is God-ordained, the enjoyment of sexual relations is not a matter of good versus evil, but of the timing and context, which always includes marriage. This is because intimacy is a sacrament that connects you to each other, and to God and His eternal purposes. Simply put, sex before marriage is wrong, and sex after marriage is good because you are authorized by Deity, for the first time in your existence, to use your gender to further God's purposes. You may now use your reproductive powers not only to bless each other but to bring your own children, members of the Father's family, to mortality.

Making It All Worthwhile

A few years ago Elder Vaughn J. Featherstone shared the following story. A man told him that his son had been attending college for a year following his mission. During the course of that year the son became engaged and was preparing for his upcoming marriage. A week before the wedding day, this son drove home to visit his parents. The father noted that while home, their son, who was usually happy and filled with enthusiasm, seemed somber and serious. After about half an hour of superficial visiting, the son asked his father to meet him in the study. Instead of the father sitting behind the desk in the big chair, the son took his place there, and invited the father to sit in the smaller, hard-backed chair. The father related that this was truly a role reversal and wondered why he was in trouble. He prepared himself for a grilling. Elder Featherstone continues the story:

> Then the son said, "Dad, you know I am getting married next week."
>
> The father thought tenderly about his son's wedding and responded, "Yes, I know that, Son."
>
> Then the son said, "Dad, I thought you and Mom would like to know I am as clean and pure as the day you brought me into this life." Tears glistened in his eyes, then tears glistened in the father's eyes. He went to his son, hugged him, and kissed him on the cheek. He couldn't speak because his heart was full. The father later said, "I would rather have heard those words than to have been called to the high place in which I now serve. I would rather know what my son told me than to have been given a promotion in my company." Home is where the greatest blessings come.
>
> Home is where we learn purity of heart (Vaughn J. Featherstone, *Purity of Heart* [1982], 42–43).

As fathers, we cheered as our sons made touchdowns and shot baskets at the buzzer. We watched them become Eagle Scouts and serve honorable missions. We watched our daughters place in track meets and make the Honor Roll. We watched them earn their Young Women's Recognition Award, receive a mission call, and do well in school. However, we agree that nothing would rank higher in most parents' hearts than a conversation like that between this father and son. There is nothing any parent in the Church would rather hear than, "Mom and Dad, I am getting married next week. I want you to know that I am as clean and as pure as the day you brought me into this life." Go then and do likewise!

Questions to Consider

Consider the following question as it applies to your situation. If you are dating someone, discuss the applicable question between the two of you. If you are not currently in a relationship, decide where you stand on an issue before you start dating someone and how you would like to improve.

1. Read the following statement by President Kimball and then complete the question afterward.

> [Wise] young people will discipline themselves early in youth, charting long-range courses to include all that is wholesome and nothing that is ruinous. The bridge builder, before starting construction, draws charts and plans, makes estimates of strains and stresses, costs and hazards; the architect, even before excavation, makes a blueprint of the building from the foundation to the pinnacle. Similarly, the smart person will plan carefully and blueprint his own life from his first mental awakening to the end of life.
>
> "Just as a builder will wish his structure to stand through storm and disturbances of the elements, so the young and old alike will wish a life unharmed by adversities, calamities, and troubles throughout eternity. Having planned such a course, prudent men will gear their lives, activities, ambitions and aspirations so that they may have every advantage in total fulfillment of a righteous destiny." . . . Thus our young people should drive down stakes early, indicating their paths. The stakes are of two kinds: *"This I will do,"* and *"This I will not do."* These decisions pertain to general activities, standards, and spiritual goals, and personal programs. They should include anticipations for marriage and family. Very early, youth should have been living by a plan. They are the wise young man and the wise young woman who will profit by the experience of others, and who early set a course in their education, a mission, the finding of a pure, clean sweetheart to be a life's companion, their temple marriage and their Church service. When such a course is charted and the goal is set, it is easier to resist the many temptations and to say . . . "no" to the car ride which will take one into the dark, lonely and hazardous places, "no" to the first improper advances which lead eventually to immoral practices (Spencer W. Kimball, *The Miracle of Forgiveness* [1969], 234–236).

Discuss the following things that you will do and not do to set some sensible limits on physical affection and appropriate behavior before marriage.

<u>**This We Will Do:**</u>   <u>**This We Will Not Do:**</u>

1.   1.

2.   2.

3.   3.

4.   4.

CHAPTER 7

Building Strong Relationships Through Communication

"It isn't that we can't or don't know how to communicate with others as much as it is that we don't feel like risking our deep-down feelings with someone who is likely to stomp on them. It is never enjoyable to approach a parent, spouse, or colleague who is domineering, overwhelming, always right, angry, came from the "true-family," has all of the answers, is smothering, critical, sarcastic, puts you down, disagrees, or is negative. The inability to risk at personal and validating levels of communication leads to a shallow relationship or one that cannot last."[1]

The plan of salvation calls for us to leave our family of origin—father, mother, and siblings—to fashion a new life with a member of the opposite sex, someone who comes from a totally different background and upbringing than we do. That is what makes marriage such an interesting adventure!

We marry hoping that our union will satisfy the most intimate longings of our soul. Couples want marriage to satisfy their deepest yearnings for emotional and physical intimacy within the context of love, commitment, and sacred covenants. We believe that through marriage we will develop a oneness and closeness that will lead to an intimate physical and emotional exchange known only to happily married couples. To achieve this ideal, you must begin now, in your premarried state.

Unfortunately, many couples never reach this ideal. Sadly, we recognize that many married pairs live rather superficial lives together, sharing only those essential matters necessary to carry out the business side of marriage. Too few ever get around to sharing their deepest thoughts and feelings with each other, or exchanging personal dreams and ambitions. It is troubling to see couples function more like roommates with an occasional sexual exchange instead of committed, covenant partners, searching and exploring life together in a journey that includes an enriching, complementary sexual dimension. Some couples, it seems, never quite come to know the inner feelings and workings of their spouse, for they never fully engage in the profound adventure of companionship that marriage can provide. It is surprising to us that individuals often have friends outside of marriage who are closer to them and know more about them than their spouse does.

This is not the kind of marriage or companionship that most people desire. Our society already has too many sterile marriages. In such unions there is usually a quiet longing for a marriage that is much deeper, richer, fuller, and more meaningful than what exists. But they are content to settle for less. Sadly, we find some individuals looking outside their own marriage to seek what they are unable to achieve within it. Our view is that marriage is a mutual commitment to share life in depth, to plumb the depths of a kindred spirit and exchange secrets and dreams in an environment of safety and emotional security. We extend to each other respect and affection, and share intimate moments in a relationship nestled in eternal covenants. Surely that is what God designed marriage to be. And, when a marriage is bound together by feelings of gratitude and frequent and heartfelt expressions of love and appreciation, marriage and family difficulties and setbacks become mere stepping stones to personal growth and development—rather than stumbling blocks. As a person preparing for marriage you want to be sure that you and your spouse-to-be are good friends. "Marry your best friend" is still a wonderful bit of advice. We want to outline for you some ideas about communication that will bring you joy and satisfaction in your coming marriage.

Levels of Communication

Human beings communicate at three basic levels that we will label here as superficial, personal, and validating. Let's discuss them in that order.

1. ***Superficial Level:*** This is the level of communication that we use most often with others throughout the course of a day. Perhaps ninety-five percent of our daily communication occurs at this level. It is the level we use in normal conversations. It is a relatively safe, nonargumentative, information-processing level where we exchange information, ideas, observations, and comments with each other. This surface conversation is usually light in nature, descriptive, and where we discuss events and observations without much personal risk on our part. It is generally the first level of interaction between people. Perhaps you recognized this level of communication when you think back to your first dates, which are notorious for being superficial. You did not yet know each other well enough to risk your inner feelings and emotions without fear of self-exposure. On that first date, most couples end up jumping from topic to topic because they have no history of interaction to allow them to share anything intimate or private with a new acquaintance. Silence is not comfortable in new relationships, and therefore couples become quite proficient at exchanging information at a superficial level.

   This level of communication, however, is not necessarily shallow or simplistic (college courses, for example, often cover complex subjects, yet discussing such doesn't generally require personal risk). It is an essential level of exchange between human beings, but it is not a level of sharing that builds feelings of love in an emotional connection—"It's a nice day." "I love the fall colors; the air smells so clean and fresh." There is little personal risk involved in these expressions. Most of us would not expect any argument on such comments because there is little chance of controversy. Most people do not become emotionally involved over weather comments unless they are meteorologists. We assume that the other person agrees with our observations. "What did you think of the game?" "So, what ward are you in?" "How was your vacation?" "I think the temple is beautiful." Most meetings we attend (testimony meeting, hopefully, an exception), classes we take, information we receive, are superficial in function and form.

2. *Personal Level:* The second level of communication involves more risk on our part. It requires us to go beyond a superficial level of exchange to a deeper level of thought and feeling. Here we risk more of ourselves as we put our personal ideas and thoughts on line for inspection by others who may or may not agree with us. We do not want to be embarrassed or have our ideas rejected or seriously ridiculed, even by friends. We want our personal views to be treated gently and with respect by others, even if they see things differently than we do. We guard against emotional hurt. Thoughts and feelings about topics such as religion, politics, or philosophical positions may be of such a nature that we are hesitant to openly expose our views to others if we are unsure of their reaction. A personal level of communication is crucial in courtship because that is when we share opinions, beliefs, and learn about human sensitivity levels. It is how we determine, to some extent, our compatibility. When we share our ideas and feelings on issues, we usually find our relationship progressing; we begin to develop feelings of attraction, affection, and connection. Those who cannot share personal feelings typically move on to other relationships, unaware of why they don't build close relationships with others.

    Generally, a couple who finds compatibility in ideas, thoughts, and feelings will say something like this: "The two of us can discuss any topic." "We think so much alike." "We're comfortable with either one bringing up practically any subject." Of course, these feelings may change later as they become engaged or married, and more important subjects surface. It is important that both individuals respect personal thoughts and feelings if they are to forge strong emotional bonds.

3. *Validation Level:* This level of communication involves positive messages between individuals that convey worth, value, appreciation, and acceptance. This level of communication, by definition, is *always* positive and may be either verbal or nonverbal. "Wow, you look stunning in that outfit," is a verbal validation, while a wink, a glance of approval, a thumbs-up signal, or a kind touch, all convey positive messages in nonverbal ways. "I love being your fiancé." "I'm so glad we met. I feel like we are developing a fun relationship." "I love the way you take charge and solve problems." These are validating verbal statements. A squeeze of the hand, an arm around each other, an expression known only to the two of you, convey positive meanings in a nonverbal way.

Validation generally involves more risk than either a personal or superficial level of communication, because there is always the fear of rejection. As human beings, we are somewhat fragile and sensitive to how others react when we express our ideas and feelings. What guy has not wondered just what he said or did to make his fiancée cry? What girl has not been frustrated that her fiancé did not seem to understand her feelings on a particular issue? There will be many opportunities during the engagement period and early marriage to realize that you have different opinions about many things—things that were relatively unimportant in the dating and courtship stages.

To understand how traumatic rejection can be, and what great lengths we go to avoid it, let's use an example. Suppose a guy places his arm around his date while at the movies. If she leaves his arm there, it signifies to him her approval and he will no doubt leave it there until his circulation is cut off! However, if his date was not prepared for that level of commitment and did not expect or want it, she may gently lift his arm off her shoulder or excuse herself to go to the restroom, sending the message that she was not ready for that level of closeness. As a result, he will not likely try the same thing again for some time. Rejection is a powerful negative emotion, something we shy away from when we can. Normally, we like to be around people who make us feel good. We don't like abrasive individuals or those who are condescending or impatient with us.

Couples who exchange validation will find their relationship moving to a deeper level of emotional attachment. Validation leads to the generation of positive feelings, further commitment, courtship, and, of course, marriage. In fact, happily married couples, almost by definition, are those who find it easy to share their deepest feelings, to risk positive thoughts and ideas easily, while couples who struggle in marriage generally find it difficult to be genuine and complimentary.

Married couples have the added dimension of sexual relations. The Lord designed marital intimacy to be a validating experience for husbands and wives through intimate exchanges of touch and expression that convey trust, desirability, and other strong emotional feelings. Though the world refers to it only as "making love," marital intimacy is also a way for married couples to share feelings and *commitment* at a most profound level of exchange. The act of marriage is wrapped in erotic and tactile stimulation designed to be an important source of validation for both spouses. It supports and deepens verbal validation.

The intimate union of a couple is a way for sweethearts to express feelings of love and trust in verbal and nonverbal ways. We will discuss marital intimacy in more detail in chapter eleven.

Understanding and Meeting Personal Needs

The reason validation and personal levels of communication create positive feelings has to do with human needs. We all have in common basic needs such as air to breathe, food to eat, shelter from the elements, and clothing for our bodies. We also have psychological and emotional needs that include acceptance, independence, creativity, worth, value, and a desire to be loved and included, along with many more. We are not hermits living in a vacuum. We interact with each other and are open to emotional reactions. When our needs for love and acceptance, worth and competence are met by another individual, we develop positive feelings and emotions for them. If those needs are met for both individuals, feelings of attachment and affection begin to form.

Let's combine both the concepts of human needs and the three levels of communication into a meaningful model. Obviously, communication carries a stimulus value, creating either positive or negative emotions. We react to what others say, and they react to our ideas. "Please pass the salt," has little emotional content, whereas "Why are these clothes all over the place?" may have great emotional significance depending on the context.

You have already discerned that a superficial level of communication contains little emotional content because what information is exchanged requires little risk. A personal level, or a validation level of communication, on the other hand, has more "risk value" because if a message is ignored, rejected, or treated roughly, we usually seek safety and less vulnerability by falling back to a more superficial level of exchange. There is less chance of our looking inadequate or inept when we are superficial or quiet. However, the problem with this level of communication is that little emotional bonding can take place.

To illustrate the principle of risk and its effect on us, let's take a common situation. Assume that you are in a Sunday School class and the teacher asks the class members if they have any comments about the subject under discussion. If you have been thinking about the topic and have something to share, you understand the concept of risk. You want to contribute, but you do not want to embarrass yourself in front of everyone. Oh how we guard against being embarrassed! Maybe what you say will be normal and reasonable, maybe even insightful, but you are not sure if you can say it in such a way that it will be appreciated, or if you can really say what you mean. There is always the fear that your personal insights may reveal something about the way you think or believe, and others may be exposed to your faulty logic. To avoid making yourself look less than brilliant, even before you raise your hand to make a comment, you very quickly rehearse in your mind what you would like to say out loud. You mentally evaluate, in your own private screening room, the impact of your comment on class members before you raise your hand. We do it in an instant.

How we react in any social situation often depends on our history of making comments in public, and the outcomes that took place. If the teacher or class members handle our personal comments positively, we are encouraged to risk again. If the stake president happens to be visiting the class that day, you may sit quietly back and let the teacher do his/her thing, or, if you do jump in with any comments at all, they may be safe, superficial, and quite orthodox.

If your experience in risking was positive you may even raise your hand again in the future. On the other hand, if the teacher does not acknowledge your comment, or simply says, "Well, we need to get back to the lesson," you might be a little stunned. You may hesitate to risk again, at least in that class, on that day, or with that teacher. The context of your comments, your personal feelings, and your self-worth, all play a part in public episodes of sharing and risking. There are individuals who never raise their hand in a public setting. They would rather just listen to what everyone else has to say and come to their own conclusions. They don't want to say anything that might embarrass them. Perhaps they have concluded through past experiences that their ideas or opinions don't sound very bright or articulate, or that their judgment is faulty, and so have learned to just keep their ideas to themselves. They do not volunteer much information for fear of personal embarrassment. Remaining quiet, for them, is more comfortable than sticking their neck out and risking. Our personalities can be shaped by our past experiences with risking.

Now, let's apply the principle to dating and courtship. Dating is designed to be positive and validating. We might ask this question: "How are your own personal needs for love, acceptance, appreciation, and value met on a consistent, ongoing basis in your present relationship?" Most likely, your answer may be that you've developed feelings of love, worth, and acceptance between you and your fiancé as you communicated together at *personal* and *validation* levels. Of course, the opposite is also true: If you feel rejected, unloved, worthless, or frustrated, it is because personal and validation levels of communication are not taking place effectively. To build a healthy, vibrant, affectionate relationship with another human being, personal and validating communication *must be exchanged.* A relationship that cannot rise above a superficial level of communication will not develop into a healthy, vibrant relationship, where feelings and positive emotions are created and sustained. Healthy relationships both before and after marriage require personal and validating communication. If these two levels are not present, it is unlikely that the relationship will develop outside of a superficial friendship.

Let's diagram these patterns. The first illustration shows what happens when we risk and receive a negative response to our risk attempts. In these instances, we stop sharing our feelings and move to a more superficial level of communication.

Risk-Taking in Communication with a Negative Response

RISK FEELINGS/IDEAS→NEGATIVE RESPONSE→STOP SHARING

•Lose confidence in each other
•Withdraw from interacting
•Less risking of personal ideas/opinions
•Stop sharing personal feelings
•Mistrust develops
•Anger and frustration increase
•Feelings of closeness dissipate
•Emotional void
•Start to avoid each other
•May seek the company of others
•Personal and validation levels cease
•Feelings of affection dissipate

Of course, single episodes of risk with a negative response take place in any couple's short-term interactions. But if this pattern were to become the norm rather than the exception, the relationship would suffer very negative consequences.

Let's look at the positive model of communication, the model we want you to develop:

Risk-Taking in Communication with a Positive Response

RISK FEELINGS/IDEAS → POSITIVE RESPONSE → RISK AGAIN

•Feelings of trust develop/continue
•Emotional closeness is strengthened
•Feelings of love intensify
•The relationship is strengthened
•Being together is enjoyable
•Affection is expressed naturally
•Enjoy exchanging personal ideas/comments
•Mutually therapeutic
•Loyalty/commitment to each other is strengthened
•We like each other; affection grows

When you risk personal feelings, ideas, and validation with your fiancé and they risk back, positive emotional bonds develop. When you can be yourself, when you can be genuine and comfortable around a good friend, and he or she reciprocates, a mutual friendship develops.

The point is that most people think that relationships do not develop because there is not enough communication between the couple to make them work well. (They would not be thinking of marriage, or be close enough to marriage if they were not quite proficient at communicating together.) The real problem is that individuals don't feel like risking their deepest feelings and ideas with someone who is critical, negative, or puts down their cherished views.

Can you imagine a young woman telling her parents, "My fiancé is so sarcastic, he talks down to me, and sometimes he won't even talk to me. But I can hardly wait till we're married in the temple!" Of course not. Who would want to be around, much less marry, someone who is domineering, overwhelming, always right, angry, came from the "true family," has all the answers, and is smothering, critical, sarcastic, demeaning, argumentative, or negative? No one would. No one wants to remain in a negative relationship. It is this negative communication pattern that is most responsible for people not wanting to marry, or wanting out of marriage.

You want to marry someone with whom you can share almost everything. No one wants a date or spouse who has fun at our expense. President David O. McKay counseled new couples:

> I do not know who wrote this, but it is good advice: "In the first solitary hour after the ceremony, take the bridegroom and demand a solemn vow of him (this is to the wife) and give a vow in return; promise each other sacredly never, not even in jest, to wrangle with each other, never to bandy words, or indulge in the least ill-humor. Never—I say never! Wrangling in jest, putting on an air of ill-humor, merely to tease, becomes earnest by practice! Mark that!
>
> Next, promise each other, sincerely and solemnly, never to keep a secret from each other, under whatever pretext, and whatever excuse it might be. You must continually, and every moment, see clearly into each other's bosom. Even when one of you has committed a fault, wait not an instant, but confess it. And as you keep nothing from each other, so, on the contrary, preserve the privacies of your house, marriage state, and heart, from father, mother, brother, sister, aunt, and from all the world. You two, with God's help, build your own quiet world. Every third or fourth one you draw into it with you will form a party and stand between you two. That should never be. Promise this to each other. Remember the vow at each temptation. . . . Your souls will grow, as it were, to each other, and at last will become as one. Ah, if many a pair had, on their marriage day, known the secret, how many a marriage were happier than, alas, they are!" (*Gospel Ideals*, 472).

It is important that you learn now to communicate at levels that build feelings of love. Here is how one wife felt about her husband:

> Being married to my husband is one of the most frustrating experiences of my life! I grew up with a bunch of sisters and we talked and yakked about everything late into the night. When I got married, I assumed that my husband and I would talk about everything too. WRONG! Trying to get my husband to discuss even superficial things is tough. When I got married, I expected that my husband and I would talk about anything and everything as a way to keep our marriage strong and viable. How can I draw my husband into conversations that are meaningful and therapeutic to me (and hopefully to him) when he hides behind the newspaper or television? Whenever I try to ask him how he

feels about something, or get his input on an important issue in our family or our life, he says, "Oh, I don't care. Do whatever you think best," and then he goes back to whatever he was doing. It is so exasperating!

It isn't always just husbands who have a difficult time communicating. Here is an example of a frustrated husband whose wife will not discuss issues that are threatening to her.

> I have a hard time talking about anything meaningful with my wife. We really do have a superficial relationship when it comes to discussing issues that I think are important. Whenever I bring up something that looks or sounds a little serious to her, she wants to change the subject. How can I bring up topics that I think need our attention when she is simply unwilling to discuss issues that I feel need joint input? It is so frustrating to want to share ideas and thoughts with her on specific issues, but she is uninterested or unwilling to talk to me about them. For example, I feel we need to talk about our children and how we discipline them, our finances, our intimacy, but she just refuses to get involved. She will get up and walk out of the room, change the subject, or ignore me. I really don't know what to do!

Now, while you are in the premarital arena, check to see that your communication patterns and your ability to risk together are healthy. This doesn't mean that you will never use superficial communication in your marriage. Of course you will, and lots of it. But the point is that happily married couples are comfortable moving back and forth between these three levels. They do not have to begin each exchange with each other at a superficial level (walking on eggshells) to determine their spouse's mood before they know if it is all right to share more meaningful information. A wife was asked: "When your husband comes home from work, do you stop what you are doing and give him a hug and a kiss and tell him you are happy to see him?" (That is validating behavior.) She said, "Heck no!" When asked why not, she said, "If I were to do that, he would probably push me away and ask me 'What have you been up to today?'" If that reaction were typical of his response, would you not predict that the wife would cease attempting to validate her husband? That is exactly what she did. The penalty they both paid was missing a wonderful opportunity to enrich each other and their marriage. You can be sure that her husband is also aware of the lack of validation, but he is unwilling to make any corrections himself. This is a terrible pattern we see in so many relationships! Don't ever allow this negative pattern to get a foothold in your relationship now or later in your marriage. Now is the time, in your engagement period, to make sure that your relationship allows you to risk with each other in ways that are comfortable, enjoyable, and therapeutic.

Summary

Communication itself is neutral, positive, or negative, depending on how it is used. We use positive communication, for example, when we pray, propose, or when we are in a good mood. ("Thanks for a wonderful dinner . . . fun evening . . . for helping me review for my test.") But, we can also use communication to punish, hurt, be sarcastic, or be hurtful ("You never seem to be able to. . ." "Why is it that you always have to. . ." "Why can't you ever. . ."). Whether we use positive or negative communication in our relationship depends on our heart, our character, and our Christlike nature (or lack thereof). We use negative communication to manipulate or cause someone else to change their behavior or feelings to suit our whim. The levels of communication we use with each other are a reflection of our own spiritual and emotional state.

We encourage you to be a positive communicator. Develop enough sensitivity to be aware of what levels of communication you use, and their effect on your relationship. If you truly enjoy your relationship now, that's a good indicator that you have been positive with each other to this point in your relationship, and that pattern is what will keep your relationship growing now and after marriage. Feelings of love and affection develop and are maintained when we communicate at all three levels of communication.

Questions to Consider

Consider the following questions as they apply to your situation. If you are dating someone, discuss the applicable questions between the two of you. If you are not currently in a relationship, decide where you stand on an issue before you start dating someone and how you would like to improve.

1. If you are dating someone, think back to your first date. What things did you talk about then? Do you remember the superficiality of the occasion? How do you both feel you have progressed in your ability and willingness to share with each other?

2. At what points in your relationship did your conversation become more personal? When did you feel like you could "risk" with each other without fear of being hurt or put down? What do you remember as the biggest risk you took with each other?

3. What can you do to ensure that you always share at personal and validating levels of communication with each other? What could happen to stop your ability to risk with each other?

CHAPTER 8

Resolving Relationship Differences

"I have often wondered what would happen if a perfect man married a perfect woman. I'll bet he would shoot her inside of a week if she didn't poison him first."[1]

Although you were initially attracted to each other because of things you found in common (could talk easily together, similar values and beliefs and opinions, enjoyed the same music, foods, etc.), as you progress through your courtship and engagement, differences in personality, character, manners, and habits no doubt will emerge in one way or another. Unfortunately, many individuals who feel that their relationship has potential often "pull the ejection handle" when any type of friction or differences surface. In fact, many engaged couples who experience a few differences as their relationship progresses become nervous and wonder if they are marrying the right person. Often, they begin to waver as the time of their marriage nears. They go back and forth questioning themselves over and over. Unfortunately, there are too many people who believe that if you are happy with each other, you simply wouldn't ever have any disagreements.

We are reminded of the scene in the *Father of the Bride* when Annie is about to call off the marriage because Brian gave her a blender as a premarital gift. To Annie, the blender implied that she was to be a stay-at-home mom, barefoot and pregnant; to Brian, on the other hand, the blender was nothing more than a useful appliance for making great shakes. Sadly, they were going to call the marriage off because of this little tiff. As you are probably aware, they did end up marrying, but not until they came to the realization that every normal couple has disagreements and problems to work through. May we repeat: *every normal couple will have problems and disagreements to work through.* Don't let minor disagreements ruin a good relationship. (There is a difference between a red flag and plain old cold feet. Obviously, if you are being put down, criticized, and your personality is being assaulted, you *are* in the wrong relationship.)

We are aware of a couple that divorced after six months of marriage. When asked why they broke up, the former bride said, "We just fought and argued too much. I lived in a home where my parents never had a disagreement. I didn't think couples who loved each other would argue that much." Years later, this same woman, more wise and mature, said, "I should have never divorced my first husband. I didn't realize until I was much older that my parents did fight and argue, they just never did it in front of me. So I grew up thinking that if you had a good marriage, you would never contend with each other. I compared my first marriage with the fantasy of my parent's marriage, and I thought my marriage was terrible." What a tragedy. If only this woman would have realized that disagreements and occasional spats are normal parts of marriage. Perhaps it could be argued that her parents did a disservice to her by hiding all of their problems. The issue is not *if* you will have disagreements any more than the issue is *if* you might get sick—everyone does. The issue will always be how you handle the inevitable differences that arise in every marriage. Elder Bruce C. Hafen put it this way: "The difference between a successful and an unsuccessful marriage is not in whether there are such times of tension, but in whether and how the tensions are resolved" (*The Broken Heart* [1989], 49).

Judith Viorst has humorously described dealing with such differences:

> Before my husband and I got married, we never had fights about anything. What was there, after all, to fight about? On every fundamental issue—war, peace, race relations, religion, education, the meaning of the universe—we were in total, sweet accord. Surely we had no reason to think that this mellow state of affairs would not continue for the next 40 or 50 years.

From the moment we were married, we have managed to have fights about almost everything. What isn't there, after all, to fight about? We're still in total accord on those fundamental issues—but so what? That still leaves clothes, cooking, driving, sex, money, inlaws, children, and who gets to read the newspaper first. And there isn't the slightest possibility that this embattled state of affairs will not continue.

I hadn't planned it this way. My marriage, as I too frequently informed people in my premarital innocence, was going to be a mature, intelligent relationship. If, perchance, some small disagreement happened to trouble the serenity of our days, it would be resolved promptly by rational discourse. This was a swell plan.

Unfortunately, it had nothing to do with reality. Reality, I found out in the course of our honeymoon, was my getting resentful about having to lend him my hairbrush and his getting huffy about the way I left the soap in the washbasin instead of the soap dish. Honestly, I didn't know until then that we even had positions on hairbrushes and soap dishes—but we do indeed. . . . We have, it turns out, passionately held positions on hundreds of subjects too lowly ever to have been thought of until we started living, day in and day out, with someone who failed to share our cherished views.

He thinks a comfortable house temperature is 68 degrees. I think a comfortable temperature is 84.

He thinks a safe speed on the New Jersey Turnpike is 90 miles an hour. I think a safe speed is 45.

He thinks it's unnecessary to enter checks in the checkbook. I think that not entering each check should be punishable by death in the electric chair. . . .

Any couple is capable of escalating dumb disagreements to ferocious fighting. In our household, escalation often happens when it's too early in the morning or too late at night. Take 7:15 A.M. when, according to my youthful dreams, my husband and I were going to awake smiling warmly at each other, and then launch immediately into a vivacious discussion of [current events]. Instead, I grope my way out of bed feeling exceedingly crabby and put-upon, while he coldly informs me that there isn't a single pair of matching socks in his drawer. . . . Theoretically, it might . . . be possible to see his remark as something other than an attack. But 7:15 A.M. is not one of my finer moments—and it is definitely no time to talk to me about socks. So, I point out to him that just because his parents catered to all his infantile needs doesn't mean that I have to perpetuate this kind of crippling emotional dependency. The morning deteriorates from there. . . .

On countless occasions, in the afterfight afterglow, we both have made the most beautiful resolutions. I won't complain anymore when he's not on time. He won't complain anymore if I use his razor. I won't tell him he just went through a stop sign. He won't tell me I just destroyed the fried eggs (Copyright © 1970 by Judith Viorst. Originally appeared in *Redbook;* condensed by *Reader's Digest;* as cited in D.E. Brinley, *Toward a Celestial Marriage* [1986], 97–99).

The Reality of Differences

Most married couples, and even many who are engaged, can relate to the above story. As you prepare for marriage, you will find that you actually have a large number of differences. They may not be important to either one of you yet, and may be unknown at this point in time because you are not living together. Your commitment is not yet complete, so the investment in each other's behavior is not quite as great as it will be after you marry. Couples tend to overlook a lot of little things until they reach a position where *things* really matter. One of the great myths in marriage is that disagreements, quarrels, and contention only occur in bad marriages. This simply is not true. Disagreements, quarrels, and contention are present in *all* marriages. In fact, our experience has taught us that couples who divorce do not have any more problems than those who stay married. In other words, couples who stay together have as many problems as those who terminate their marriages; but the couples who stay together simply *place a higher value on their commitment to each other* and have a great desire to work through their problems. Dr. James Dobson explained:

> Two people are not compatible simply because they love each other and both are professing Christians. Many young couples assume that the sunshine and flowers that characterized their courtship will continue for the rest of their lives. . . . It is

naive to expect two unique and strong-willed individuals to mesh together like a couple of machines. Even gears have multiple cogs with rough edges to be honed before they will work in concert. . . . A good marriage is not one where perfection reigns: It is a relationship where a healthy perspective overlooks a multitude of "unresolvables."[2]

Indeed, a healthy perspective will help you overcome many differences. To borrow the analogy from Dr. Dobson, most couples have "cogs" that don't mesh. Our colleague, Brent Barlow, had such an experience. After he and his wife and been married for just a few weeks, Brent's parents telephoned one Saturday morning to indicate that they were passing through town and would like to stop by. Brent began to tidy the place up while his new bride, Susan, began to cook breakfast. Unknown to Brent at the time, and to most of the male population in America, making the first meal for the in-laws is a stressful rite of passage for new brides. So, when Susan dropped the first egg in the frying pan, the yolk broke, and instantly she began to cry. Brent was insensitive to her tears and began to tell her to quit crying over broken eggs. This only made matters worst. Brent didn't understand that his new wife wanted the meal to be just right. An argument ensued, and then, the doorbell rang.

Brent and Susan went into "Mormon Delay" (the ability of Latter-day Saints to rant and rave at their families, and then answer the phone with a perfect and dignified, "Hello") as they greeted their family and had a good visit. However, soon after their family departed, they were able to resume their argument almost right where they left off. As the day wore on, three week's worth of problems surfaced. By 11:00 P.M., Brent and Susan were discussing the finer points of their relationship, such as "Why did we get married in the first place?" and "How will our marriage survive?" Remember, all of this over one lousy egg.

The next day Brent and Susan found themselves in fast and testimony meeting in their new ward. They were still feeling somewhat depressed from the night before and were wondering if their marriage had a chance. During the course of the meeting, an older gentleman bore his testimony. He let everyone in the congregation know that he and his wife had been married over fifty years and never had an argument or expressed a cross word to each other. This only drove the Barlows into deeper despair. Here was a man saying that he and his wife hadn't had a disagreement in fifty years and Brent and Susan couldn't even make it three weeks (which would actually double most people's record). They left the church more depressed and dejected than when they arrived.

Later that afternoon, Brent phoned his sister who had been married several years. He asked her if she and her husband had ever been in an argument before. She let Brent know that of course they had arguments and disagreements—all normal couples do. Brent then related the story of the old man in church who hadn't argued with his wife in fifty years. His sister assured him that a) either the old man was a liar, or b) he was forgetful, and c) if it really were true, what a dull and boring marriage they must have had.

With the encouragement of his sister, Brent and Susan were able to mend their differences. He apologized for not being as sensitive as he should have been, and she admitted that crying over broken eggs may have been overreacting. Thankfully, they were able to move forward and put their "egg-issues" behind them (See B.A. Barlow, *Just for Newlyweds* [1992]). However, there is an important point here. Like many couples, the Barlows believed that those who have good marriages don't have differences or disagreements. Elder Joe J. Christensen, however, has wisely stated:

> Occasionally we hear something like, "Why, we have been married for fifty years, and we have never had a difference of opinion." If that is literally the case, then one of the partners is overly dominated by the other or, as someone said, is a stranger to the truth. *Any intelligent couple will have differences of opinion. Our challenge is to be sure that we know how to resolve them. That is part of the process of making a good marriage better* ("Marriage and the Great Plan of Happiness," *Ensign,* May 1995, 65; emphasis added).

One of the main objectives in coming to mortality was to experience problems and to learn how to solve them. In 2 Nephi 2, we are taught that there is opposition in all things. Why would marriage be any different? The earth is filled with a host of mortals with a bunch of problems. No one is excluded—no one. The life cycle assures that. No matter what stage of life you are in, there will always be obstacles glaring at you. Even the people we most admire, even Church leaders, must deal with marital problems. Case in point: One morning when Joseph Smith was translating the Book of Mormon, his wife, Emma, did something that caused Joseph to take offense. After the disagreement, Joseph went upstairs to continue the work of translation. However, he found that he could not translate a single syllable. So what did he do? He went out into the orchard and prayed. About an hour later Joseph got up from his prayer, went into the house and asked Emma to forgive him. Only then was he able to commence the translation of the Book of Mormon (See B.H. Roberts, *A Comprehensive History of the Church,* 1:131.)

Another example comes from the life of current Apostle Jeffrey R. Holland. He and his wife, Pat, shared the following humor with the BYU student body:

> Pat: Do you want to know what I have told him he does that irritates me the most? It is that he walks everywhere in a hurry—first five, then ten, then fifty feet in front of me. I have learned now to just call out and tell him to save me a place when he gets where he's going.
>
> Jeff: Well, as long as we are telling secrets, do you want to know what irritates me? It is that she is always late and that we are therefore always running to get somewhere, with me first five, then ten, and then fifty feet in front of her.
>
> Pat: We have learned to laugh about that a little, and now compromise. I watch the time a bit better, he slows down a stride or two, and we actually touch fingertips about every other bounce.
>
> Jeff: But we don't have everything worked out yet—like room temperatures. I used to joke about LDS scripturalists who worried about the body temperature of translated beings. I don't joke anymore, because I now worry seriously about my wife's body temperature. She has an electric blanket on high for eleven months of the year. She suffers hypothermia at the Fourth of July picnic. She thaws out from about 2:00 to 3:30 on the afternoon of August 12; then it's bundle-up time again.

> Pat: He ought to talk. He throws the window open every night as if he's Admiral Peary looking for the North Pole. But let someone suggest a little winter morning's jogging and he sounds like a wounded Siberian sheepdog. Mr. Health here can't tie his shoelaces without taking oxygen (Jeffrey R. & Patricia T. Holland, "Some Things We Have Learned—Together," in *On Earth As It Is In Heaven* [1989], 103-104).

Since marriage *is* a series of adjustments, even the best adapted couples will have issues to resolve. After the glamor of the wedding and the drama of the honeymoon is over, you two will have to settle into real life. President Kimball wisely counseled:

> Some think of happiness as a glamourous life of ease, luxury, and constant thrills; but true marriage is based on a happiness which is more than that, one that comes from giving, serving, sharing, sacrificing, and selflessness. Two people coming from different backgrounds soon learn after the ceremony is performed that stark reality must be faced. There is no longer a life of fantasy or make-believe; we must come out of the clouds and put our feet firmly on the earth. Responsibility must be assumed and new duties must be accepted. Some personal freedoms must be relinquished, and many adjustments, unselfishness adjustments, must be made.

> One comes to realize very soon after the marriage that the spouse has weaknesses not previously revealed or discovered. The virtues which were constantly magnified during courtship now grow relatively smaller, and the weaknesses that seemed so small and insignificant during courtship now grow to sizable proportions. The hour has come for understanding hearts, for self-appraisal, and for good common sense, reasoning, and planning" (Spencer W. Kimball, *Marriage and Divorce* [1976], 13).

Differences Can Destroy

Frankly, the ability to resolve differences will determine whether your marriage goes well or not. Differences that go unresolved can bring disagreement, conflict, anger, a loss of the Spirit, and frustrated relationships. In the state of Utah, for example, 54% of all divorces occur within the first five years of marriage; 18% occur within the first year.[3]

Regardless of why divorces occur, we are more interested in prevention. Remember our premise: fences are preferable to ambulances. It is important that you understand and anticipate that differences will surface as you two interact. Some of your differences will be minor and some may be quite major. The Association of Mormon Counselors and Psychotherapists (AMCAP) reported on the most common problems facing newly married couples. The therapists ranked unrealistic expectations about marriage or spouse as the number one problem facing LDS couples entering marriage (71%), followed by communication (69%), money management/ finances (58%), decision making/problem solving (54%), power struggles (53%), and sex (50%).[4] Unfortunately, couples who are not prepared, or who have no experience in confronting problems, often end up bailing out of their marriages. You can prevent such damage ahead of time by preparing yourselves to deal with any differences now, before you say "I do."

According to the study mentioned, unrealistic expectations may be the most obvious problem you will face in marriage. All who come into marriage will need to be prepared to deal with each other's expectations. Some individuals expect a lot out of marriage (high maintenance), while others do not (low maintenance). It might be a good idea to discuss some of the expectations that you have for each other now and as marriage partners. You might want to discuss friends, recreation, money management, sexual intimacy, in-law relations, children, housekeeping, religious rituals and practices, job/career issues, and anything else that you might feel is important. The idea is to learn what you two expect of each other in various areas of marriage and family relations. If you can discuss these issues now and develop a healthy system for dealing with differences, you will be well on your way to a successful enterprise. (We have included a form to help you in this analysis at the end of this chapter.)

We all come into marriage with high expectations that we will please each other. However, when you merge two families, you quickly learn that there are many differences that can surface, as Judith Viorst indicated. Every couple must understand that they will have differences, but that they can handle those differences in appropriate and relationship-building ways. Learn from each other what your expectations are for spousal behavior. Obviously it will not be essential to discuss every little detail, but some of the "big" issues that are listed above need your attention now so they don't surprise you after marriage. If you can do this now then you will be much more prepared for marriage.

Let's take an example. One of the major areas that usually causes problems in new marriages is the house. Take a peek on the chart entitled "Marital Expectations." You will notice house is number 7 on the chart. "House" may imply anything from what color you want the interior or exterior to be, to whether or not you have a sprinkler system. But that isn't the issue. We want you to think as broadly as you can about each of these areas. However, to lead you just a tad, let's examine the housekeeping role. Who will do the dishes, for example? Vacuum? One of the top marriage stressors today in many families is the division of household labor. You can probably understand why. More women are in the workforce than ever before, yet once they come home from their jobs, they are still expected to do 90 percent of the housework. This can be a "hot button" for working wives, and it is better to discuss this issue now than two weeks after you marry. One author reported that household responsibilities are the number one area of family disagreement in contemporary marriages. Young and old husbands, be prepared to grab a broom and help out. It's easier to sweep a kitchen floor than keep stressing the marriage relationship.

Complete together the following worksheet.

Marital Expectations

Instructions: Fill in what you wish would happen in your marriage and what you would like your future spouse to do in each category:

	I would like to:	I would like my future spouse to:
1. Socializing		
2. Recreation		
3. Money Management		
4. Sexual Intimacy		
5. In-law Relations		
6. Children		
7. House		
8. Religious Practices		
9. Job or Career		
10. Other		

Adapted from John Narcisco, Ph.D. and David T. Seamons, Ph.D.

Another area that can cause trouble for newly married couples is misunderstandings in communication. We devoted an entire chapter to communication to help you learn how important it is to share and risk with each other. The idea is to marry someone who will become a therapist to you, and you to them. Marriage was designed for complete sharing. Those who can't risk with each other will generally have shallow marriages and unexamined relationships. Apply the principles of the gospel to your relationship now. Be empathetic. Share feelings with each other in calm, rational ways. Take time for talking together now. Don't walk around the room when your friend or fiancé is trying to talk with you—give them your full attention. Developing healthy communication patterns now will serve you well after you are married and provide a healthy model for your future children. President David O. McKay cautioned the men of the Church:

> No member of this Church—husband, father—has the right to utter an oath in his home or ever to express a cross word to his wife or to his children. . . . You have to contribute to an ideal home by your character, controlling your passion, your temper, guarding your speech, because those things will make your home what it is and what it will radiate. . . . Say nothing that will hurt your wife, that will cause her tears, even though she might cause you provocation. . . . He is a weak man who flies into a passion. . . . A man of the priesthood should not fly into a passion. Learn to be dignified (as cited by Stephen R. Covey, *Spiritual Roots of Human Relations* [1993], 190–191).

This counsel applies equally to the sisters of the Church. None of us has the right to speak anything to each other unless it is positive and edifying. Then, the Holy Spirit can increase our ability to be kind, tenderhearted, and forgiving towards each other (see Eph. 4:29–32).

Resolving Differences—A Scriptural Example

An example of how to handle ourselves in resolving marital conflict comes from an account in the Book of Mormon record. It may be that this is the only account of a marital disagreement found in the scriptures. In 1 Nephi 5, we learn of a contention that arose between a prophet and his wife. The Lord told Lehi to send his sons back to Jerusalem to obtain the set of brass plates. They were gone far longer than Sariah expected them to be, and she began to lose faith in the journey to which Lehi had committed the family. She raised four major complaints against her husband: 1) his visions had led them into the wilderness and were the cause of much grief and sorrow, 2) they lost all of their possessions and now the family estate was gone (they had literally left everything to escape Jewish persecution), 3) their boys were probably dead by now, and 4) if that were so, the entire family was doomed to die without the protection their older sons could provide.

How Lehi handled these major issues is a testament of his Christlike nature. It also serves as a model of how couples should deal with their own disagreements and how they should treat each other when they see issues differently. Regarding Sariah's first concern about her husband being a visionary man, Lehi essentially said, "Dear, I know that I have had some unusual experiences. If it weren't for what the Lord showed me, I would agree with you. However, I know what the Lord has taught me; it is important that we left Jerusalem; otherwise, we would have been destroyed in our home." (see 1 Ne. 5:4) Notice that Lehi did not attack Sariah and her family ("you're a doubter just like your mother"), or spend time criticizing her weaknesses ("you've been a wimp ever since I married you!") Lehi didn't pull rank by saying, "Hey, who's the prophet here anyway?" There were no temper tantrums or threats to sleep outside the tent. In fact, there was no defensiveness on his part whatsoever. Lehi appears to graciously and humbly listen and demonstrate empathy, as if to say: "Sweetheart, I know this is tough on you. I don't blame you for being discouraged. I can only tell you what I know and what I have experienced; and I know that the Lord's hand is in this. He has shown me what would have happened had we remained in the city."

Sariah's second objection concerned the loss of family estate, creature comforts, resources, wealth, and their possessions. Lehi responded to her concern with kindness. In effect, he said: "I know that we have lost everything of a material nature. 'But, behold, I have obtained a land of promise, in the which things I do rejoice' (v. 5). We are on the Lord's errand, and He will compensate us well for the loss of our property and home." Once again, no defensiveness, no criticism, no withdrawal. Lehi dealt with Sariah's concerns patiently and humbly.

Her third objection was that their sons were probably dead already. Lehi responded with his testimony: "I know that the Lord will deliver [our] sons out of the hands of Laban, and bring them down again unto us in the wilderness" (v. 5). It is as if Lehi said to his wife: "Yes, it is a dangerous mission. Their travel may not be easy and is certainly fraught with danger. But I am confident that the Lord will inspire them and they will return unharmed."

Finally, Sariah feared that the rest of the family would be killed as well. Joseph and Jacob were born in the wilderness and there were daughters. Lehi's reassurance that the boys would return solved this final problem. He didn't respond with "Why don't you ever listen to me? Can't you hear what I am telling you? We'll get through this if you'll just relax." No, none of that stuff. Lehi was compassionate and understood his wife's concerns.

Nephi described the outcome of Lehi's charitable treatment of his wife. "And after this manner of language (resolving her concerns, to use missionary jargon) did my father, Lehi, comfort my mother, Sariah, concerning us" (v. 6). Lehi did so with kindness, faith, and testimony. No nasty lectures. No talking down to her. When their sons made it back to camp Sariah "was exceedingly glad" (v. 1). Nephi recorded that "their joy was full, and my mother was comforted" (v. 7). Because Lehi acted as you would expect a man of God would, he treated his wife in such a way that the Lord's Spirit touched her heart. She received her own witness: "Now I know of a surety that the Lord hath commanded my husband to flee into the wilderness; yea, and I also know of a surety that the Lord hath protected my sons, and delivered them out of the hands of Laban, and given them power whereby they could accomplish the thing which the Lord hath commanded them" (v. 8).

It is a credit to Sariah that she never wavered or attacked her husband after this experience. From that point on she was committed to the cause. We learn something of her stature when a few days later the Lord spoke to Lehi and commanded him to send the boys *back* to Jerusalem to obtain wives. A lesser woman than Sariah might have said angrily, "Look Buster, you lucked out the first time you sent these kids off. You're not sending them back again unless it's over my dead body! Once was enough. I let you have your way the first time, but they are not going back there again, do you hear?" No, none of that nonsense that you and I might come up with. Never a word of complaint, ever again.

Perhaps the next time you find yourself gearing up for battle, remember Lehi and the way he handled an unhappy spouse.

Effective Problem Solving

There is no secret or rocket science to resolving concerns. Like anything else you do in life—it will take some effort, thinking, and inspiration on your part. The key is being Christlike so that your heart is softened and you can amicably resolve differences together. You both need to have help from the Holy Ghost. We would like to help you think through issues that may come up now and later in your marriage. After you have accomplished a degree of softening your heart living the gospel, we suggest a three-step process for effective verbal problem solving. You'll notice that the process (diagramed below) is divided into two parts, a steps side and a skills side. The person who feels a need to bring up a problem should focus on the **steps** side of the diagram, while the spouse can help solve the problem by focusing on the **skills** side.

Steps (The one bringing up the issue)	**Skills** (The one trying to help resolve it)
Step 1. **Deal with Facts**	
• Tactfully state the problem without attacking the other person.	• Focus on solving your partner's concerns and don't be defensive. • Ask questions that get at the "why" and restate what you hear to verify you understand correctly.

Steps (The one bringing up the issue)	Skills (The one trying to help resolve it)
Step 2. Deal with Feelings	
• Use "I" statements—not "you" statements—to reflect how you feel (e.g. "I feel upset when this happens," not "You make me mad when . . .") • Make sure your partner understands your true concerns	• Show empathy for partner's concerns, and express interest in resolving the issue. • Focus on understanding and solving the issue at hand.
Step 3. Resolve the Concern	
• Brainstorm together • Ask your partner what they think would resolve the issue.	• Collaborate on solutions that fit your needs and address your partner's concerns.
Step 4. **Commit to a Solution:** Decide together the best solution, and then state and clearly commit to a plan of action.	

The following is a demonstration of how this model of communication should work. Let's take Carrie and Blake, for example. They have been engaged for three months and will be married in a few weeks. They are both college students at BYU and returned missionaries. Carrie's entire family lives in Provo, while Blake's lives in Washington state. Carrie's family is big and they like to get together often. None of them have ever lived outside of Utah Valley, despite job offers to different places. They could never leave their family. Blake's family is a little more transient. They graduate and take jobs all over the country. Blake has brothers and sisters in Texas, California, Florida, Kansas, Utah, and Washington.

One of Blake's concerns is that every single Sunday he and Carrie have to spend the entire afternoon over at Carrie's house with her family, eating, playing games, and discussing the BYU linebacking core for the next season. Blake feels that visiting Carrie's parents' house is fine every now and then, but he is getting tired of this routine. He would like some time just to be with Carrie by himself. Furthermore, he is concerned that once they are married, they will visit with her family even more often. Blake fears that he and Carrie will never have their own identity, be their own family, and have their own traditions. Additionally, once Blake graduates he is hoping to attend graduate school on the eastern seaboard. He is unsure of how Carrie will feel about leaving her family.

So, let's see how this model works. Blake has just picked Carrie up from church in his car, and they are driving over to her parents' home for the traditional Sabbath activities. This is when Blake decides to bring up the issue.

Step 1: Deal with Facts

Blake: "Carrie, I don't want to make you mad, but there is something I want to talk to you about. Do you mind if we pull the car over and talk for a minute?"

Carrie: "I don't mind. What are you thinking about?"

Blake: "Carrie, I'm just not sure if I want to continue going over to your parents' house *every* Sunday. I just feel that there are certain things I would like to do on Sundays, like discussing our goals and progress as a couple, reading scriptures, writing in our journals, taking walks, or talking and reading. You know, things like that. I like going over to your parents, but like I said, just not every Sunday." (**Notice how he tactfully states the problem without attacking Carrie**).

Carrie: "OK, Blake, so what you're saying is that you would rather do other things on Sunday, and they aren't just excuses—you like my family, right? Are you *feeling* something else I don't know about? (**Notice that they deal with facts. Carrie doesn't let her agenda get in the way, she is not defensive, and she focuses on Blake**).

Step 2: Deal with Feelings

Blake: No, I do like your family, but when you want to spend every Sunday over there it makes me feel like you would rather be with your family. So, in a way I feel rejected, or that I come second in your life. (**Blake is careful to use "I" statements so Carrie doesn't feel attacked or put on the spot**).

Carrie: Blake, I'm sorry if I have made you feel that way. I didn't mean to. In fact, I just assumed that you loved being with my family as much as I do. You seem to be right in the middle of those BYU football discussions and playing computer games with my little brother. (**Notice that Carrie shows empathy by helping Blake identify his feelings because he isn't sure what they are. Once feelings are brought in, they can help isolate a problem and find a solution. Also, notice that as Blake discusses his feelings it creates an appropriate moment for Carrie to apologize**).

Step 3: Resolve the Concern

Carrie: So, what do you think we need to do here?

Blake: I don't know. I don't want you to feel that you can't see your family anymore. I want you to be close to them. I don't want to get in the way of that..

Carrie: Well, what do you think would work?

Blake: What if we continued going over, but instead of saying for six hours, we only stayed for two?

Carrie: OK, I think I'll be alright with that. How do you feel about it?

Step 4: Commit to a Solution

Blake: I feel good about it. If we just stay for a couple of hours, I promise that I won't complain or gripe about going over there.

Carrie: Sounds great.

What might have happened if Carrie and Blake didn't use this model to work through their problems? Consider the following scenario:

Blake: Carrie, I'm just not sure if I want to continue going over to your parents' house every Sunday.

Carrie: Why?

Blake: Well, I just feel that there are certain things I would like to do on Sundays, and I don't think that spending all day at your parents' house is the best way to spend our time. I like going over there, just not every Sunday.

Carrie: Blake, I can't think of a better way to spend the Sabbath than with my family. Sunday is family day. If you really love me, then get used to spending Sundays with my family. (**Blake may see this as an attack on him by placing conditions on his love for Carrie. He may also feel that his feelings about the situation aren't being considered.**)

Blake: It's like you think your family is the only "true family" on the earth. We never do anything with my family. (**He's defensive now**)

Carrie: What do you want to do, hop in the car and drive to Seattle to visit them? It's not my fault they live twelve hours away! (**She's defensive now**)

As you can see, this is going nowhere fast. When couples are focused on themselves, they will never be able to resolve their differences. Tiny molehills can become mountains. There will be occasions in your lives when this model will not work. If this model doesn't work, then let your partners talk for five uninterrupted minutes while you just listen. When they are finished, take your turn. If things get really out of hand, write each other a letter—not a bad thing to do regularly anyway.

President Spencer W. Kimball gave a simple formula in this observation about resolving marital difficulties:

> [I]t is certain that almost any good man and any good woman can have happiness and a successful marriage if both are willing to pay the price. . . . The formula is simple; the ingredients are few, though there are many amplifications of each.
>
> First, there must be the proper approach toward marriage, which contemplates the selection of a spouse who reaches as nearly as possible the pinnacle of perfection in all the matters which are of importance to the individuals. And then those two parties must come to the altar in the temple realizing that they must work hard toward this successful joint living.
>
> Second, there must be great unselfishness, forgetting self and directing all of the family life and all pertaining thereunto to the good of the family, subjugating self.

Third, there must be continued courting and expressions of affection, kindness, and consideration to keep love alive and growing.

Fourth, there must be complete living of the commandments of the Lord as defined in the gospel of Jesus Christ.

With these ingredients properly mixed and continually kept functioning, it is quite impossible for unhappiness to come, misunderstandings to continue, or breaks to occur. Divorce attorneys would need to transfer to other fields and divorce courts would be padlocked. . . .

I am convinced that almost any two good people can get along together and be reasonably happy together if both are totally cooperative, unselfish, and willing to work together. I realize that sometimes there are personality clashes which make the difficulty greater. . . . I want to tell you that there are no marriages that can ever be happy ones unless two people work at it. . . . The hard thing, when problems arise, is to swallow pride, eat humble pie, analyze the situation, accept the blame that is properly due and then grit one's teeth, clench one's fists, and develop the courage to say, "I'm sorry" (Spencer W. Kimball, *The Teachings of Spencer W. Kimball* ed. Edward L. Kimball [1982], 306-307).

Questions to Consider

Consider the following questions as they apply to your situation. If you are dating someone, discuss the applicable questions between the two of you. If you are not currently in a relationship, decide where you stand on an issue before you start dating someone and how you would like to improve.

1. How well do we resolve differences so far in our relationship?

2. How should two Christlike people resolve their differences in helpful and healthful ways?

3. What is the most important attribute that a couple needs in resolving differences—whether married or single?

4. Briefly summarize the main points of President Kimball's formula for building a successful marriage.

CHAPTER 9

Temporal Preparation, Goals, and Plans for Marriage

*"In reviewing the Lord's counsel to us on the importance of
preparedness, I am impressed with the plainness of the message.
The Savior made it clear that we cannot place sufficient oil
in our preparedness lamps by simply avoiding evil. We must
be anxiously engaged in a positive program of preparation."*[1]

A few years ago a young man from BYU was getting ready to drive home for the holiday season. His new fiancée was worried that the drive would be too long and treacherous for him to make by himself. Since they both lived in Texas, the young coed convinced her parents that she should drive home with her future husband to help keep him awake and assist in the driving duties. Although her parents were reluctant at first, after some gentle persuasion they consented.

Immediately after their final exams they began their cross-country trek late on a Friday afternoon. As they reached southern Utah, the snow began to fall. In fact, the snow fell all night as they drove cautiously along the horizon. When morning came, instead of being in Texas, they were just across the border into New Mexico. By 9:00 A.M., their car had slipped off the interstate highway twice. The young man had to pay two different tow services in order to be pulled out of two separate snow banks (only about two miles apart). These were expenses he had not planned for.

They finally arrived in Albuquerque about the time they should have reached Houston. They called their parents to let them know they were fine, but the weather conditions were terrible. The young woman's parents made them promise that they would not travel another mile until they purchased chains for their tires, another surprise expense. Obedient to the parent's request (the young man wanted to make a good impression), they drove to a local hardware store and bought chains and other necessities that would be useful for the remainder of the trip. They left the store, drove the car to an empty parking lot, and spent the next several hours learning how to chain tires, not a simple task for two college students from the southwest.

Getting those chains on the tires proved to be more formidable than the rest of the trip. Each time the young man laid the chains out on the snow-covered pavement, he would instruct his fiancée to put the car in reverse and roll slowly over them. Because the parking lot had become a sheet of ice, she would accidently spin the tires, causing the chains to get caught up in the axle. Consequently, the young man would slide under the car without a coat or gloves (he figured he would not need them in Texas for Christmas). With his bare hands on the ice cold steel, he would pry the chains loose and lay them back down on the ice. This process was repeated at least three times on each wheel. By the time the young man came back to the car, his lips were purple, matching the color of his hands. He could not get mad and yell at his fiancée because, well, she was his fiancée. Everyone knows that you cannot get mad about stuff like that until after you are married.

Eventually he climbed back into the car and began the painful process of thawing out. By the time they reached the Texas border, the young man had spent all of his funds on chains, extra food, and tow truck services. His fiancée had to purchase gasoline for the remainder of the trip. Finally, they arrived in Houston three days after they left Provo; a trip that usually can be made in twenty-four hours.

Could this couple's problems have been prevented? What could they have done differently? Could checking the *Weather Channel* before the trip have been helpful to them? Bringing extra money for emergencies would have been wise. Packing warm clothing would have been smart too. Preparing for matrimony is not unlike preparing for a long trip cross-country. Just as safe and successful trips across the Rocky Mountains during winter snows require planning and preparation, so successful marriages require planning, goal setting, and execution.

The Savior taught:

> For which of you, intending to build a tower, sitteth not down first, and counteth the cost, whether he have sufficient to finish it?
>
> Lest haply, after he hath laid the foundation, and is not able to finish it, all that behold it begin to mock him,
>
> Saying, this man began to build, and was not able to finish (Luke 14:28-30).

We probably all agree that no one should set out on a trip across the country without the proper amount of food, clothing, money, and emergency equipment, yet that is exactly what some people do when it comes to marriage preparation. Creating a successful marriage is a little more complex than a cross-country trip, and it is silly to believe that we can establish a celestial marriage without specific planning.

Goals Are Essential

In order to succeed, couples need goals and a plan. A well-ordered marriage just doesn't happen because two outstanding people are joined together in a ceremony. If there is one key ingredient to successful marriages, it is *working to achieve your goals.* Elder Jeffrey R. Holland has written:

> Where do we think "good marriages" come from? They don't spring full-blown from the head of Zeus any more than does a good education, or good home teaching, or a good symphony. Why should a marriage require fewer tears and less toil and shabbier commitment than your job or your clothes or your car?
>
> Yet some couples spend less time on the quality and substance and purpose of their marriage—the highest, holiest culminating covenant we can make in this world—than they do in maintaining their '72 Datsun. And they break the hearts of

> many innocent people, including perhaps their own, if that
> marriage is then dissolved (*However Long and Hard the Road*
> [1985], 122).

The good news is that almost any couple can have a successful marriage if they are willing to pay the price. Yes, it will require tears and toil and commitment, but anything worthwhile usually does. However, commitment alone is not enough; couples also need direction and planning. We have observed that most couples who come for counseling often lack both commitment and direction. In fact, most of them do not have joint goals. We often must take time with them to teach them how to set goals and make plans together in their marriage.

Relationships can be rejuvenated as couples discuss and set goals together. We find ourselves reminding couples that if goals are good for personal improvement and professional success, then they are certainly needed to strengthen marriages. President Spencer W. Kimball declared, "Goals are good. Laboring with a distant aim sets the mind in a higher key and puts us at our best" (Spencer W. Kimball, [address delivered at regional representatives' seminar, 3 Apr. 1974]).

Elder Joseph B. Wirthlin gave this counsel:

> You should look ahead now and decide what you want to do
> with your lives. Fix clearly in your mind what you want to be
> one year from now, five years, ten years, and beyond. . . . Write
> your goals and review them regularly. Keep them before you
> constantly, record your progress, and revise them as circum-
> stances dictate. Your ultimate goal should be eternal life—the
> kind of life God lives, the greatest of all the gifts of God
> ("Running Your Marathon," *Ensign,* Nov. 1989, 73).

Goals should bring us closer together and point us in the direction of the celestial kingdom. Furthermore, goals should be specific rather than general. For instance, instead of writing as a goal, "become more spiritual," you should write down how you will accomplish your written goal. How are you going to become "more spiritual"? Are you going to read the scriptures more often? If so, how many pages are you going to read? What time of day will you actually read them? When will your goal be completed? Breaking goals down in this way allows them to be observed and measured. It is difficult to evaluate "become more spiritual." However, you can determine whether you read two pages every day at 6:30 A.M. Making goals specific allows them to be observed and measured. Moreover, each goal must have a plan of action to accompany it. Once married, you and your spouse may wish to read your own and each other's patriarchal blessings so that you can help each other become what Heavenly Father wants you to be.

Set goals as couples, weekly, monthly, and yearly. It is good to get away together, at least annually, to review your progress as a couple. Your anniversary might be the perfect time to decide the direction and speed you both want to go. It doesn't matter when you get off together, but it does matter that you do it. Remember, babysitters are always cheaper than divorces. A retreat helps you retain and regain perspective, stay on track, and recharge your marriage and parenting batteries.

Take Time to Write Them Down

A few years ago Sister Margaret Nadauld shared the following experience. As she was speaking at a fireside given at BYU, she held up an envelope and showed it to the audience. The letter was so old that a six-cent stamp was fastened in the top right-hand corner. Sister Nadauld related that the letter belonged to a young married couple years ago. They were excited and optimistic about their future together. The young man was in graduate school and his new bride taught school to support them.

On a beautiful fall day in New England they decided to picnic near Walden Pond, close to Boston, and a favorite location of author Henry David Thoreau. Their purpose was to ponder their future and decide what to do with the rest of their lives. They were seeking a road map for the future. Their partnership was promising, and they wanted to make a great life together. They agreed that with God's help, nothing would be impossible. They talked about future careers, how many children they would have, where they would live, how they would share the talents they had been given. They wanted to make the world a better place, and they wanted to "seek . . . first the kingdom of God" (Matt. 6:33).

Since this couple believed in setting goals, they eventually put aside their philosophical discussion and simply wrote down on the back of an envelope their goals, dreams, and aspirations. Later that day, they drove away from that beautiful pristine setting at Walden Pond with a renewed determination to become what God wanted them to be.

All too soon, the husband graduated and they found themselves in a new location. Like most other couples, life became busy and hectic. The husband worked hard at his career; the wife worked hard raising the children the Lord had blessed them with. They served in the Church and in the community. More children came. Soon the envelope was forgotten as life became busier and busier. But, they were happy.

The years passed by, complete with challenges, obstacles, and trials. They faced their difficulties together as they held tightly to each other. Eventually, they moved to a new city where the husband accepted a very responsible position. In the process of moving some boxes, the wife unexpectedly came across the Walden Pond envelope. By now it was old and yellowed. However, those goals that had been written so many years earlier were still legible on the back.

As the wife silently read each goal for the first time in many years, tears filled her eyes. She pondered over the many things that had happened in their lives since Walden Pond. As she went down the list, item by item, she realized that almost every goal on the list had come to fruition. It was interesting that her husband's new job was the fulfillment of the final goal they had set at Walden Pond. It was now time to get a new envelope and start making a new list (see "Prepare Today for Tomorrow," *Brigham Young University 1997–1998 Devotional and Fireside Speeches* [1998], 49–50).

Goals and dreams not written down are simply wishes. If you fail to plan for your future, you can expect to fail. The converse is also true. Like the couple at Walden Pond, if you take time to plan now, you can fulfill your dreams as your lives become a self-fulfilling prophecy. Although these sayings are trite, they are true. Brenton Yorgason has written, "Becoming the right person to marry, a task we pursue in our youth, becomes of paramount import as we think of saddling someone with what and who we are for eternity" (Yorgason, Baker, & Burr, *From Two to One* [1981], 19). Certainly goals can help you "become the right person." All of us should have a plan for self-improvement. Goals should become an important part of your coming marriage and parenting relationships. They will assist you in leading your family to the "promised land." Much like the path alongside the rod of iron, they will support you in the charge to lead your family to the Savior. If you have not made goal-setting a part of your life at this point, it is never too late. Find a quiet place and select short, medium, and long-range goals. Areas of consideration for goal setting include, but are not limited to, the following: social, recreational, financial, intimacy, in-law relations, children, housekeeping, religious practices, careers, academics, spirituality, exercise and fitness, etc. (At the end of this chapter is an exercise that you and your sweetheart can complete. It will provide a structure and a format for goal-setting and planning.)

Positive Program of Preparation

Although there are numerous areas of improvement that each couple can make, we would like to concentrate on the following areas: education, health, employment, financial management, home storage, and discovering resources. Each one of these areas can be worked on as an individual, during engagement, and later as a married couple. Since some of these areas have been addressed in previous chapters, we will brush over them lightly here.

Education
President Hinckley has counseled the youth of the Church to "be smart about training your minds and hands for the future . . . You have an obligation to make the most of your life. Plan now for all of the education you can get, and then work to bring to pass a fulfillment of that plan." ("Words of the Prophet: Put Your Shoulder to the Wheel," *New Era*, July 2000, 4). He wisely noted that an education prepares one to serve effectively in society.

The Lord has enjoined upon this people the responsibility to train their minds that they may be equipped to serve in the society of which they will become a part. The Church will be blessed by reason of their excellence. Furthermore, they will be amply rewarded for the effort they make.

I read from a clipping I made the other day: "The latest Census information . . . indicated the annual wage for someone without a degree and no high school diploma stood at little more than $16,000 nationally [in 1997]. The jump wasn't much higher for a high school diploma—$22,895 annual average income. As the level of education increases, however, so does the span. The holder of a bachelor's degree earned, on average, $40,478 that year. Finally, the holder of an advanced degree typically bumped up their annual earnings by more than $20,000 to a nationwide average of $63,229, according to [these] Census figures" (Nicole A. Bonham, "Does an Advanced Degree Pay Off?" *Utah Business,* Sept. 2000, 37; as cited in "Great Shall Be the Peace of Thy Children," *Ensign,* Nov. 2000, 52).

Plan to get all of the education you can. Your education will help you acquire the talents and skills to contribute to society and the kingdom of God. Remember, education is important for future brides as well. President Howard W. Hunter stated: "There are impelling reasons for our sisters to plan toward employment also. We want them to obtain all the education and vocational training possible before marriage" (Howard W. Hunter, *Teachings of Howard W. Hunter* [1997], 149). Follow your dreams. Don't ever sell yourself short or change your educational path because another field looks easier or will propel you through the graduation line sooner. Together, you will be able to accomplish anything as long as you are in agreement and the Lord is your partner. Are you satisfied with the career path you have chosen.[2] How do you feel about additional education? Are you making progress in your present educational goals?

Health

President Spencer W. Kimball explained: "We teach our people to live the laws of health. It is paying important dividends in longer and more healthy lives" ("Why Call Me Lord, Lord, and Do Not the Things Which I Say?" *Ensign,* May 1975, 6). There are several areas to consider when discussing health. How healthful are your eating habits? College students are notorious for locating convenience stores where they can purchase three hot dogs and a drink for a buck—calling that dinner. Although such diets are great for the wallet, they are terrible for the digestive system, not to mention the lack of nutritional value. Can you cook your own meals and shop economically? What about your living area? Do you keep your residence clean? All of these skills are just as important for men as they are for women. Some Latter-day Saint family scholars explained:

> When you consider being healthy, you should primarily concern yourself with developing and maintaining good habits in the areas of eating, sleeping, exercising, and physical strain. You should also be sensitive to the needs and limitations of your body and strive to maintain a balance that will not only allow you to be healthy the day of your wedding but will also insure a long life of health and vitality. It is not surprising that when you are healthy and taking good care of your body, your mental and emotional well-being is affected as well (Yorgason, Baker, & Burr, *From Two to One*, [1981], 27).

What are some "health" areas you could improve in? Consider several goals to write down at the end of this chapter. What about your partner? How is he or she doing health-wise? How could you help or provide encouragement to each other?

Employment

In today's high-tech world people change jobs and careers often. Young people who enter the work force today can plan on three to four career changes and ten to twelve job changes throughout their work life. There is a need to be marketable. What skills can you develop that will be unique and can command a price? Work in fields and areas that will bring you happiness and where you can use your God-given gifts. President Howard W. Hunter gave this helpful counsel:

> The employment we choose should be honorable and challenging. Ideally, we need to seek that work to which we are suited by interest, by aptitude, and by training. A man's work should do more than provide adequate income; it should provide him with

a sense of self-worth and be a pleasure—something he looks
forward to each day ("Prepare for Honorable Employment,"
Ensign, Nov. 1975, 122).

Be prayerful about your career choice. Review your patriarchal
blessing and look for the gifts and talents Heavenly Father has blessed
you with, and then find a career where you can use your skills. Choose
a career field in which you can look forward to going to work every
day. Choose a field of endeavor that is family friendly so that you will
have time to be a spouse and a parent. How are you preparing for your
future employment skills currently? What skills do you need to
acquire? What goals have you set for yourselves in these areas?

Financial Management

You can increase your chances of having a successful marriage if
you can become self-reliant in several areas, especially finances. Elder
J. Thomas Fyans maintained that "members of the Church [are] to
use their own gifts and abilities, their financial and personal resources
in becoming temporally self-reliant and then reaching out to help
others to gain that same capacity for self-reliance" ("News of the
Church: Individual and Family Self-Reliance Features in Leadership
Session," *Ensign,* May 1983, 84). This does not mean that we all need
to become millionaires, but we certainly need to be able to take care
of ourselves. One of the epidemic problems in our society is that of
consumer debt. In 1991 the Federal Reserve Board reported that 85
percent of households owed an outstanding balance on a credit card.[2]
In a study conducted by Bae, Hanna, and Lindamood, it was
reported that "40% of American households spent more than their
take-home incomes and 25% of the sample spent at least 127% of
their take-home income."[3]

Avoid debt. You probably receive five to ten applications for credit
cards in the mail each month. Financial institutions are eager to lend
you money that you will have to pay back at 21 percent interest. Rip
those envelopes in half and throw them in the garbage without
reading them. It is difficult to begin a marriage when your finances
are sinking. Consider the warning and advice of Elder J. Reuben
Clark and Elder Jeffrey R. Holland:

> [Debt] never sleeps nor sickens nor dies; it never goes to the hospital; it works on Sundays and holidays; it never takes a vacation; . . . it is never laid off work; . . . it buys no food; it wears no clothes; it is unhoused; . . . it has neither weddings nor births nor deaths; it has no love, no sympathy; it is as hard and soulless as a granite cliff. Once in debt, [it] is your companion every minute of the day and night; you cannot shun it or slip away from it; you cannot dismiss it . . . and whenever you get in its way or cross its course or fail to meet its demands, it crushes you (J. Rueben Clark, in Conference Report, Apr. 1938, 103).

And then,

> [W]e encourage, if necessary, plastic surgery for both husband and wife. This is a very painless operation, and it may give you more self-esteem than a new nose job or a tummy tuck. Just cut up your credit cards. Unless you are prepared to use those cards under the strictest of conditions and restraints, you should not use them at all—at least not at 18 percent or 21 percent or 24 percent interest. No convenience known to modern man has so jeopardized the financial stability of a family—especially young struggling families—as has the ubiquitous credit card (Jeffrey R. Holland, *However Long and Hard the Road* [1985], 106).

You shouldn't expect, nor do you need to begin your life together with all of the amenities your parents enjoyed. You can wait for the entertainment center and a nice car. Men, don't mortgage the farm to buy an engagement and wedding ring. Be simple but elegant in your choice of wedding rings and first living arrangements. Here is some good counsel to engaged couples:

> As you move through the engagement period, it would be well for you to discuss finances and to begin to plan for the needs of tomorrow. Those couples who have a nest egg when they marry . . . do themselves a great favor, as they are never at the end of their financial rope (Yorgason, Baker, & Burr, *From Two to One* [1981], 26).

Elder M. Russell Ballard suggested that self-discipline is the key to avoiding financial mishaps. Specifically he counseled the Saints to:

- Avoid debt where you can—exorbitant fees are charged.
- Tell yourself, "We can't afford it."
- Make a budget and stick to it.
- Cut expenses by distinguishing between wants and needs.
- Increase homemaking skills and have family members do repairs.
- Invest wisely. Avoid speculations and get-rich quick schemes. (See "Providing for Our Needs," *Ensign*, May 1981, 85–87.)

Perhaps the three most important things you could do at this juncture is to live by a strict budget, spend less money than you make, and avoid consumer debt. What goals do you have in these areas? Have you made a budget recently just for yourself? How can you get out of debt if you are in it? What plan could you implement so that by the time you marry you could be debt free?

Home Storage

Temporal preparation for marriage includes knowing how to produce and prepare food, and food storage basics. Although you may think that such an idea is absurd at this point in your lives, consider the following example. A young couple who was engaged to be married made a frugal decision. Instead of spending hundreds of dollars on expensive dates, they decided to keep their dates rather inexpensive. Then, they took the money they had saved each week and bought food items to store. By the time they married they had an entire year's supply of food which was stored in their extra bedroom. All they really had to buy was milk and produce. The use of their food storage allowed them to continue their schooling without getting into debt or taking on extra jobs. (See Yorgason, Baker, & Burr, *From Two to One* [1981], 26)

The habit of storing food for a rainy day is a good practice. Couples who can practice food storage while young will continue throughout their marriage. It will be much harder to begin storing food later in life. Elder L. Tom Perry warned:

> As long as I can remember, we have been taught to prepare for the future and to obtain a year's supply of necessities. I would guess that the years of plenty have almost universally caused us to set aside this counsel. *I believe the time to disregard this counsel is over. With events in the world today, it must be considered with all seriousness* ("If Ye Are Prepared, Ye Shall Not Fear," *Ensign,* Nov. 1995, 36; emphasis added).

Remember the words of President Benson: "The revelation to produce and store food may be as essential to our temporal welfare today as boarding the ark was to the people in the days of Noah" ("To the Fathers in Israel," *Ensign,* Nov. 1987, 49). You do not have to do much in this area at this point, but you should do something. What could you do in the area of home storage? What about storing a box of cereal each week under your bed? How about preparing a 72-hour emergency kit? What goals can you two come up with in this area?

Discovering Resources

There are many things that both of you can do in order to temporally prepare yourselves for engagement and marriage. Consider the following ideas:

- Graduate school will increase your earning power.

- Purchasing an older home and remodeling it is often cheaper than buying a new one.

- Invite your parents to teach you practical skills that have helped them over the years.

- Go to the local hardware store and sign up for classes that teach you how to tile a floor, paint, wallpaper, frame, build decks and fences, and put in sprinkler systems.

- Be sure to match your housing expense to your income. We both know of couples who live in 4,000-square-foot homes but cannot afford to furnish them. Half of the rooms are empty and probably will be for some time because they have strapped themselves financially. Start slowly. Assess the market where you would like to live and see what you can qualify for. Then exercise some self-restraint, look at homes that may cost a few thousand *less* than what you qualify for, and decide what you can live with. How much better would it be to have a little money left over to furnish your home, perhaps get another car, and put some money away in savings.

You would also be surprised to learn how much money you can save when you learn to change the oil in your car and fix appliances. Service repair people usually charge at least $90 just to visit your home, and that is before they even take a look at what is wrong with your dryer! Use people in your ward who know how to fix things in case you don't. Exchange with them. Trade babysitting where you can. Plant gardens, bottle fruit, hunt and/or fish, teach classes in your specialty where you can get paid for your expertise. Elder Joe J. Christensen shared the following experience:

> When we moved to Pullman, Washington, to attend graduate school, we had three children and Barbara was expecting our fourth. Major appliances did not come with the "temporary" World War II surplus housing apartments available for married students. . . . In a used-appliance store, we found a stove and refrigerator that cost a fraction of what we would have paid for them new. Even though we had to work with a little innovation to make the latch of the refrigerator door function, the appliances served our needs very adequately for the three years it took to finish graduate school. We then sold them to incoming married students who were delighted to pay as much as we had paid for them originally. Instead of leaving graduate school with our five children and a lot of debt, we had saved enough— through part-time work, a fellowship, and a wife who knew how to make ends meet—to place a down payment on a big, old, modest home near the University of Idaho (*One Step at a Time* [1996], 45).

Take advantage of the time you have now to improve. Develop celestial habits that will remain with you for the rest of your life. In a coming day, you will have a spouse and children to take care of; but now is the time, while you are still single, to focus on improving your own skills.

Consider the following vision, or expectation, from Sister Margaret Nadauld:

> You young men out there, do you know what I see in you? I see more than bulging biceps or computer geniuses. I see men who want to be husbands, men who love little children and who want to communicate effectively with their wives and sons and daughters. I see men who are taking full advantage of available educational opportunities, who are preparing to be providers, and who take seriously that God-given responsibility.
>
> I also see something else! I see men who should know how to care for a yard—mow, edge, fertilize, make it look like a million bucks! I see men who should know what to do with a tool chest, who should know the difference between pliers and a pipe wrench, and who should know how to use tools to make home repairs. . . .
>
> Now, young women, let's focus on you. For you this is a time of unprecedented opportunities and options. You have important choices to make, and I'm sure you're aware of that. Please, for yourself and for your future family, choose a fine education. I can see in you women who are educating themselves and who are preparing to bless others through that education. . . .
>
> I see souls preparing to create a beautiful, loving environment for raising a family. I see women who can cook delicious, balanced, and healthy meals. I see women who find satisfaction from following recipes handed down by mothers and grandmothers. I see women who understand the importance of having a family put their feet under the dinner table every day. I see in you women who love children and look forward to the day when you will be mothers, nurturers of precious sons and daughters. I see women who will learn to make a budget and understand provident living, who look forward to establishing a home of love, a home of order, a home of faith ("Prepare Today for Tomorrow," *Brigham Young University 1997–1998 Devotional and Fireside Speeches* [1998], 53–55).

Set goals. Dream together. Plan for a wonderful future together. Be prayerful, and Heavenly Father will direct you in your lives. He wants you to succeed and be happy. He will help you develop the talents and abilities that will enrich your lives and help you succeed.

Questions to Consider

Set some specific goals in each of the areas listed. If you are dating someone, discuss your goals together. If you are not currently in a relationship, set your own personal goals before you start dating someone and decide the areas in which you would like to improve.

Goals: Planning for Our Future

Consider the following areas of improvement. Remember, in chapter two you ranked yourselves in some of these areas. Now is the time to set goals in the suggested areas and make specific plans to accomplish the goals you set. In the form of a chart, outline these areas of improvement, goals you set in each area, and the plans you make to implement these goals.

Area of Improvement	Goals	Plans for Implementation
Spirituality		
Education		
Current job		
Health/exercise		
Financial management		
Home storage		
Discovering resources		
Social/friendships		
Recreational		
Relationship with spouse		
Children		
Career		

CHAPTER 10

Money Matters in Marriage

"Overindulgence and poor money management place a heavy strain on marriage relationships. Most marital problems, it seems, originate from economic roots—either insufficient income to sustain the family or mismanagement of the income as earned."[1]

It is no secret that one of the major sources of marital discord is selfishness as it pertains to acquiring and managing money. Not that money itself is bad, but the misuse of it is often where trouble begins. "The American Bar Association has indicated that 89 percent of all divorces can be traced to quarrels and accusations over money. . . . Others have estimated that 75 percent of all divorces result from clashes over finances. Some professional counselors indicate that four out of five families are strapped with serious money problems" (Marvin J. Ashton, *One for the Money: Guide to Family Finance* [pamphlet, 1992], 1–2). President Gordon B. Hinckley has observed, "I am satisfied that money is the root of more trouble in marriage than all other causes combined" (*Cornerstones of a Happy Home* [pamphlet, 1984], 8). Without question, money *can* become the source of much conflict and strife in a marriage, but it doesn't have to. If you are prepared to handle money, you can avoid much of the heartache that accompanies mismanaged or insufficient funds. The parable of the ten virgins applies just as much to temporal matters as it does to spiritual ones—if you are prepared, you have nothing to fear.

Several years ago, Elder Marvin J. Ashton counseled a couple who were engaged. Overall they had prepared well for their future marriage. Both had graduated from college, came from good homes, and had rich cultural experiences. For the most part they had prepared for their marriage, except for one crucial area. When Elder Ashton asked, "Who is going to manage the money in your marriage?" the future bride responded, "He is, I guess." The prospective husband then countered, "We haven't talked about that yet." Elder Ashton was rather shocked that such an important topic had not been addressed by a couple so close to marriage (Marvin J. Ashton, *One for the Money: Guide to Family Finance* [pamphlet, 1992], 1). Perhaps too few couples do much in the way of discussing money management before marriage. Some may analyze their sources of income, but few actually discuss and then agree on where the money will be spent.

Discuss Financial Management Before Marriage

As you begin married life, you probably won't have a great amount of money to manage initially. Don't worry, you're in good company. Few couples start out with a nest egg. In fact, most couples hardly have a nest. When President and Sister Kimball were married, for example, Spencer had six dollars to his name, that is, until he paid the two-dollar-and-fifty-cent fee for their marriage license. They began their marriage on three dollars and fifty cents (see E.L. Kimball & A.E. Kimball, Jr., *Spencer W. Kimball* [1977], 70). Elder Russell M. Nelson shared a similar experience.

> For a short time during the first year of our marriage, Sister Nelson maintained two jobs while I was in medical school. Before her paychecks had arrived, we found ourselves owing more than our funds could defray, so we took advantage of an option then available to sell blood at twenty-five dollars a pint. In an interval between her daytime job as a schoolteacher and her evening work as a clerk in a music store, we went to the hospital and each sold a pint of blood. As the needle was withdrawn from her arm, she said to me, "Don't forget to pay tithing

on my blood money." (When her mother learned I was bleeding her daughter between two jobs, I sensed at that time she may not have been too pleased with her new son-in-law) (Russell M. Nelson, *The Power Within Us* [1988], 112).

Whether you have a large sum of money to manage or a little does not matter. The issue is never the amount of money anyway, but how you will manage it. There are people who are millionaires who have declared bankruptcy, and school teachers who live debt-free, happy lives. Visit with some couples who have been married for a while. See if they don't confirm the fact that no matter how much money they've made, it's always a struggle to balance needs and wants with the income. They will probably tell you that when they made $15,000 a year they barely survived; when they made $30,000 a year they still struggled; and now as they make $80,000 a year they must still budget and watch their expenditures. Why? What makes the difference? There are probably two reasons for this tendency. First, the older we get and the more children we have, the more "life" seems to cost. Second, most of us seem to spend what we make. Janene Wolsey Baadsgaard wisely wrote, "We want Hostess Cupcakes, lavish homes in the best neighborhoods, and twenty-seven pairs of designer-name athletic shoes with inflatable soles and blinking shoelaces. The problem with most wants is, once we get them, we usually want more" (*Family Finances for the Flabbergasted* [1995], 41). Along the same lines, Brent Barlow contends:

> Most newlyweds should realize that more money will not solve their problems. We often assume that if we had just a few thousand dollars more each year, our financial troubles would vanish. Many are surprised to find that couples earning two hundred thousand dollars or more are sometimes among those who have the greatest money problems, simply because they haven't yet learned to manage their income. *No amount of money will suffice if husband and wife have an inadequate means of handling it.* Successful couples of lesser means are those who have learned to manage what they do have—and they are much happier than those who have or earn vast amounts of money and yet are inept managers (*Just for Newlyweds* [1992], 64–65).

So the issue, it seems, is not how much money but "how will we manage our money?" That is where both the source of conflict lies, and where the solution can be found. Some couples argue over how to spend their meager funds; others disagree on how to save money. A husband may feel that his wife spends too much while the wife feels that her husband is a tightwad. Nevertheless, couples must be careful and cooperative. Paul warned the Saints that "the love of money is the root of all evil . . . while some coveted after, they have erred from the faith, and pierced themselves through with many sorrows" (1 Tim. 6:10). Not that money is the root of all evil, but the *love* of it, the coveting of it, and always wanting more—is where problems can develop.

Prophets have warned us that the acquisition of wealth could become a hindrance to our spiritual growth. Specifically, Brigham Young declared:

> The worst fear I have about this people is that they will get rich in this country, forget God and His people, wax fat, and kick themselves out of the Church and go to hell. This people will stand mobbing, robbing, poverty, and all manner of persecution, and be true. But my greater fear . . . is that they cannot stand wealth (in James S. Brown, *Life of a Pioneer* [1900], 122–23).

If that was President Young's worst fear, then perhaps we should consider our own attitude about finances. The major problem that arises isn't the money itself, but how people perceive the money—that is the core issue. We know of couples who are quite well off financially, but their marriage and family relationships are a disaster. We know couples with little money who are extremely happy. It is not necessarily the amount of money a couple has, but the meaning money has to both partners. How individuals feel about money in terms of spending it, earning it, saving it, using it, etc., tells a great deal about them in general—especially in a relationship where there is little agreement on its use. How a couple acts toward each other in situations involving money may be a tip off as to how they relate to each other in other areas of the marriage.

How we view money can be seen as an extension of our personality. Is it your observation, for example, that when an individual is stingy or tight with money, they are also tight with other resources such as time and emotions? Some individuals view money as a source of power; hence the rule: "He that has the gold, makes the rules." Others view money as a gift from God for righteous living. Those who have money are favored of God, so the thinking goes, so those who don't have much must have done something wrong in the pre-earth life! Others view money as a kind of status-giver. For others, spending money is like hemorrhaging or giving away vital parts of their bodies. They can feel the blood dripping. Other individuals exercise control through allocating money to family members. Some feel that money is simply for fun and enjoyment. Just as people differ in personalities, so they differ in their beliefs on how money should be earned, spent, saved, and how much should be given away. For this reason, it is important that you discuss your beliefs about money and other financial issues before marriage so you can evaluate that part of your personalities.

For example, before his marriage a friend of ours wanted to be a teacher. His fiancée, on the other hand, came from a wealthy family who convinced him that such a profession was beneath his dignity. The young man gave up his dream of teaching to make his future wife happy. Unfortunately, after fifteen years of marriage he is still professionally miserable. Although he makes an adequate living in the corporate world, his heart is still set on the classroom. In this case, his wife's beliefs of equating happiness with income and assets won out. Driving nice cars, shopping in upscale malls, and living in a large home were at the top of her chart. He grew up in a home where his father was a teacher and was extremely happy, but he was pressured to follow the counsel of his in-laws. You can imagine that there has been some friction and unfulfilled dreams in their marriage.

The Importance of Wise Resource Management

"Thou shalt be diligent in preserving what thou hast, that thou mayest be a wise steward" (D&C 136:27). The Lord gave this counsel to Church members encamped at Winter Quarters in 1836 at a time when the Saints had little to preserve in the first place. How much more relevant this counsel is for us today as we try to accumulate and preserve family income and resources. Our standard of living can easily be threatened by poor management, increases in living costs, higher taxes, a fluctuating economy, crop disasters, a sometimes fragile employment picture, a droopy stock market, and our own peculiar lifestyle as Latter-day Saints (tithing/fast offerings, etc.).[2] Good financial practices are certainly necessary in our day to "preserve what thou hast."

As Latter-day Saints, we have unique expenditures that demand good management practices. After you pay the Lord, pay yourself. Besides the primary contributions to the Church, such as tithing and fast offerings, our lifestyle requires additional income. You may be blessed with a few more children than your neighbors, which will necessitate a slightly larger home, a larger vehicle perhaps, and more funds for music lessons, athletics, and college. You need to anticipate future expenses to prepare for emergencies. We also have things like missions and food storage that take much of our income.

Financial Priorities

Elder Marvin J. Ashton wisely advised engaged couples, "A prospective wife could well concern herself not with the amount her husband-to-be can earn in a month, but rather how he (and she) will manage the money that comes into their hands. Money management should take place over money productivity" (Marvin J. Ashton, "One For The Money," *Ensign,* July 1975, 2). Agreeing on financial priorities is a key to marital success. Consider this counsel in the following areas:

- *Pay your tithing.* When you pay tithing and fast offerings you have a sense of well-being because you know you are building Zion and pleasing Heavenly Father. Joseph Smith taught that one aspect of faith is "an actual knowledge . . . that the course of life which he pursues is according to the will of God" (Joseph Smith, *Lectures on Faith,* comp. N.B. Lundwall [1985], 57). When you are disciplined to the extent that you return to the Lord one-tenth of your earnings, you have an inner peace, an assurance that you are in harmony with the "will of God." Some young couples have the mistaken notion that paying tithing will make them financially rich. That isn't the promise. Prosperity doesn't always mean cash flow, but "growth in a knowledge of God, and in a testimony, and in the power to live the gospel and to inspire our families to do the same. That is prosperity of the truest kind" (Heber J. Grant, *Gospel Standards*, comp. G. Homer Durham [1941], 58). One woman couldn't understand why her family was having so many financial problems. After all, they paid their tithing faithfully. When would the windows of heaven be opened? One day as she was watching her husband and children playing together, she realized that her family was the greatest blessing her Heavenly Father had given her, and that was something that money couldn't buy. (See James E. Faust, "Opening the Windows of Heaven," *Ensign*, Nov. 1998, 59.) Blessings, you will learn throughout your life, don't always come as a check in the mail. President Gordon B. Hinckley promised that if the Saints would pay their tithes and offerings, no matter how poor they were, they would always have food "in their bowls and clothing on their backs and shelter over their heads" ("Inspirational Thoughts, Solution for Poverty," *Ensign*, Aug. 1997, 7).

- *Meet current expenses and bills.* When you two undertake a financial obligation, your word must be "as good as your bond." Latter-day Saints, in past decades at least, were known for their honest work ethic, as men and women of integrity. Let's not ruin that reputation. Pay your debts, and if you can't, contact the debtor and make arrangements to make payments agreeable to both of you. Elder Marvin J. Ashton said: "Latter-day Saints who ignore or avoid their creditors are entitled to feel the inner frustrations that such conduct merits, and they are not living as Latter-day Saints should!" (Marvin J. Ashton, *One for the Money: Guide to Family Finance* [pamphlet, 1992], 6).

- *Have an emergency fund.* Short term savings are essential to meet life's little surprises! Putting aside a little money each payday will help you save for emergencies. Most couples do not have an emergency fund. In fact, they live so close to the financial edge that when emergencies occur (and they will) they are not prepared. Transmissions, washing machines, and mechanical parts have a way of wearing out—always at an inconvenient time. You might want to have what we term "tiered savings." The amounts are simply to illustrate the point. Suppose your first goal is to acquire $500–$1,000 in emergency funds. This is money that you could get your hands on this afternoon if you needed to. Another $1,000–$2,000 is in the second tier, money that you would rather not touch unless there is a more serious problem, but you could, if the need existed get to it. Perhaps you have $5000–$10,000 tucked away in a longer-range resource for use if you had to touch it. This is money you hesitate to use unless it is an emergency and you both agree to tap it. Usually having some money set aside in a credit union account, money deducted from each paycheck, is the best way to begin building up savings in the beginning.

- *Have insurance.* Insurance is a vehicle to preserve your assets against risks that could deplete your savings quickly. You need health and life insurance (cheaper through group rates with employers), and car insurance along with home or renter's insurance to safeguard against catastrophic losses. Newly married couples often have no medical coverage for their first pregnancy. If there are complications at birth with either the mother or baby, costs could be astronomical. We know of a newly married couple—and their case is not uncommon— who had their baby delivered by an emergency C-section. The hospital bill was close to $20,000 dollars—a large sum of money for a young couple in college to pay off. Insurance is to protect your assets. Premiums are generally cheaper than paying the costs yourself. However, shop around, as insurance rates vary dramatically between companies.

- *Exercise self-control.* One of the most common mistakes young couples make is overspending. Often, newly married couples want to furnish their apartments with all of the "gadgets" their parents have—computers, big screen TVs, Palm Pilots, DVDs, CD players, new cars and appliances. As instructors of college-age students, we are always amazed at what kinds of cars our students drive. Some wheel around in vehicles costing $30,000 or more. Perhaps parents are providing these vehicles for their college-age children (which could be another book altogether). If these students are in debt for these vehicles, it could become a financial albatross around their necks. Young couples should recognize that it would be unwise to think that they can maintain the same spending patterns and lifestyles to which they were accustomed as part of their parent's family. Married couples manifest a level of maturity when they consider the needs of their spouse and family members before their own.

- *Avoid debt.* It is rather easy to get into debt these days. A multitude of credit card applications arrive in the mailbox almost daily. Everywhere you go, whether an appliance store or lumber yard, institutions are anxious to lend you money—especially at 19 to 21 percent interest (What this means is that if you only pay the minimum amount due on your bill, it would take you thirty to forty years to complete the pay-off schedule. That is exactly what the credit company wants!) Avoid using credit cards for purchasing consumer items such as groceries and clothing. We know that you may not be able to avoid debt to purchase a home, a car, or education. But, aside from those essential expenses, avoid debt when you can. J. Golden Kimball, a General Authority beloved by the Saints for his candid humor, made this point: "An honest man is in hell when he is in debt" (in Conference Report, Oct. 1931, 56).

- *Budget.* One of the best ways to manage your income is to budget. Keep a careful record of both income and expenses. There is an old adage that says that what couples do in the first six months of their marriage tends to be perpetuated throughout the marriage. This also applies to financial matters. Developing a good budget system early in your marriage will be a blessing to you your whole lives. Budgeting is a process of preplanning your income and making sure it accomplishes what you want your resources to do for you. Both of you should understand how the budget in your home operates. It may not always be possible to keep track of every penny like Scrooge did, but you ought to have an idea of what your income is and where it is needed to meet your financial obligations. Many people do not like to be restricted by a budget, but it can be a positive experience in your marriage. Budgets are quite painless, and when you see the results of managing your spending, you will appreciate the principle of budgeting. Financial decisions must be made anyway, so why not have a system that will work well for both of you. Budgeting requires wisdom, self-control, goals, a sense of direction, a firm hand, and a desire to save money.

A simple way to budget is to go back through your checkbook(s), ledger, or software program to see what your expenditures have been for the past three months (disregard the holiday season). That will give you a larger view of what categories you typically must spend money in over a period of time. Then, calculate the average monthly cost of each category by dividing the total amount for three months by three (in this case) to obtain the *average monthly expenditure* for each category. You now have a pretty good idea of the average amount of money that you spend for each of the budget categories. The first principle of budgeting is to know exactly where you have allocated your funds in the past and how you need to continue or change directions in the next budget period.

Setting Reasonable Limits for Living Expenses

The following expenses are typical for most married couples. Once married, make a comparison of your actual living expenses with the percentages given below.

Our Family Budget

To determine the percent for each category, divide each total by the income. As an example, $200/$1000 = 20%; $100/$2000 = 5% of income spent on an item.

Items/Categories	% Allotted	Joint Goal	Actual Spent
Food	20–30%		
Housing	15–35%		
Clothing	10–15%		
Personal	2–5%		
Transportation *(inc. ins.)*	10–25%		
Medical *(inc. ins.)*	3–15%		
Education/Recreation	0–10%		
Gifts/Contributions	10–15%		
Emergency/Misc.	2–10%		
Savings/Investments	0–10%		
Life Insurance	0–10%		
Debts*	0–20%		

* Debts should never exceed 20% of your net income.

Summary

Let's review some basic financial principles.
- Pay an honest tithing; first meet your obligations to the Lord.
- Learn to manage money by having a budget that works well for both of you
- Exercise self discipline and restraint in money matters—don't let *wants* overpower *needs*. We can all think of things we would like to have no matter how much money we've amassed.

- Make education a lifelong experience. Knowledge in your field of expertise will change over time and you will want to keep up.
- Save toward home-ownership down payments, for your home will be one of your most important assets..
- Educate yourself on the principle of insurance and learn how it can help you preserve your assets in case of a loss; compare programs and premiums carefully.
- Understand how the United States economy functions in general. Then you can understand external forces such as inflation, fiscal and monetary policy, and be somewhat aware of what the future economic picture will be. You will be better prepared for making investment decisions for the long term.
- Appropriately involve yourself in a food storage and emergency preparedness program.

Questions to Consider

Consider the following questions as they apply to your situation. If you are dating someone, discuss the applicable questions between the two of you. If you are not currently in a relationship, decide where you stand on an issue before you start dating someone and how you would like to improve.

1. Who handled the finances in our families? What did we like about the system in our home(s) and where could we make some improvements?

2. How do we see finances being managed in our marriage? Which one of us has a better grasp on the principles of managing money? How could we set up a system of managing money that will work well for us?

3. What plans are we making now to manage money? Have either of us taken a class on personal finance, or been involved in living by a budget so far? (It would be a good idea for you to visit with both sets of parents to obtain their counsel on how to manage money in your marriage.)

CHAPTER 11

Preparing for Marital Intimacy

*"Many marriages have been wrecked on the dangerous rocks of ignorant
and debased sex behavior, both before and after marriage. Gross
ignorance on the part of newlyweds on the subject of the proper place
and functioning of sex results in much unhappiness and many broken
homes. Thousands of young people come to the marriage altar almost
illiterate insofar as this basic and fundamental function is concerned. . . .
Some sound instruction in this area will help a man to realize
the numberless, delicate differentiations and modifications in the life
and reactions of the normal woman."*[1]

If you're engaged, you are about to begin one of the great adven-
tures of your lives—marital intimacy. Most of you up to this point
have abstained from sexual relations. Therefore you have surely antici-
pated this aspect of marriage with both trepidation and excitement.
The wedding night and subsequent honeymoon are always interesting
experiences for Latter-day Saint couples. This is because throughout
life, parents, teachers, and Church leaders may have emphasized the
"don'ts" of the law of chastity, and now it is time for the "dos." What
was once off limits, now becomes a wonderful opportunity to share
your heart and soul with each other in an intimate embrace. As one
of our students said, "Until now it has been 'no, no, no,' and now it is
time for 'yes, yes, yes.'"

You may feel some anxiety as you approach marital intimacy
because of the expectations you bring to marriage. Due largely to the

influence of the media and perhaps a few braggart friends, most couples anticipating marriage have some misconceptions about the purpose and function of sexual relations. Although most expect that everyone will enjoy this aspect of marriage, there is a danger that we may set ourselves up for disappointment. One of the most obvious discoveries you will make together after your marriage is that the movies don't portray the reality of sexual intimacy very well. One young bride cautioned, "I think a lot of people don't realize before they get married how powerful a thing sexual intimacy really turns out to be within marriage."

Most couples learn soon after marriage that there is an important connection between the quality of the marital relationship and the quality of their sexual experience—emotionally and physically. The Lord designed marital intimacy to be a positive expression of feelings between spouses. Those feelings are dependent on how well the nonsexual areas of your marriage are functioning. Many individuals learn this the hard way. Generally, a good sexual relationship is the product of a good marriage.

Sadly, for many, marital intimacy is not a positive factor in their union. Instead, this part of the relationship turns into a source of frustration and conflict. President Spencer W. Kimball gave this explanation:

> If you study the divorces . . . you will find there are one, two, three, four reasons. *Generally sex is the first.* They did not get along sexually. They may not say that in the court. They may not even tell that to their attorneys, but that is the reason. . . . Husband and wife . . . are authorized, in fact they are commanded, to have proper sex when they are properly married for time and eternity. That does not mean that we need to go to great extremes. That does not mean that a woman is the servant of the husband. It does not mean that any man has a right to demand sex anytime that he might want it. He should be reasonable and understanding and it should be a general program between the two, so they understand and everybody is happy about it (Spencer W. Kimball, *The Teachings of Spencer W. Kimball,* ed. Edward L. Kimball [1982], 312; emphasis added).

Like anything else worthwhile, learning to enjoy each other physically requires time and effort on both your parts. We do know this: For most couples, this sexual aspect of marriage will be an important component of your happiness. Just as marriage is ordained of God, so are sexual relations. The Lord grants each person this divine power in mortality so that they may express, in a profound way, their deep feelings of love for each other. Let's look at four major purposes of marital intimacy.

A Profound Expression of Love; A Sacrament

Few things can so aptly express your love for each other as will physical and emotional closeness. President Kimball explained that,

> *Sex is for procreation and expression of love.* It is the destiny of men and women to join together to make eternal family units. In the context of lawful marriage, the intimacy of sexual relations is right and divinely approved. There is nothing unholy or degrading about sexuality in itself, for by that means men and women join in a process of creation and in an expression of love (Spencer W. Kimball, *The Teachings of Spencer W. Kimball,* ed. Edward L. Kimball [1982], 311).

Elder Jeffrey R. Holland has provided the following additional insight:

> Sexual intimacy is not only a symbolic union between a man and a woman—the uniting of their very souls—but it is also symbolic of a union between mortals and Deity, between otherwise ordinary and fallible humans uniting for a rare and special moment with God Himself and all the powers by which He gives life in this wide universe of ours. . . .
>
> Sexual union is also, in its own profound way, a very real sacrament of the highest order. . . . Indeed, if our definition of sacrament is that act of claiming and sharing and exercising God's own inestimable power, then I know of virtually no other divine privilege so routinely given to us all—women or men, ordained or unordained, Latter-day Saint or non-Latter-day Saint—than the miraculous and majestic power of transmitting life, the unspeakable, unfathomable, unbroken power of procreation ("Of Souls Symbols, and Sacraments," *Brigham Young University 1987–88 Devotional and Fireside Speeches* [1988], 82-83).

To Gain Emotional, Physical, and Spiritual Closeness with a Spouse

Sharing your sexual natures as husband and wife is designed to strengthen your emotional, physical, and spiritual bonds as a couple. Recall our discussion of validation in an earlier chapter. Sexual relations were ordained by Deity so as a couple you could complement each other and meet each other's needs for touch, acceptance, and validation. When you meet each other's needs you are able to achieve a level of intimacy that expresses love, renews your relationship, and strengthens the most tender feelings of your soul. Regarding this closeness, Elder Boyd K. Packer taught: "In marriage all of the worthy yearnings of the human soul, all that is physical and emotional and spiritual, can be fulfilled" ("Marriage," *Ensign*, May 1981, 15).

Elder Parley P. Pratt described the purpose of marital intimacy in these words:

> Our natural affections are planted in us by the Spirit of God, for a wise purpose; and they are the very main-springs of life and happiness—they are the cement of all virtuous and heavenly society—they are the essence of charity, or love. . . . There is not a more pure and holy principle in existence than the affection which glows in the bosom of a virtuous man for his companion (Parker P. Robinson, *The Writings of Parley Parker Pratt* [1952], 52).

To Fulfill God's Command to Have Children

Of course, this intimate expression of masculine and feminine traits becomes the way you naturally expand your family. You will find it a sacred privilege to bring children into the world—those spirits whom the Father will assign you. Your love for each other will be made holy as you join to create a physical body for a premortal brother or sister, a son or daughter of Heavenly Parents who will be sent to join your little kingdom. Does this privilege not give a sacred context to parenthood? Thus, procreation becomes a most holy sacrament. Elder Richard G. Scott expressed these sentiments about the command to have children.

> Within the enduring covenant of marriage, the Lord permits husband and wife the expression of the sacred procreative powers in all their loveliness and beauty within the bounds He has set. One purpose of this private, sacred, intimate experience is to provide the physical bodies for the spirits Father in Heaven wants to experience mortality ("Making the Right Choices," *Ensign,* Nov. 1994, 38).

Some couples, especially in today's environment of selfishness, are hesitant to have children. They want to live together and have sexual relations without the accompanying responsibility of parenthood. May we say to you that no greater blessing will come into your lives than that of children. President J. Reuben Clark, Jr. cautioned that marital intimacy is not just for physical enjoyment without the obligation of parenthood:

> There is some belief, too much I fear, that sex desire is planted in us solely for the pleasures of full gratification; that the begetting of children is only an unfortunate incident. The direct opposite is the fact. Sex desire was planted in us in order to be sure that bodies would be begotten to house the spirits; the pleasures of gratification of the desire is an incident, not the primary purpose of the desire.
>
> As to sex in marriage, the necessary treatise on that for Latter-day Saints can be written in two sentences: Remember the prime purpose of sex desire is to beget children. Sex gratification must be had at that hazard. You husbands: be kind and considerate of your wives. They are not your property; they are not mere conveniences; they are your partners for time and eternity (in Conference Report, Oct. 1949, 194–195).

Of all people, Latter-day Saints should be enthusiastic about bringing children into the world. In this way we fulfill the measure of our creation, the Lord's purposes, and the reasons why the Lord created the earth (see D&C 49:15–17). The work of our Heavenly Father, thereby, moves forward.

To Provide Pleasure and Joy to Each Other—A Therapeutic Aspect of Marriage

Again from Elder Pratt:

> The object of the union of the sexes is . . . for mutual affection and cultivation of those eternal principles of never-ending charity and benevolence which are inspired by the Eternal Spirit; also for mutual comfort and assistance in this world of toil and sorrow and for mutual duties toward their offspring (*Key to the Science of Theology* [1978], 105).

In a similar vein, Elder Boyd K. Packer taught this concept to a Relief Society gathering:

> It is interesting to know how man is put together—how incomplete he is. His whole physical and emotional, and for that matter, spiritual nature, is formed in such a way that it depends upon a source of encouragement and power that is found in a woman. [When man] has found his wife and companion, [he has, in a sense], found the other half of himself. He will return to her again and again for that regeneration that exalts his manhood and strengthens him for the testing that life will give him ("Church Relief Society Conference," *Salt Lake Tribune,* 2 Oct. 1970, sec. B, p. 1).

A similar concept holds true for women, for without a kind and loving husband, a wife cannot find fulfillment in her sacred roles as wife and mother. Neither one of us can reach our ultimate potential alone. We need each other to progress towards exaltation. Remember Paul's instruction to the Corinthian Saints "Neither is the man without the woman, neither the woman without the man, in the Lord" (1 Cor. 11:11).

Marital intimacy will require charity, kindness, and selflessness, the most important Christlike attributes that you possess. There will be times, for example, when you as a husband will need to exercise self-control in your sexual desires, especially when your wife is exhausted from her responsibilities as a mother and homemaker. Likewise, there will be occasions when a husband is in need of the type of therapy that comes only from intimate relations, and as a wife you will want to be sensitive to such occasions. As a couple, you will find that marital intimacy has the power to rejuvenate your lives and regenerate feelings for each other when the strains and pressures of life challenge you both. God designed this union as a therapeutic exchange for married sweethearts. Learn to be sensitive to each other's needs on those occasions when you express your feelings for each other in emotional and physical ways.

Elder Richard G. Scott provided the following counsel to the priesthood:

> I would speak of something that is most sacred. When we were created, Father in Heaven put in our body the capacity to stir powerful emotions. Within the covenant of marriage, when properly used in ways acceptable to both and to the Lord, those emotions open the doors for children to come to earth. Such sacred expressions of love are an essential part of the covenant of marriage. Within marriage, however, the stimulation of those emotions can either be used as an end unto itself or to allow a couple to draw closer in oneness through the beautiful, appropriate expression of these feelings between husband and wife. There are times, brethren, when you need to restrain those feelings. There are times when you need to *allow their full expression.* Let the Lord guide you in ways that will enrich your marriage ("The Sanctity of Womanhood," *Ensign,* May 2000, 37; emphasis added).

As a husband, you will learn that there will be times when your wife may feel the need for more intimate contact than you do, especially as she moves out of her childbearing years. She may enjoy the closeness of marriage more than she did in her earlier years, and you want to be there for her. It is usually in the early years of marriage that a husband appreciates more intimate contact with his wife than perhaps she does, and his attitude also may change in the later years. The key from Elder Scott is "to let the Lord guide you" in this aspect of your marriage. Unfortunately, many of our young men and women have attended too many R-rated movies, so when they marry, they think they can demand sexual relations whenever they want. Maybe that happens in Hollywood, but that is not the way it happens in most marriages. There will be bills to pay, floors to mop, babies to burp, tests to study for, cars to fix, rooms to paint, and clogged toilets to deal with. We would all like to believe that married life will always be filled with romance, sexual relations, and exotic getaways. However, "strong couples also enjoy peanut-butter-and-jelly sandwiches while sitting in their backyard. They enjoy working together pulling weeds, painting walls, and washing dishes. Romance alone cannot sustain a continuing relationship" (H. Wallace Goddard, *The Frightful and Joyous Journey of Family Life* [1997], 49). There are times when you will be unable to be intimate together.

President Spencer W. Kimball declared:

> [Love in marriage] is deep, inclusive, comprehensive. It is not like that association of the world which is misnamed love, but which is mostly *physical attraction*. When marriage is based on this only, the parties soon tire of one another. . . . The love of which the Lords speaks is not only physical attraction, but spiritual attraction as well. It is faith and confidence in, and understanding of, one another. It is a total partnership. It is companionship with common ideals and standards. It is unselfishness toward and sacrifice for one another. It is cleanliness of thought and action and faith in God and His program. It is parenthood in mortality ever looking toward godhood and creationship, and parenthood of spirits. It is vast, all-inclusive, and limitless. This kind of love *never* tires or wanes. It lives on through sickness and sorrow, through prosperity and privation, through accomplishment and disappointment, through time and eternity (Spencer W. Kimball, *Faith Precedes the Miracle* [1972], 130–31).

Elder Jeffrey R. Holland offered this profound insight about the sacred nature of marital intimacy:

> Human intimacy is reserved for a married couple because it is the ultimate symbol of total union, a totality and a union ordained and defined by God. From the Garden of Eden onward, marriage was intended to mean the complete merger of a man and a woman—their hearts, hopes, lives, love, family, future, everything. Adam said of Eve that she was bone of his bones and flesh of his flesh, and that they were to be "one flesh"

in their life together. This is a union of such completeness that we use the word seal to convey its eternal promise ("Personal Purity," *Ensign,* Nov. 1998, 76).

Newlyweds and Intimacy

Because you have been properly taught that sexual relations are only appropriate within the bonds of marriage, as a newly married couple you should be inexperienced in sexual matters, and that is right and proper. It is much better to go on a honeymoon and discover together the joys of marital intimacy. Oftentimes we see sexual intercourse become nothing more than exploiting another person for one's own personal gratification. However, it is when intimacy is coupled with the commitment of marriage that this act of love retains its purity and beauty. Outside of marriage, sexual relations become an abomination, an excuse for the selfish use of another for one's own personal gain. Surely that is one of the primary reasons God limits, by command, sexual intimacy to marriage. It is in mortality that we first have the power to create physical bodies, and He commands that His children be born in homes where a father and mother reside. Children are to be born under the protection of the family umbrella.

Premarital Exam for the Wife

Inasmuch as you will soon be sexually active as a married couple, it is important that as a future bride you have a premarital exam a month or two before your marriage date, preferably with an obstetrician/gynecologist (OB/GYN), a specialist in female sexual anatomy. He or she can explain the physical demands of sexual intercourse and by physical examination tell you of the ease or difficulty you may have in consummating sexual relations. In most cases women are pronounced physically fine for this new adventure. Sometimes it is necessary, however, for the hymenal ring of tissue that surrounds the vaginal opening to be stretched or dilated to ensure that sexual relations can take place with minimum discomfort. If any procedures are necessary before the honeymoon and beyond, you may need a little time to heal before your wedding night. Also, the doctor can help the two of you learn about different approaches to birth control. You will want to decide as a couple what you will do about children and possible health issues before and after pregnancy. (We are not advocating the use of birth control here. That decision can only be made by the two of you as you seek heavenly wisdom and inspiration.)[2]

Emotional Preparation

Aside from physical preparation for sexual relations, you will also want to consider the emotional aspects. As you may both need some sex education after the wedding, we recommend a book entitled *Between Husband and Wife: Gospel Perspectives on Marital Intimacy.*[3] You won't need a great deal of material on this topic before marriage, but this volume will give you some basic things to think about and consider after you marry. The honeymoon experience and first few months can be difficult for both of you if you are mentally and emotionally unprepared for sexual relations.

In the temple ceremony you will hear the command to consummate the marriage and become parents, which implies sexual intimacy. Your marriage will soon be consummated. Though it will be somewhat new and strange to you at first, most couples have made the adjustment rather easily since the days of Adam and Eve. We will assume that you too will find this a fulfilling part of your marriage. We recommend that on your wedding night you take time and be very patient with each other. Too many couples rush away from the wedding reception and arrive at a hotel after midnight, supposing they are going to experience something quite marvelous as they consummate their marriage. They soon learn that a day filled with an endowment session, the marriage ceremony, hours of pictures, a brunch, a reception, and opening presents can be emotionally, spiritually, and physically exhausting. Take your time with each other. Couples who end up having their first sexual encounter at 1:00 A.M. usually conclude, "So, that was it?" If you are set on consummating your marriage on the wedding day, as most do, try to schedule the day so that there is uninterrupted time for both of you. If you get to the hotel at a late hour, you might want to save yourselves for the next morning. You have the rest of your lives to work at this relationship. Listen to some comments by newly married individuals:

> One thing that my husband and I had to deal with that we really weren't expecting was the guilt associated with having sexual relations for the first time. We were not prepared for the feelings that we experienced after being celibate for so long. The morning after our honeymoon night was such a strange feeling, something that really surprised me.

Another newly married person said this:

> I think many Saints have sexual compatibility problems with their spouse because they have been programmed all their lives that sex is evil [off-limits], and all of a sudden one day you are married and now everything is okay. So my husband and I talk frequently about our sexual relationship.
>
> I admit that the first couple of times we discussed it, we were both embarrassed. [Individual feelings about] sexuality are . . . extremely personal. Talking about sexuality and intimacy is taking a huge risk. But we have gotten better at sharing sexual feelings and preferences and it is wonderful! It is so comforting to me that I can talk to my husband about anything.

In *A Parent's Guide,* a manual the Church published as a help for parents in preparing their children for marital intimacy, we receive the following perspective and counsel:

> The courtesy and friendship the couple have shown during courtship are vital on their wedding night. The first night requires nearly perfect courtesy, consideration, and, in many cases, a gentle sense of good humor. They must be the very best of friends on this first occasion when they are able to begin to know one another completely. They may be ill at ease, even awkward, and would do well to smile at their awkwardness. Each must remember that the other person is vulnerable to embarrassment. And, they must realize that the greatest passions of

marriage lie ahead, to increase over the years through experience and growth. A truth not generally known to newly married couples is that in virtuous marriages passions increase over the years between the couple. Couples can find great joy through fidelity, childbirth, rearing and teaching their children, providing a home, and striving to live gospel truths. President McKay explained:

"Let us instruct young people who come to us, first, young men throughout the Church, to know that a woman should be queen of her own body. The marriage covenant does not give the man the right to enslave her, or to abuse her, or to use her merely for the gratification of his passion. Your marriage ceremony does not give you that right.

"Second, let them remember that gentleness and consideration after the ceremony is just as appropriate and necessary and beautiful as gentleness and consideration before the wedding.

"Third, let us realize that manhood is not undermined by the practicing of continence, notwithstanding what some psychiatrists claim. Chastity is the crown of beautiful womanhood, and self-control is the source of true manhood, if you will know it, not indulgence. Sexual indulgence whets the passion and creates morbid desire.

"Let us teach our young men to enter into matrimony with the idea that each will be just as courteous, and considerate of a wife after the ceremony as during courtship. . . ." (As cited in Conference Report, Apr. 1952, 86-87)

We also learn from President Kimball:

The honeymoon ought to be a time when the partners learn about one another's minds, emotions, bodies, and spirits. It is not a time for sexual excess. It is not a fling of worldly diversions that is scheduled between the temple wedding ceremony and a return to serious living. For Latter-day Saints, the honeymoon and early weeks of marriage are a time for private discovery on all levels: physical, social, emotional, and spiritual.

In sexual matters, as in all other aspects of marriage, there are virtues to be observed: "If it is unnatural, you just don't do it. That is all, and all the family life should be kept clean and worthy and on a very high plane. There are some people who have said that behind the bedroom doors anything goes. That is not true and the Lord would not condone it" (Spencer W. Kimball, *The Teachings of Spencer W. Kimball,* ed. Edward L. Kimball [1982], 312).

A Parent's Guide also explains that

> Both husbands and wives have physical, emotional, psychological, and spiritual needs associated with this sacred act. They will be able to complement each other in the marriage relationship if they give tender, considerate attention to these needs of their partner. Each should seek to fulfill the other's needs rather than to use this highly significant relationship merely to satisfy his or her own passion.

> Couples will discover differences in the needs or desires each partner has for such a relationship, but when each strives to satisfy the needs of the other, these differences need not present a serious problem. Remember, this intimate relationship between husband and wife was established to bring joy to them. An effort to reach this righteous objective will enable married couples to use their complementary natures to bring joy to this union.

> The intimate relationship between husband and wife realizes its greatest value when it is based on loving kindness and tenderness between the marriage partners. This fact, supported by valid research data, helps newly married couples recognize that the so-called sex drive is mostly myth. Sexual intimacy is not an involuntary, strictly biological necessity for survival, like breathing and eating. Sexual intimacy between a husband and wife can be delayed or even suspended for long periods of time with no negative effect (for example, when the health of one or the other requires it). Husbands and wives are not compelled to mate because their genes or hormones order them to do so. Sexual powers are voluntary and controllable; the heart and mind do rule. While sex drive is a myth, husbands and wives do have physical and emotional needs that are fulfilled through sexual union. If they perceive and appreciate their masculine and feminine natures as important, complementing, but not controlling, parts of their lives, becoming as one flesh can be one of life's richest and most rewarding experiences.

> There are times within the marriage when complete abstinence is appropriate for extended periods of time, such as during ill health, difficult pregnancy, separation due to employment

away from home, or a need to restore respect and mutually decent emotional and spiritual relationships. There also are times when a spouse's emotional and physical needs would make it desirable for the other to be especially affectionate. Throughout the marriage, the husband is expected, in the name of simple decency, to understand and sustain his wife as she literally gives her body to create life. Although no significant physical changes are likely for men after marriage, bearing children evokes very significant changes for women. These changes are so profound and complex that each couple should seek reliable medical information about them. Ideally, both will study this information before and then again during pregnancy. This study should provoke within pure hearts gratitude for the human body and its godlike parts. The objective is to increase virtue, not carnality. (*A Parent's Guide:* Ch. 6: "Mature Intimacy: Courtship and Marriage," [pamphlet, 1985], 47–49).

Keeping Intimacy Appropriate and Sacred

Because the sexual relationship should be a new experience for you, it will be necessary that you *learn* how to enjoy this part of your marriage, thereby enhancing your overall marriage relationship. (Even if you have been married before, or sexually active in the past, sexual relations will be different with a new spouse and there is much to learn from each other.) Because this is such an important issue in determining marital happiness, and is dramatically affected by all aspects of life—health, gender, age, individual need, etc.—you will want to learn as much as you can about the sexual functions of the human body, and especially those of your spouse in particular. Though your best sex manual as a married couple will be *each other*, we again strongly recommend that you read an appropriate book on the subject after marriage.

You will need to learn how to communicate with your spouse about what works best for each of you, and you will need to be extremely sensitive to your spouse's individual fears, insecurities, wants, and needs. Most importantly, however, you will need to maintain intimacy's sacred nature while meeting those needs. You will learn from each other, of course, and from the Spirit as you exchange mutual feelings concerning intimacy.

You will need to know that not everything of a sexual nature is to be participated in with each other as marriage partners. As Latter-day Saints, we do not believe in the worldly notion that behind closed doors, "anything goes." Hopefully, the two of you will have a spiritual sensitivity to know what is appropriate. Spiritual promptings will come to you from the Lord concerning what is right and what is not. The prophets have given some counsel on this issue without being specific about the dos and don'ts. We can learn from their instruction.

"It is not love if it manipulates; it is selfishness . . . it is irresponsibility," said President Spencer W. Kimball on one occasion. "If sex relations merely become a release or a technique and the partner becomes exchangeable, then sex returns to the compulsive animal level" (*Love Versus Lust* [1975], 15).

President Howard W. Hunter gave this counsel in a Church priesthood meeting: "Tenderness and respect—never selfishness—must be the guiding principles in the intimate relationship between husband and wife. Each partner must be considerate and sensitive to the other's needs and desires. Any domineering, indecent, or uncontrolled behavior in the intimate relationship between husband and wife is condemned by the Lord" ("Being a Righteous Husband and Father," *Ensign*, Nov. 1994, 51).

You must focus on not allowing this sacred privilege to be degraded by worldly ideas. Much of what the world sells as sexuality is merely pornographic in nature—it isn't even related to the true nature and purpose of this divine act of love. Victor Cline, a psychologist specializing over the years in pornography and its victims, put this in perspective years ago:

> As I personally see it, the big problem with pornography is that it presents sex out of context. It presents sex in an untrue manner and creates an image that sex exists as an entity all by itself. This, of course, is not the way real life usually is. . . .
>
> Pornography is counterfeit sex. It's sex without affection and tenderness and dedication; and most of all, for Latter-day Saints, pornography is without an understanding of the purpose of sex and how it relates to the eternal scheme of things. And that's the great problem with some kinds of publications. Women are presented as things to be exploited and used rather than as people.

> Love is presented as a physical thing and nothing more. Movies legitimize adultery, infidelity, and immorality because "the physical attraction is so beautiful." All they are doing is justifying irresponsibility, telling us that passion overwhelms and justifies all. Well, in my view this is an antisocial message, destructive and Satanic in impact. It degrades love, and it is destructive of human personality and male-female relationships ("A Conversation on Things of the Spirit, Pornography, and Certain Kinds of Movies, Books, and Magazines," *New Era,* May 1971, 11).

You must remember to hold the marriage relationship sacred—and everything that comes with it. You honor each other in all ways. Remember that infidelity is not limited to *sexual* relationships outside of marriage. Now that you are close to marriage, and especially after you are married, you should close the door to flirting or having any intimate contacts—physical or *emotional*—with members of the opposite sex. President Ezra Taft Benson explained:

> If you are married [or committed], avoid flirtations of any kind. . . . What may appear to be harmless teasing or simply having a little fun with someone of the opposite sex can easily lead to more serious involvement and eventual infidelity. A good question to ask ourselves is this: Would my spouse be pleased if he or she knew I was doing this? Would a wife be pleased to know that her husband lunches alone with his secretary? Would a husband be pleased if he saw his wife flirting and being coy with another man? My beloved brothers and sisters, this is what Paul meant when he said: "Abstain from all appearance of evil" (1 Thess. 5:22) ("The Law of Chastity," *New Era,* Jan. 1988, 6).

President Hunter summed up the dangers in walking any lines when it comes to keeping the spirit of our marital covenants. "Be faithful in your marriage covenants in thought, word, and deed. Pornography, flirtations, and unwholesome fantasies erode one's character and strike at the foundation of a happy marriage. Unity and trust within a marriage are thereby destroyed" ("Being a Righteous Husband and Father," *Ensign,* Nov. 1994, 50). And, as the prophets have stated, unwholesome activities even within marriage can do the same—degrade the uplifting nature of intimacy and impede healthy feelings of unity between husband and wife.

Summary

Let us say, in conclusion, that this sacred privilege of sexual intimacy will be a great blessing to your relationship. The marriage bed will be a wonderful retreat and a haven when life deals you some unexpected blows, to say nothing of the positive, marriage-strengthening qualities it will provide. The Lord designed sexual relations for married couples as a way for them to strengthen mutual feelings and to increase their family. It was *not* designed to *solve* marital problems, but it was intended to be an expression of the love that already exists between the two of you. How you treat each other in areas of your marriage will have a profound influence on how well you enjoy sexual relations, and vice versa.

Questions to Consider

Consider the following questions as they apply to your situation. If you are dating someone, answer the applicable questions by yourself, and then come back and discuss them together at a later time. If you are not currently in a relationship, decide where you stand on an issue before you start dating someone and how you would like to improve.

1. In what ways can a bride prepare herself for marital intimacy? What can a husband do to prepare himself?

2. Have I been sensitive to my future spouse's needs to this point? How can I improve this before marriage?

3. What would be a wise plan for intimacy following our wedding reception? (Consider distances and trying to do everything in one day. Some of this depends on how far you have to go to find a temple, and then how far it is to the hotel you will be staying at.)

CHAPTER 12

Anger—the Great Destroyer of Family Relations

*"Don't lose your temper. Anger is
a corrosive thing that destroys, breaks
hearts, destroys peace and happiness
and brings sadness and regret. Curb your anger."*[1]

Do you feel that you are almost ready for marriage? Hopefully from our cautions, you have looked closely at the strengths and weaknesses of your prospective spouse as well as your own inadequacies. The purpose of your engagement has been to scrutinize each other's personality and character traits to determine if you really want to live with each other now—and for eternity! This has been your time to screen for potential flaws and major pathologies that are simply irreconcilable.

Specifically now, there is one area we would like you to carefully review—temperament. We are asking that you make sure you are comfortable with your own temperament and tendencies to become angry as well as those of your fiancé. From our experience in working with married couples, especially as we watch people go through a divorce, it seems that the great destroyer of marriage and family relations is anger and ill-temper on the part of one or both marriage partners. These fraternal twin emotions can destroy even the strongest relationships. The unfortunate aspects of anger and temper are that they usually don't rear their ugly heads until after the marriage ceremony; they are difficult to detect during courtship because both individuals have been on their best behavior. In fact, an angry outburst during dating or courtship could be enough to end the relationship right there. Therefore, because of its importance, we are devoting an entire chapter to the topic.

The Great Destroyer of Marriage

Please note that most people allow themselves to become angry when their expectations aren't met. Perhaps they feel that their fiancé should be there to console them when they have a bad day. Perhaps a husband feels that the new baby should sleep through the night on the evening before final exams are scheduled. However, when the baby decides that the night before finals would be a great time to scream, cry, and get an earache, then anger can rise in immature hearts and overwhelm usually calm, more sanguine feelings. Perhaps a husband lashes out in frustration at his wife because he feels she should take care of the baby and keep things quiet while he studies, knowing he has finals the next day. Perhaps a wife will give her husband the silent treatment for several days because she has to take care of the baby most of the time while her husband provides little assistance in taking care of the apartment. Carlfred Broderick explained the damage that can be done by our carelessness:

> The explosive expression of anger has a doubly bad effect. First it is hurtful to others and destructive of trust and intimacy. Second, it feeds upon itself within the person expressing it. That is, expressing anger breeds more anger; it does not eliminate it . . . The Lord's position on this matter is unambiguous: there is no permission for losing one's temper in the circle of those who love and attempt to follow the Savior. The only righteous response to our own temper is to root it out as we would root out any other lust or excess in order to be worthy of the kingdom (*One Flesh One Heart* [1986], 40-41).

As a couple you need to realize that anger can arise in your mortal, fallen heart. Anger is a natural emotion that is common to mortals. But before you act on such inward feelings with an outward display of immaturity, understand that the Lord gave agency to decide how you'll react when you feel provoked or choose to take offense. The philosophies of the world would have us believe that the anger model should be diagramed this way:

Stimulus⟶Response

However, the gospel perspective adds one more word to the diagram. It should look like this:

Stimulus⟶Agency⟶Response

Do you believe that agency plays a role in controlling anger? If you are having a difficult time with this issue, let us give you an example. Let's say you are playing a friendly softball game in the backyard with your family. You are the pitcher when your little brother swings at a pitch and accidently lets go of the bat, and it hits you right in the shin. After you hop around on one leg for a few minutes and eventually regain the use of your limb, you will probably hobble around the yard chasing your sibling while yelling a few words that cannot be repeated in church. What if the very same thing happened in a ward softball game? And to make it more realistic, let's assume that the bishop is the batter. He swings at your pitch, lets go of the bat, and it accidently hits you in the shin. Now, how do you react? Do you chase him around the diamond, waving the piece of broken bat, shouting "an eye for an eye, and a tooth for a tooth"? Probably not. In fact, when you're able to walk again, you would probably hobble over to him and say, "Don't worry about it, my brother does that all the time," or "Hey, accidents happen." Do you see the point? Anger is a choice we make given the circumstances as we interpret them. We decide how we will react in a particular setting because we do not want to make fools of ourselves in public. Christlike people, because of their understanding of the principles of the gospel, choose to respond in mature ways, no matter what the setting.

Now, we're not going to tell you that there aren't cases where righteous indignation is merited, where wrongs should not be righted.

There are some things that ought to get our dander up, such as unfairness, injustice, inhumanity to man, and suffering by the innocent. Some would argue that anger provides individuals with the incentive to fight for humanitarian causes. Anger, others contend, is justified where civil rights are violated, or against those who prey upon children, the elderly, and others who need society's protection. Even the Savior became angry when His Father's house, the temple, was being desecrated. But as we read the scriptures, undisciplined anger is always—100 percent of the time—cankerous, destructive, and, in reality, a primary tool of Satan to destroy marriages and family relations. You need to know that when anger is habitually directed toward family members, it is like a cancer that destroys the relationship. Thus, the critical issue for you to consider is one of anger management. That you will get angry may be a moot point. Most mortals do. But how you control your anger will determine the type of relationship that will exist between you and your family members, spouse, and children. Feelings of anger that arise within you, and a public demonstration of that anger, are two different things. Consider the experience of the following young woman, and how she learned that anger can destroy relationships:

> I wanted so much to be loved by my father. Everyone loved him. He was always making crazy jokes and being the life of every party. All of my friends wanted him to be their dad. They never understood why I didn't like to play at my house. They didn't understand why I was so afraid of him. My dad could be very loving and affectionate, but he had a horrible temper. Everyone at church considered my family the ideal family. Whenever my dad would get upset I would cry. He did not accept tears from anyone, especially one of his own kin. He told me more times than I can count to "buck up and be a man." Maybe my dad really wanted me to be a boy, I don't know. Maybe that is why he threw me against the walls and hit me with his belt, and screamed at me, and humiliated me, and never believed me. I was not a boy!

What a tragic experience. How can children who live under the roof of such hatred, hostility, and hypocrisy turn out to be normal? Anger *always* destroys or negatively affects human relationships. It never builds them up or strengthens them. Not only does anger bring negative feelings into a relationship, but it can be transmitted through generations, from angry fathers, to soon-to-be-angry sons. Over the years we have read student accounts of how parents treat their children, and it seems that many Church members must not realize that manifesting anger is a *sin* (JST, Eph. 4:26). There is little doubt that an uncontrolled temper corrodes human character of both the giver and the recipient. It is a truism that when you lose your temper, you lose the Spirit of the Lord. Without the Lord's Spirit, you will have a difficult time being charitable, and without charity, your relationship or marriage will not be what it ought to be. Let us say it bluntly: Mortals do not have enough wisdom to use anger constructively! Only the Savior possessed that wisdom. No wonder the Lord counsels us to reprove betimes with sharpness, *when moved upon by the Holy Ghost*" (D&C 121:43; emphasis added). It is only on rare occasions that the Spirit of the Lord would advise us to be sharp with others, much less display anger and ill-temper in private or in public.

One of the serious problems with anger is how it negatively affects our willingness to communicate with each other. When we become angry, we often say things that cause further frustration and difficulties. Without the Spirit of the Lord, most of us make very poor rational decisions. Perhaps the long-term penalty of anger directed toward family members is a loss of exaltation. We can think of no justifiable reasons for temper outbursts in family relationships. We are reminded of President David O. McKay's counsel that the only justification for yelling in the home is if the house is on fire. (see David O McKay, *Stepping Stones to an Abundant Life*, comp. Llewelyn McKay [1971], 294). The Lord was clear with the Nephites: "Behold, this is not my doctrine, to stir up the hearts of men with anger, one against another; but this is my doctrine, that such things *should be done away*" (3 Ne. 11:30; emphasis added). The Savior referred to Satan as the "father of contention, and he stirreth up the hearts of men to contend with anger, one with another" (3 Ne. 11:29). It is Satan who loves contention.

Temper and a Lack of Affection

Over the years in our classes we have asked our students to write a paper on their family background. More will be said about this later in the chapter, but suffice it to say, the most negative dimension of family life they reported was their father's temper. In fact, they mention their father's anger more often than they do their mother's, though there are surely numerous cases of mothers who yell and scream in their homes too. The sad part of reading these student comments is that even though their fathers are active in Church callings, read scriptures, lead out in family home evenings and give charitable service on many occasions, their father's display of temper and angry outbursts of yelling are unsettling to them. Many children are confused about their father's private religious worship (prayer and scripture study) and their public displays of temper. We think that if these men can act like saints at church, then they certainly should be able to act that way at home too. Put another way, if these men are yelling and screaming in a church setting, head-butting the deacons and knocking people down in the hallways, then we might understand their behavior at home. The fact that they can be so pleasant during three hours of church meetings gives encouragement that they really can do better on the home front.

Let us mention a distinction between anger and discipline—tough love. There are very few children who take time to thank their parents for the correction they received and the family rules that were used to help train them. When you are in the trenches as a child, it is hard to view your parents disciplinary actions very objectively. However, college-age students can look back with a little more impartiality at their home life and can appraise both the good and the bad. A few of them admit that they wished their parents had been more strict with them. However, there are too many young people who bear the emotional, psychological, and sometimes physical scars caused by angry parents. One young woman recalled:

> We heard Dad coming home, and we all ran away and hid. Some of us crawled under our beds and others climbed in closets and hid. My little sister had broken the guardrail [that kept] the baby from falling down the stairs, and we all knew Dad would be

mad. He screamed his rage, and everyone stayed quiet and hidden. Then he found one of my little sisters and he screamed at her and threatened to spank her hard unless she told him who did it or who was the oldest child at home. I was the oldest one home at the time and I could hear her screaming "Daddy, I didn't do it. I didn't do it." She told him she didn't know who did it. She told him where I was and I got a spanking so bad the marks lasted for weeks. Then he wanted me to tell him I loved him. I didn't love him. I hated him for being so mean and unfair. I hadn't caused it and it was just a little thing that could be fixed quickly. I think he just spanked us because he was angry and didn't want to fix anything.

Contrast this approach with the feelings of President Gordon B. Hinckley concerning his father: "I will be forever grateful for a father who never laid a hand in anger upon his children. Somehow he had the wonderful talent to let them know what was expected of them and to give them encouragement in achieving it." Then the prophet commented on how fathers impact their children: "I am persuaded that violent fathers produce violent sons. I am satisfied that such punishment in most instances does more damage than good. Children don't need beating. They need love and encouragement. They need fathers to whom they can look with respect rather than fear. Above all, they need example" ("Save the Children," *Ensign*, Nov. 1994, 53).

Displays of temper seem more serious when viewed from an eternal perspective. "Anger against *things* is senseless indeed!" said Elder ElRay L. Christiansen, "Because a wrench slips and we bruise our hand is no reason for throwing the wrench halfway across a wheat field. Having a flat tire on a busy downtown street will not be remedied by a tirade of words. Anger against *things* is bad enough, but when it is directed against people and it flares up with white-hot fury and caustic words, we have the makings of a tragedy!" ("Be Slow to Anger," *Ensign*, June 1971, 37).

President Gordon B. Hinckley gave this warning to men who treat their wives and children in un-Christlike ways: "Unfortunately a few [women] may be married to men who are abusive. Some of them put on a fine face before the world during the day and come home in the evening, set aside their self-discipline, and on the slightest provocation fly into outbursts of anger." We might ask what might qualify as a "slight provocation?" Could it be that dinner is not ready when Dad comes home from work? Is the house a little cluttered from the play of *his* children? Maybe the sprinklers were left on too long or the thermostat was set too low or too high? Perhaps his wife was on the phone when he walked in the door? Then President Hinckley chastised immature husbands who fly into a rage over trivial matters:

> No man who engages in such evil and unbecoming behavior is worthy of the priesthood of God. No man who so conducts himself is worthy of the privileges of the house of the Lord. I regret that there are some men undeserving of the love of their wives and children. There are children who fear their fathers, and wives who fear their husbands. If there be any such men within the hearing of my voice, as a servant of the Lord I rebuke you and call you to repentance. Discipline yourselves. Master your temper. Most of the things that make you angry are of very small consequence. And what a terrible price you are paying for your anger. Ask the Lord to forgive you. Ask your wife to forgive you. Apologize to your children ("Women of the Church," *Ensign,* Nov. 1996, 68).

One young woman wrote this about her father:

> After a day's work, my father comes home, demands dinner (complaining about whatever it is that my mom fixes), and then he sits down and watches TV—for the rest of the night, completely ignoring everything and everyone around him. I consider my dad to be emotionally abusive. He is very degrading in his comments to his family. I don't think it's because he doesn't love us, just that he is extremely selfish. He is always attacking someone's self-esteem. He likes to order the family around from his TV chair. I think President Kimball was speaking of my father when he said: "We have heard of men who have said to their wives, 'I hold the priesthood and you've got to do what I say.' Such a man should be tried for his membership. Certainly he should not be honored in his priesthood" (Spencer W. Kimball, *The Teachings of Spencer W. Kimball,* ed. Edward L. Kimball [1982], 316). Yet at church, my dad comes across as a capable person, and somehow he gets a temple recommend every year.

Contrast those comments with this young man's feelings about his father:

> I have never ever heard my father curse. To me this is a great source of strength because my father is my greatest living example of how to live a good Latter-day Saint life. Having had such a good example to follow makes making all the little decisions in life all that much easier. When I catch myself doing things that I saw my father do, I am even more thankful for a righteous father who lived the gospel of Jesus Christ every single day. I will forever be in the debt of my dad for showing me the way that Christ would have been my father.
>
> If I could only say one thing about my dad, it would be that he was always there for me. When I felt that the world was against me as a young boy and felt a lack of love from brothers and sisters, dad was my anchor. He has always been the silent motivator in my life. When we'd win a game and I thought I played poorly dad always comforted me. My father was there at every single game that I played. I know it was a sacrifice to make some of the two and three hour trips each way, but somehow, he did it. I could count on him to be waiting outside the locker room to give me his impressions of how well I had played. Being there would not have been as special to me unless you realize that I am the second of eleven children and my dad has worked two full-time jobs since I was a baby. There was always something else that he could have been doing, but he chose to be my biggest fan and has been for the other ten as well.
>
> I think that the single most sad day of my life will be the day that my father passes away. He has been so much more than just a man to me. He has been a peacemaker in our home, a spiritual leader, my greatest fan, my finest example, a community leader, and uncompromising on values. If I end up being half the father that my dad is and has been to me, then I can consider my life a success. I never could be able to tell him quite how he has touched my life and spirit, and changed my life for the better. Maybe the best way I could show him how much he means to me would be by living a life like he has led and striving to be the type of person that he believes I can become.

Parents have an immense influence on their children. You will be not only a husband or wife, but before long a father or mother of your own children. How blessed will be your children if you are the kind of father or mother who cared; who loved, taught, and yes—chastened, but who influenced the lives of their offspring to become better people, who in turn will become better husbands and wives, fathers and mothers in their own right.

In the classes we teach, one of our assignments is to have students write a paper on their family background. We ask the students to do the following:

1. Describe your father. What kind of individual, husband, and dad is he? How do you assess his strengths and weaknesses now that you're away from home and can look back at your family life with some objectivity?

2. Describe your mother. Now that you are an adult, what are her strengths and weaknesses as an individual, wife, and mom as you now look back with some perspective?

3. What did your parents do in their companionship that you would like to emulate in your marriage and what things would you not want to carry over into your own family life?

In general, about one out of three students say: "If I could have a marriage like my parents, I'd take it in a heartbeat." Another third say things like, "My parents were okay together, but I want to do things differently in my own family (read scriptures, observe FHE, be more consistent in family prayer, etc.)." But most notable were the last third; those comments reflecting how even minor anger (lack of affection, the cold shoulder, the silent treatment, and general insensitivity) created an uncomfortable and hurtful family atmosphere. Comments ranged all the way from, "I'm going to show more affection to my spouse in front of our children than my folks did," to, "My parents are so different—I'm not sure how they ever got together in the first place!" Students would go on and on about what poor role models their parents were: "They don't really like each other and have very different interests. They never showed much affection to each other while I was growing up. I'm not really sure how I got here!"

Lack of affection, unkindness, and insensitivity can go a long way in destroying individual self-esteem, and eventually the marriage relationship. Small acts of anger, like the silent treatment or ignoring hurt feelings, can eventually create barriers between couples that are no longer surmountable. Even an innocent lack of attention can create the feeling that an individual no longer loves, respects, or even thinks about his/her spouse. This perception drives a wedge of mistrust and emotional distance between a couple—which can lead to a "falling out of love," and eventually find permanent expression in divorce.

About one in three students live in step-family situations, came from single-parent families, or their parents were going through a divorce. There are always a few who write in their summaries that although their parents live together, they sleep in separate beds, or even separate rooms. When we ask why their parents stay married when they obviously don't like each other, the students will usually respond: "They stay together because of us kids," or "Because they were married in the temple."

And our immediate reaction to this is always, "Well, if they don't like each other in this life, do they think that death will somehow change their feelings? Do they actually believe that if they don't like each other in this life that when they die they will hardly be able to keep their spirit hands off each other?" Our informal data collection reveals that great damage can come to a family member through displays of anger or a lack of affection.

Not only does anger destroy feelings of love and trust in the hearts of wives, husbands, or children, but it fills that empty space with negative feelings that bring heartache, and memories of an unpleasant childhood ingrained in the soul of a those on the receiving end of the temper tantrum. These negative emotions, as well as their result—a negative sense of self and family relations—are, more often than not, passed to the next generation as the children themselves become parents. Wisely, the Prophet Joseph Smith revised the scripture in Ephesians 4:26 from "Be ye angry, and sin not" to "*Can* ye be angry, and not sin?" In Proverbs we read: "He that is slow to anger is better than the mighty" (16:32).

Anger and temper lead to caustic remarks, or even verbal or physical abuse—behavior that must not become a part of your personality as you prepare yourself for marriage and family relationships. These two emotions should never be manifested in relationships with those who live with you. Of course, as mortals we all slip on occasion (sin), but our goal must be to eliminate temper and demonstrations of anger in our lives. Perhaps the ultimate example would be our Heavenly Parents. Can you imagine them being mad at each other and throwing fits around the universe? And, of course, our goal is to become as They are.

Controlling Anger

Have you ever imagined what the world, or even your home, would be like if anger were eliminated? Burton Kelly has written:

> Imagine, for a moment, a world where few, if any, marriages end in divorce, few children shout at their parents, no parents abuse their children. Imagine a world of safe neighborhoods, peaceful governments, and healthy citizens—largely without hypertension, headaches, or backaches.
>
> Sound like never-never land, unpeopled by mortals? Yet I have just described some of the probable effects of a world absent only one simple emotion—anger ("The Case Against Anger," *Ensign*, Feb. 1980, 9).

What a wonderful world it would be with such a scenario. No doubt that is what heaven is like; or a little closer to home—the temple. However, if individuals could learn to control and eliminate their anger, could that not be the result in our homes? Here are a few suggestions for you to review as you think about temper and anger in your own life:[2]

- *Be responsible for your anger.* Often we will hear people say, "I just tell people how it is," as if expressing anger is a good thing. We are not sure that "telling people how it is," is a good thing. Expressing anger always carries dangerous overtones. Moreover, we often act as if we believe that anger is something beyond our control. Many say, "I lost my temper," or "my husband makes me so mad." No one can make you mad or angry. Anger is a choice. You can choose to be angry, or you can choose not to be (see Lynn Robbins, "Agency and Anger," *Ensign*, May 1998, 80).

- *Identify "trigger points."* Trigger points are those cues and prompts that lead to angry outbursts. You know that the combination of spilling milk on your dress at 8:08 A.M., getting your hand slammed in the car door at 8:15 A.M., and then ramming into the trash cans with your car at 8:16 A.M. will probably lead to a loud yell or scream at 8:17 A.M. Couples need to identify what leads them to be angry and hostile. What is it that contributes to the steam that's building and about to blow?

- *Withdraw from the situation if you feel anger welling up in your heart.* Don't stay in the ring—get out quick. Take a walk, go to the bathroom, exercise, chop down a tree, do something else. Richard L. Evans declared: "One of the safest tonics for temper is time. Many centuries ago, Seneca said, 'The best cure for anger is delay.' And the idea of the counting to ten has been traced back at least as far as Thomas Jefferson, who wrote, 'When angry, count ten before you speak; if very angry, an hundred'" (Richard L. Evans, *Richard L. Evans: The Man and the Message,* comp. Richard L. Evans, Jr. [1973], 301). One of the most important reasons to withdraw is to collect your thoughts. Richard Mower has written: ". . . the times we get angry are the times when it is hardest to think rationally and gain control; in initiating new responses that are as powerful as old habits, we must use a lot of advanced preparation and creativity" (*Overcoming Depression* [1986], 129-130). Brigham Young said "I charge myself not to get angry. . . . No, Brigham, never let anger arise in your heart, never, never!" (*Discourses of Brigham Young,* sel. John A. Widtsoe [1941], 265).

- *If you find yourself in a confrontation, respond softly.* Often, a soft answer will defuse the situation. President Hinckley has said that a cornerstone to marriage is the "soft answer," and that "quiet talk is the language of love, it is the language of peace, it is the language of God" (*News of the Church*, "Make Marriage a Partnership," *Ensign*, Apr. 1984, 76).

- *Use humor.* Humor can often defuse tense situations. Sometimes a comment at the right time can change the feeling in a relationship or room. Part of humor involves keeping a proper perspective on mortal matters. What benefit comes from getting angry? Whenever does anger change people or motivate them to do something better or differently?

- *Pray.* Ask the Lord for help. He wants you to control your emotions. He wants you to eliminate anger. Said Brigham Young:

> Many men will say they have a violent temper, and try to excuse themselves for actions of which they are ashamed. I will say, there is not a man in this house who has a more indomitable and unyielding temper than myself. But there is not a man in the world who cannot overcome his passion, if he will struggle earnestly to do so. If you find passion coming on you, go off to some place where you cannot be heard; let none of your family see you or hear you, while it is upon you, but struggle till it leaves you; and pray for strength to overcome. As I have said many times to the Elders, pray in your families; and if, when the time for prayer comes, you have not the spirit of prayer upon you, and your knees are unwilling to bow, say to them, "Knees, get down there"; make them bend, and remain there until you obtain the Spirit of the Lord. If the spirit yields to the body, it becomes corrupt; but if the body yields to the spirit it becomes pure and holy (Brigham Young, *Discourses of Brigham Young*, sel. John A. Widtsoe [1941], 267).

Anger can be controlled. Learn to manage it before it manages you. Who would not want to be married to someone who is in control of their emotions? On the other hand, who would want to marry someone who can't seem to control their emotions? Consider the following letter President Hinckley read to a group of Saints in England:

> Dear President Hinckley, my husband is a righteous priesthood holder. That is the highest compliment I can pay him. When he is around it is as though the Savior Himself is directing us. He is kind and gentle, always finding ways to help me and the children. He has always been the one who gets up with the children during the night. He has never raised his voice or hand to me and has been a big help during my various health problems. Although we have had our difference of opinion, we have never had an argument and I know it is because he is so careful in the way he communicates with me. He guides us through family Book of Mormon study and prayers and has now instigated a few minutes of gospel study together in the evening after the children are in bed. He is just the best man that could ever be. I feel it is an honor to be married in the temple to such a man. We are happy and in love and life is good (Gordon B. Hinckley, *Teachings of Gordon B. Hinckley* [1997], 329).

What a nice tribute from a wife to a husband. We can all have similar relationships. Why? Because how we respond to stimuli is our choice to make. We counsel you to look at each other's temperament in the dating and courting period and especially before you make the final decision to marry. If you see red flags in your fiancé's emotional makeup, please look more closely, or rethink your decision to continue the relationship. Most of us have a hard time changing our temperament. On the other hand, if you both have excellent control of your emotions, count your blessings. You are already on the path that leads to a great marriage.

Summary

Anger and abuse are destroyers of family relationships. They cause great misery, and they have no place among Latter-day Saints, either in our marriages or in our homes. They are typical components of broken marriages and tension-filled houses. They are not part of the plan. The gospel is designed to bring joy and peace and happiness to married couples and their children, not anger and contention. Think back. Have you ever seen a friendly divorce? They are few and far between! Instead we usually observe bitterness and rancor that spills its poisonous venom over both families, vitriolic attacks that bring cankerous sores and open wounds that often persist over a lifetime. Divorce is the antithesis of the love and harmony which are the principal fruits of the Spirit of the Lord.

Questions to Consider

Consider the following questions as they apply to your situation. If you are dating someone, discuss the applicable questions between the two of you. If you are not currently in a relationship, decide where you stand on an issue before you start dating someone and how you would like to improve.

1. Who in my family is known for temper outbursts? What do they usually do to display their anger? How do I feel about it when they behave that way?

2. How have I learned to control my anger in the past? Give an example of a time when you were angry and what you did about it.

3. How can I make sure that anger and the resulting loss of the Spirit is not one of the terrible sins I commit in my marriage?

CHAPTER 13

The Marriage Triad: You, Your Spouse, and the Savior

"Now, the most important principle I can share: Anchor your life in Jesus Christ, your Redeemer. Make your Eternal Father and His Beloved Son the most important priority in your life—more important than life itself, more important than a beloved companion or children or anyone on earth. Make their will your central desire. Then all that you need for happiness will come to you." [1]

A few years ago the Church aired a satellite broadcast hosted by Elder M. Russell Ballard of the Quorum of the Twelve. Elder Ballard interviewed prominent members of the Church regarding their testimonies of the gospel, personal experiences with the scriptures, and their feelings about the Savior. One of the experiences shared that evening came from the life of Wayne Osmond, one of the Osmond brothers.

Wayne explained that he had been recently diagnosed with a malignant brain tumor. Although the prognosis was grim, his faith and that of his wife and children in the Lord Jesus Christ was the turning point that pulled him through. Wayne further related to Elder Ballard that when he was on the gurney to be wheeled into surgery, he held his wife Kathy's hand and told her "I love you honey. Don't you worry; the Lord is with us." Wayne then shared this testimony: "If we didn't have that rock to hold on to, where would we be? We'd just be floundering. We'd have nothing."

Think of that statement. *"If we didn't have that rock to hold on to, where would we be?"* Here was a man who some might think had it all—fame, fortune, and a well-known family. Yet, when it came down to the bottom line, Wayne Osmond was saying that the most important thing in his life and in the life of his family was the Savior, Jesus Christ. And so it is with each of us. Just as He is with Wayne Osmond, the Savior should be the centerpiece of our lives.

Building on the Sure Foundation of Jesus Christ

In Matthew 7 we are told of two men, one wise and one foolish. The wise man built his house upon a solid foundation, a rock. When the rains fell and the floods came and the winds blew, his house (and his family) stood strong. On the contrary, when the storm came upon the foolish man's house, one built upon sand, he lost all he had. President Howard W. Hunter declared that the formula for success is quite simple. He said, "Please remember this one thing. If our lives . . . are centered upon Jesus Christ . . . nothing can ever go permanently wrong. On the other hand, if our lives are not centered on the Savior and His teachings, no other success can be permanently right" ("Following the Master: Teachings of Howard W. Hunter," *Ensign*, Apr. 1995, 21).

Helaman taught his sons this principle:

> And now, my sons, remember, remember that it is upon the rock of our Redeemer, who is Christ, the Son of God, that ye must build your foundation; that when the devil should send forth his mighty winds, yea, his shafts in the whirlwind, yea, when all his hail and his mighty storm shall beat upon you, it shall have no power over you to drag you down to the gulf of misery and endless wo, because of the rock upon which ye are built, which is a sure foundation, a foundation whereon if men build they cannot fall. (Helaman 5:12)

Jesus is the sure foundation upon which we should build our lives; we should center our lives on the Savior and His teachings, and He should be the focal point of all that we think, say, and do (see D&C 6:36).

Symbolically, the majestic Salt Lake City Temple stands squarely in the center of Salt Lake. In fact, the entire city was built around the temple. The streets are numbered according to where they stand in relationship to the temple; in fact, a person's address can tell them where their home stands in relation to the temple. Each time we drive past that temple, or any temple for that matter, we can be reminded that just as the Salt Lake Temple is the centerpiece of the city, so should the Savior be the center of our lives. C. S. Lewis once said "I believe in [Christ] as I believe that the Sun has risen, not only because I see it, but because by it I see everything else" ("Is Theology Poetry?" in *The Weight of Glory and Other Addresses* [1980], 92). To center our lives on the Savior is to see the world through His eyes, to walk in our communities and neighborhoods with His feet, to touch those around us with His hands, to say what He would say and do what He would do.

Another concept taught from the verse in Helaman reminds us that the devil is after us. It is not a matter of *if*, but *when*. Adversity will descend upon all of us. No one is going to be exempt. Each one of us, regardless of our social status, education, or pedigree is going to experience difficulty, disaster, illness, slander, pain, grief, and sorrow. All of these things are just part of life. However, those who have built their houses on the rock will never fail. They will take what life deals them, and move forward with faith. President Harold B. Lee confirmed this idea when he said:

> The prince of this world is coming to tempt every one of us, and the only ones who will stand through these evil days are those who have founded their houses upon the rock, as the Master said; when the storms descended and the winds blew and the rains came and beat upon the house, it fell not because it was founded upon the rock. That is what the Lord is trying to say to us today (Harold B. Lee, "The Way to Eternal Life," *Ensign*, Nov. 1971, 12).

As an engaged couple, the devil does not want you to marry in the temple; he does not want you to have a happy marriage. We have covered that point. Having Christ at the center of your lives will serve as an insulation and protection against things that are evil in nature. Joseph Smith taught that "the devil has no power over us only as we permit him" (Joseph Smith, *Teachings of the Prophet Joseph Smith*, comp. Joseph Fielding Smith, Jr. [1979], 181). Certainly Satan could have no power over us if our lives were built on the rock of our

Redeemer. Elder Joseph B. Wirthlin promised, "If you build your home on the foundation rock of our Redeemer and the gospel, it can be a sanctuary where your family can be sheltered from the raging storms of life" (*Finding Peace in Our Lives* [1995], 8). This promise is true—we have seen the fruits of it in our own families.

From *The Family: A Proclamation to the World* we learn that "happiness in family life is most likely to be achieved when founded upon the teachings of the Lord Jesus Christ" (September 1995). If your engagement and eventual marriage relationship is built on the promises of the Savior and His teachings, you will be happy and successful. In a general conference address, President Howard W. Hunter reminded us that, "whatever Jesus lays His hands upon lives. If Jesus lays His hands upon a marriage, it lives. If He is allowed to lay His hands on the family, it lives" ("Reading the Scriptures," *Ensign*, Nov. 1979, 65). That is, whatever Jesus touches will thrive, grow, develop, heal, and succeed. The same promise is true for you as a couple preparing for marriage. As you focus on the Savior and make Him the center of your life, your relationship as a couple will grow and thrive and move forward. To claim such blessings, you must have your priorities clear.

Now, what does it mean to have a marriage built on the foundation of Christ? That sounds a little vague, doesn't it? Such a marriage can be characterized by a couple who pray consistently as individuals and together, and who feast from the scriptures daily. Such a couple will serve in the Church and assist their fellowmen. They seek to put each other's needs before their own. President Kimball described what such a couple actually does:

> When a husband and wife go together frequently to the holy temple, kneel in prayer together in their home with their family, go hand in hand to their religious meetings, keep their lives wholly chaste, mentally and physically, . . . and both are working together for the upbuilding of the kingdom of God, then happiness is at its pinnacle (*Marriage and Divorce* [1976], 24).

We have worked with many couples over the years, and we are confident estimating that over 90 percent of couples we have visited with did *not* follow this simple counsel. They were *not* attending the temple; they were *not* attending their meetings, they were *not* living wholly chaste lives; they were *not* working together in building the kingdom by serving their families and those in the family of the Church. How could they be happy? Their marriage appeared to start off on the right foot. They married in the temple. They loved each other and they loved the Lord. Initially they were following President Kimball's counsel and living gospel principles in their relationship. But, for a variety of reasons, that pattern changed. Perhaps they became angry and withdrew from each other. Consequently, they quit praying together and reading the scriptures. They quit serving each other and those around them because they became so preoccupied with their own problems. In doing so, they shut off the flow of inspiration, revelation, the desire to live by the Spirit, and the desire to be kind and charitable. Subsequently, the lifeblood of their marriage was gone.

Such marriages need not be. Marriage is not the place to get careless in spiritual matters. That is why it is important to begin habits of righteousness now, during your courtship and engagement. That is why you should look closely at each other's testimony and commitment to the gospel plan. Although we suggest that you wait until you are married to pray together, individually you should be kneeling in prayer, living chaste lives, serving in the Church, and attending the temple where you can. Once married, you will have the opportunity to participate in these activities together, and they will help you find peace and strength in each other and your daily rituals.

Common Distractions

Centering your lives in Christ is not as simple as it sounds due to the many distractions. There are always different forces pulling at you and trying to keep you away from doing what is right. Sometimes your own choices can drive away the Spirit of the Lord. In *The Divine Center*, Stephen R. Covey speaks of these distractions, or, as he labels them, distortions. These distortions, ironically, are deceptive because they appear to be good things. It is not easy, at first, to see how they can distract us from righteousness.

He contends that some people are *work-* or *making-money-centered*. This suggests that such individuals gain their personal sense of worth from income and assets. Others are *possession-centered*, which implies that these people find meaning in life from the things they acquire. Still, others are *pleasure-centered*. They find fulfillment having fun and in not taking life too seriously. They seek personal gratification, and they will most often do whatever it takes to obtain it. Some individuals are *friend-centered*, which describes those who derive purpose and meaning in their lives from their social relationships. Another "center," *self-centeredness*, is the foundation for each of the previous "centers" mentioned, and might be thought of as the plaguing sin of our culture. Elder Richard G. Scott warned that "selfishness is at the root of all sin. It leads to unrighteous acts that bring anguish and misery" ("We Love You—Please Come Back," *Ensign,* May 1986, 10). Although each of these "centers" can provide temporary satisfaction, they cannot contribute to lasting peace and joy. Thankfully, most people can see past these distractions and seek a higher plane. They know what is important in life, and their priorities reflect that understanding. Yet sometimes these people also get caught up in a life that is *spouse-centered* or *church-centered*. Let's look at *spouse-* and *church*-centeredness a little closer.

The Spouse-Centered Life

Despite the fact that the husband-wife dyad is one of the central relationships in the kingdom of God, and the foundation unit in the celestial kingdom, there can be an overdependence on each other, as strange as that may sound.

> When a person's sense of emotional worth comes primarily from the marriage relationship, then he or she becomes highly dependent upon that relationship. That makes him or her extremely vulnerable to the moods and feelings, the behavior and treatment, of the partner, or to any external event which may impinge the relationship—a new child, in-laws, economic setbacks, social successes, and so forth (Stephen R. Covey, *The Divine Center* [1982], 23).

Please do not misunderstand. We are not saying that you can love your future spouse too much. You should love your spouse deeply and do everything in your power to nurture the marriage relationship so that your love will continue to grow. We are told very clearly in Doctrine and Covenants 42:22 that "Thou shalt love thy wife with all thy heart, and shalt cleave unto her and none else." Cleaving suggests loyalty and faithfulness. Even children do not come before the spouse. There is to be deep and committed love between married companions. But we are saying that your life should not center on them, but on your relationship—individually and collectively—with the Lord.

Remember, your future spouse was Heavenly Father's child before they were yours. It would be wrong of anyone to think they can keep their spouse only to themselves. Your future spouse is a child of Heavenly Father and has a mission to perform on this earth. No marriage partner should stand in the way of that; instead, they should help their spouse fulfill their mission as best they can. Occasionally, however, we see men who are possessive of their wife and feel that their wife's earthly mission is to serve them and be there for them. We are aware of one man who expects a four-course meal to be served for dinner every night when he comes home from work. (Not just after he gets home from work, but it needs to be on the table when he walks in the door.) If his wife chooses not to do this, or if she gets busy and occupied, she pays for her "mistake." He gets grumpy when he isn't fed. We know of another man who has a very social wife and she has many friends in the ward. However, he doesn't think that he should have to share his wife with the Church. One day someone asked him who his friends were in the ward and neighborhood. He said that he did not have any. It was suggested that maybe he should get a few friends. He needs to find someone else to discuss sports, someone with whom he could share his dreams about the "perfect sprinkler system," someone who could understand why he was depressed when his favorite mechanic moved to Laramie.

It is equally important for women to have friends outside the marriage as well. They need an outlet from rearing children all day long. They need to talk to other women who can understand what they are experiencing and who can feel what they feel. Understanding these "spatial" requirements should start while courting and during the engagement period.

Another caution about spouse-centered couples. We know a couple who have been married for some time, and still, like newlyweds, their entire world revolves around each other. When they are together, they are not even remotely aware of the world, or their surroundings for that matter. We could be invaded by China and they would be the last ones to know. Aside from continually talking baby talk to each other, the wife often takes time in fast and testimony meeting to share with the congregation how her husband is the greatest man in the world. She can be found at Church softball games cheering wildly as he rounds the bases. She holds up a sign she made at ward homemaking night that says something like "Way to Go _____; You Are the Greatest Ball Player in the Church!" Although many people would admire this relationship, especially some men, there are some red flags here that concern us.

What Stephen Covey says is true. When a partner's sense of meaning and worth is derived solely from the spouse, they become very dependent on that person. It certainly places them in a vulnerable position should the spouse die. What then, is left for either spouse. Both of them have put their entire strength and devotion for the last twenty years into a relationship that will end in this life.

One man explained that if his wife ever bore her testimony in Church and testified that he was the greatest man that she knew, he would take immediate medical precautions. After she got off the stand, he would towel her off, check her pulse and temperature, and then have her lie across the pew until the end of the meeting. When she recovered, he would then explain to her that if she thinks he is that great, she must not be getting out enough, and he would introduce her to a few people. He couldn't entertain the thought of being the greatest man she knew even for a minute. He knew he wasn't, and recognized he had a long way to go. He further explained that he and his wife are perfectly aware of each other's weaknesses and strengths, that yes—they love each other very much, but they both know they are still "under construction."

Doctrine and Covenants 42:22 says that we should love our *spouse* with all of our heart. However, there is one higher law that applies, and that is in Matthew 22:37, which teaches us that we should love *God* with all of our heart, soul, and mind. When we put God at the center of our lives and love Him more than we love any other mortal, we actually increase our capacity to love others. That is, you can love your spouse more deeply and profoundly if you will first love God. The reason is because God is the personification of love (1 John 4:8), and when we love Him first He blesses us in return. We receive an endowment and gift of charity. Charity is godlike love. When we love God first, He gives us a gift in return. He places within us a power to love our spouse and children, and neighbors the way He loves us. Without that gift, we are left on our own. We are weak, and those around us are also weak. We need God's help to become better spouses and parents.

The Church-Centered Life

As Covey says,

> [The] Church is a means to an end, not an end in itself. The Church is the instrument. It is the vehicle, the conveyer. . . . But by itself, the Church cannot be a person's effective center, because it is itself dependent. . . . It is of critical importance that we see the Church as a means to an end and not as an end in itself. Most members of the Church know in their hearts that there is a very clear and distinct difference between being active in the Church and being active in the gospel. . . . There are Church-centered people who escape from the more rigorous responsibilities in the marriage and the family by saying, "I'm going to do the work of the Church" (or "the work of the kingdom," or "the work of the Lord"). Attending meetings, interviewing others regarding their worthiness, or conducting worthwhile programs for others may be much easier than confronting and solving a difficult emotional situation at home with the spouse or the teenage son or daughter. Sometimes such a member, of whatever leadership position, will fully rationalize family neglect in the name of the Church (Stephen R. Covey, *The Divine Center* [1982], 52-53).

The warning is clear. Don't get so caught up in building the kingdom that you neglect the most important people of all—your spouse and children. It is a major problem that we see all around us. When a spouse does not have their needs met at home, they often keep busy serving in the Church. We are aware of men and women who do not want to come home to their spouses because the spouse is either critical, negative, unhappy, or extremely messy. Instead, they stay away from home and spend more time in their Church callings or their vocations. We know of a particular man who was having some struggles with his teenagers. Instead of going home after work and helping his wife with them, he decided to devote more time to his calling in the bishopric. Apparently he felt that if he spent his time helping the ward, the Lord would take care of his family. Frankly, he was probably getting more strokes from the ward members than from his own children. Consequently, he spent his time where he was more appreciated and where his needs could be met. Meanwhile, the condition of his family grew worse. Regarding this tendency, President Lee declared:

> Sometimes as I go throughout the Church, I think I am seeing a man who is using his church work as a kind of escape from family responsibility. And sometimes when we've talked about whether or not he's giving attention to his family, his children and his wife, he says something like this: "Well, I'm so busy taking care of the Lord's work that I really don't have time." And I say to him, "My dear brother, the greatest of the Lord's work that you and I will ever do is the work that we do within the walls of our own home." Now don't you get any misconception about where the Lord's work starts. That's the most important of all the Lord's work. And you wives may have to remind your husbands of that occasionally (Harold B. Lee, Address to Seminary and Institute Teachings at Brigham Young University Summer School, "Objectives of Church Education," BYU, 8 July 1966).

Family-relations scholar Glen Latham shared the following experience:

> Some years ago a prominent Church leader in the area where I lived came to me, simply beside himself over the behavior of two of his children—and he had reason to be concerned.

We grieved together deep into the night and into the early hours of the morning, and though many things were discussed and many feelings shared, nothing made a more lasting impression on me than did this good brother's reflection on his first and fundamental responsibility as a father. "Brother Latham," he said, "almost from the time I was married I have either been a counselor in a bishopric or a bishop, a counselor in a stake presidency or a stake president. I have spent the better part of my parenting years away from my family in Church service, all the while thinking that if I took care of the Saints, the Lord would take care of my family. But I was wrong. It wasn't until it was too late that I realized that my family was my first responsibility all along." Then he wept.

As I work with members of the Church far and wide, I am forever amazed at how often parents put other things before parenting, sometimes even Church service—and sometimes even to the point of hiding behind Church callings as a shield from parenting responsibilities! Not infrequently young mothers will take me aside, tears bathing their faces, with the sad lament of that of a mother I recently encountered: "My husband is a good man, but he's never home. He's thirty-four years old and the bishop. . . . He's a wonderful bishop, and the members of the ward love him. I can see why he would give more of his time and attention to his Church calling. Being adored by ward members has got to be more pleasant than dealing with dirty diapers, crying babies, and fighting kids. But they need him more as a father than the ward needs him as a bishop."

What parents in Zion must understand is that the only unit of society that will outlast mortality is the family. Not even the Church in its exact present form will outlast mortality! Though we certainly should be active in Church service, we must be active in the family, which is the most noble Church service of all. In its finest sense, that means teaching our children what is expected of them (Glenn I. Latham, "As Christ Would Parent," in D.E. Brinley & D.K. Judd (eds.) *Eternal Families* [1996], 20–21).

There are too many fathers in this church who come home from work, throw some food down their stomachs, and then run off to a Church meeting, leaving a wife with a screaming, sick child to minister to. How many times must women think to themselves, "If only you would just stay home and help me tonight." Husbands may use the excuse that they must magnify their callings or provide more money for the family's use. There must be a delicate balance. Yes, the kingdom is being constructed, but the kingdom is being built for the purpose of strengthening families. Both can be done if we have the proper perspective. Humorist Chris Crowe explained it this way:

> Once you've got a child or two, additional Church responsibilities start coming your way. A little home teaching at first, then you're thrown to the Boy Scouts or the Young Men program and the discretionary hours fly away like a pack of ravenous deacons to a buffet table. The elders quorum waits to nab you as soon as you're turned loose by the youth programs, and after that, well, stake missions, Sunday School, Primary, Cub Scouts, the activities committee, bishoprics, and, for the unlucky few, the big B-job: Bishop. You don't mind these callings, because you recognize and appreciate the blessings such service brings, but they're an added and distracting burden to your other duties.

> Committed as you are to your church duties, you smack head-on into the first of the married Mormon . . . conflicts. Do you spend a jillion hours a week with the teachers quorum and Varsity Scouts, or do you stay home evenings to read with your kids and play a little basketball with them after dinner? Do you go on camp outs every month and leave your wife alone with the kids, again and again? Do you spend your one and only precious week of summer vacation chaperoning girls' camp instead of taking your family on a trip to visit grandparents? And if you do choose to spend time with your kids instead of your church calling, how do you handle the inevitable guilt that follows? When you miss your weeknight church meetings to watch your daughters play soccer, are you a worthless slouch in the eyes of the bishop? Of the Lord?

> Of course you know the key is balance, that it's not one without the other but both together. Planning helps. So does a good attitude. And often you strike that happy balance and life seems good (*Fatherhood, Football, and Turning Forty* [1995], 3–4).

The Christ-Centered Marriage

We now come back to the main point. A life centered on God is the only sure center available to man. If we were to lose everything mortal, transitory, and temporal, we would still have our relationship with Deity. Despite the trials you will encounter in life, you can be sure that God is always available to you. The Savior will not ignore you or leave you alone. These two members of the Godhead have always been there, and they always will be. And no matter how difficult life may get, we have the assurance from a Father and a Brother that we can count on Them. Brother Covey gave this perspective:

> When a person has this map or frame of reference, the Lord and His work becomes the driving force of that person's life. It becomes the unifying and organizational principle, the center around which everything revolves. . . . In keeping with Christ's example, if the God/Christ-centered person is offended, he blesses in return. He returns kindness for unkindness, patience for impatience. If he is afflicted, he chooses a response which enables him to grow and learn from the affliction, to suffer with meaning and nobility, a response which will have a greater influence on others than perhaps any other value. . . . If the person is praised, he gives thanks. If he is blamed, he appraises the matter to see whether there may be some blameworthiness in him, and if there is he plans self-improvement. But he does not overreact and either accuse or blame in return, or condemn himself. . . . [Instead] he seeks to identify with Christ. Christ is his model. For instance, he studies scriptural accounts of the Savior's earthly life, and as he does so he visualizes each of the situations recorded. He empathizes with the people involved, sees himself as part of the action, feels himself in the more positive, disciple-type roles. He creates in his mind his response to present-day situations based on living by the principles represented by the scriptural accounts. . . . Gradually, as he comes to see the Savior as the perfect model and mentor, he identifies with that mental image and vision. In this way he acquires "the mind of Christ" and thus gradually learns to respond to life situations as He would have responded (which is as His Father would have responded) (*The Divine Center* [1982], 145, 148 149).

Seeing the world through the Savior's eyes, walking where He would walk, saying what He would say, and touching those He would touch—that is what one does who lives a life centered on the Savior. Paul exhorted the Corinthian Saints to possess the "mind of Christ" (1 Cor. 2:16). Elder Bruce R. McConkie explained that having the mind of Christ is, "to believe what He believes, think what He thinks, say what He says, and do what He does. It is to be one with Him by the power of the Holy Ghost" (*A New Witness for the Articles of Faith* [1985], 71). Our thoughts govern our behaviors; by changing our thoughts, we can have the power to change our behaviors. If our thoughts are centered on the Savior, we obtain the power to behave like Him.

A few years ago after an Education Week presentation, Dr. Brent Barlow related that a young man and his wife approached him and asked if they could talk. The man was a member of the Church in his early thirties who was a successful executive. He often worked sixty to seventy hours per week, while ignoring his wife and new baby. His job also required him to travel a great deal during the week, and on weekends. So, besides not spending time with his family, he was missing church as well.

> At first he tried to attend church at wards in the cities where he had to conduct business, but after a time he stopped making the effort. He became involved with a woman colleague at his office, spending a great deal of time with her. At first the relationship was supposedly businesslike and professional, but then they became emotionally attached to each other. A sexual encounter loomed as a likely possibility. Then, about the time he was promoted to the high-salaried position he was aspiring to, his wife filed for divorce.
>
> The young executive said he made several attempts at reconciliation. He reluctantly agreed to see their bishop, who suggested that they needed professional counseling. That avenue was pursued but to no avail—the damage had apparently been done. They finally entered the waiting period before their divorce would be final.
>
> The husband became a little tearful as he continued his story. He realized that he would lose his young wife by divorce and that subsequently his relationship with his little daughter

would be limited. The divorce and final separation seemed inevitable.

So he made a decision. As a priesthood holder and returned missionary, he still wanted to retain his membership in the Church and reestablish his relationship with the Savior. In essence, he decided not so much to "come unto Christ" as to "return to Christ." During the few weeks before the finalization of the divorce, he began praying alone and fasting periodically. He stopped seeing and traveling with the woman at his office. He attended his priesthood and other Church meetings regularly for the first time in several months. He started to study the gospel and get more involved in Church service. He examined his heart and tried to bring spirituality into his life. He did all these things fully expecting that his wife and child would soon leave him. But unknown to him, his wife was observing him. (As he was telling me about this episode in their lives, she was holding on to his arm, also in tears.)

The wife then continued the story. She said she noted some sincere and genuine changes in him as he tried drawing closer to the Lord. When the time came for her to sign the final divorce papers, she called her attorney and said that she was going to delay the action another thirty days.

The husband made major adjustments with his employment, even taking a cut in pay. He had realized the significance of the statement, "For what is a man profited, if he shall gain the whole world, and lose his own soul [and his wife and daughter]? or what shall a man give in exchange for his soul?" (Matt. 16:26). By the time the thirty days was up, the wife had decided not to sign the divorce papers.

Although their marriage nearly ended in divorce, the couple experienced something more important than their troubles as they begin to center their lives on the Savior, His teachings, and His Church (Brent A. Barlow, *Dealing With Differences in Marriage* [1993], 121–123).

There is a tremendous healing power available to us through the gospel. The Savior can inspire us in our marriage and family relationships. When He is at the center of your marriage, you succeed. If gospel principles are lived and practiced in your home, peace and happiness and harmony will abound.

Developing Christlike Character Traits

When couples fail to center their relationship on the Savior, they have no promise or guarantee of success. In fact, as mere mortals, they are unable to correct their course. Without the Savior, the power to be kind and compassionate is often lost. Human kindness and charity wane when spiritual resources are ignored or forgotten. Once couples lose the Spirit of the Lord their relationship deteriorates rapidly, for the natural man takes over. When they are sarcastic, angry, critical, defensive, or uncaring, the partnership is on the brink. In contrast, when both partners possess an eternal perspective of marriage it is much easier to be kind and considerate. The nearer we are to God, the more likely we will be to have His attributes.

As we come to appreciate the Savior's life and mission, we obtain the mind of Christ. When we begin to think as He thinks and behave as He behaves, it is amazing what we can accomplish and overcome in our marriage relationships. When we have Christlike character traits, the Holy Ghost will be with us. He will inspire us and teach us how to act and what to say.

Summary

The time to put Christ at the center of your life is now. Do not wait until you are married—begin right now. A Christ-centered approach can drive the dating decisions you will make. The Savior's love will nurture and anchor your personality and character so that you have no need to play dating games. "[You] wouldn't want in any way to not live true to the standards [you] have been taught. [You] would have moral courage to stand up for those standards and be true. Why? Because [your] security does not come from the wrong center. It comes from a divine center" (Stephen R. Covey, "Becoming Christ Centered," *Brigham Young University 1997–1998 Devotional and Fireside Speeches* [1998], 121).

Your appreciation and gratitude for the Savior will strengthen your decision to marry. You will want to be with someone who will help you become the kind of person you want to be, and you, in turn, will be more willing to assist your good friend to be prepared to be your marriage partner. Family scholar Wallace Goddard suggested that we each ask this query: "Does being with the person help you be the person you want to be? Does the person help you be peaceful, joyous, kind, and committed?" (*The Frightful and Joyous Journey of Family Life* [1997], 38). If the person you are courting helps you develop the Christlike attributes you are in need of, then you are in good company.

President David O. McKay declared "I regard it as an incontrovertible fact that in no marriage circle can true peace, love, purity, chastity, and happiness be found, in which is not present the Spirit of Christ, and the daily, hourly striving after loving obedience to His divine commands, and especially the nightly prayer expressing gratitude for blessings received" (*Gospel Ideals* 1976, 473).

Our Very Best to You

We congratulate you on desiring to follow the right path that will lead you to the greatest privilege of your mortal lives—to marry in the temple of our God. Hopefully the habits and practices that you have been working on over the past few years and months have set you in the direction of an eternal relationship. We wish you the very best as you seek to obtain the keys to the highest degree of glory in the celestial kingdom (see D&C 131:1–4).

Questions to Consider

Consider the following questions as they apply to your situation. If you are dating someone, discuss the applicable questions between the two of you. If you are not currently in a relationship, decide where you stand on an issue before you start dating someone and how you would like to improve.

1. What common problems might we face if we fall into a Church- or spouse-centered life?

2. What are advantages of living a Christ-centered life both individually and as a couple?

3. How will a Christ-centered focus affect our dating and engagement times? What choices will we make?

4. Once we are married, what can we do as a couple that would indicate that Christ is the center of our relationship?

ENDNOTES

INTRODUCTION

1. President David O. McKay, in Conference Report, Apr. 1964, 5.

2. Not everyone marries in mortality, of course. For a treatment of how the plan of salvation affects those who never marry in mortality, those who divorce and remain single despite being temple worthy, or those married to an unworthy spouse who cannot qualify for exaltation, see Douglas E. Brinley, *Strengthening Your Marriage and Family* [1994], 77-96.

3. Of all the times in the history of the world to marry, this is surely the best. We live longer, have more to eat and wear, have nicer houses to live in, and the opportunities before us are unprecedented in the history of the world.

4. Cohabitation has proven unsuccessful as a way to avoid divorce. The average duration of cohabitation in the United States is 1.3 years, and 60 percent of these relationships dissolve within the first 2 years (J. DaVanzo and M.O. Rahman, "American Families: trends and correlates," *Population Index* 59, no. 3 (1993): 350-386). By far, more cohabitant relationships—designed to prepare against divorce—break apart than do typical marriages wherein couples didn't "get to know each other" first. *

   *Virtually all research on the topic has determined that the chances of divorce ending a marriage preceded by cohabitation are significantly greater than for a marriage not preceded by cohabitation. A 1992 study of 3,300 cases, for example, based on the 1987 National Survey of Families and Households, found that in their marriages prior cohabitors "are estimated to have a hazard of dissolution that is 46% higher than for noncohabitors." The authors of this study concluded, after reviewing all previous studies, that the enhanced risk of marital disruption following cohabitation "is beginning to take on the status of an empirical generalization" (Popenoe, David and Barbara Dafoe Whitehead. "Should We Live Together? What Young Adults Need to Know About Cohabitation Before Marriage: A Comprehensive Review of Recent Research," Piscataway, NJ: National Marriage Project, Rutgers University [1999]).

5. We assume that some divorced individuals will read this volume in preparation for another marriage. We think the same principles of success that apply to first marriages apply to second marriages, though the "innocence factor" for such individuals may be greatly lessened.

CHAPTER 1

1. David B. Haight, *A Light Unto the World* [1997], 131–132.

2. William J. Bennett, Speech delivered to the *Heritage Foundation*, Washington, D.C., 7 September 1993.

3. L.L. Bumpass, "What is happening to the Family? Interactions Between Demographic and Institutional Change," *Demography*, 27 no. 4 (1990): 483-498.

4. U.S. Bureau of the Census. *Marriage, divorce, and remarriage in the 1990's*, Current Population Reports, P23–180. Washington, D.C. U.S. Government Printing Office 1992.

5. Popenoe, "American Family Decline," *Journal of Marriage and the Family* 55 (August 1993), 527–544.

CHAPTER 2

1. Spencer W. Kimball, *The Teachings of Spencer W. Kimball*, ed. Edward L. Kimball [1982], 25.

2. Stephen R. Covey, *The Seven Habits of Highly Effective People* [1990], 97.

CHAPTER 3

1. Lowell Bennion, as quoted in *Achieving a Celestial Marriage* [Church Educational System manual, 1992], 32.

2. Actually, Hugh B. Brown suggested that marriage preparation begins much earlier than age eight. It was his feeling that it begins before we are born, with our parents and our grandparents. So much of what we believe and who we are comes from them. (See Hugh B. Brown, *You and Your Marriage* [1960], 49.)

3. *Strong's Exhaustive Concordance of the Bible* [1989], "Greek Dictionary of the New Testament," 81.

4. Rice, *Intimate Relationships, Marriages, & Families* [1999], 208.

5. M. Tzeng, "The effects of social economic heterogamy and changes on marital disillusion for first marriages," *Journal of Marriage and the Family* 54 (1992): 609-619.

6. See R.A. Bell, J.A. Daly, & M.C. Gonzalez, "Affinity-Maintenance in Marriage and Its Relationship to Women's Marital Satisfaction," *Journal of Marriage and the Family* 49 (1987), 445–454; J. Lauer & R. Lauer, "Marriages Made to

Last," *Psychology Today* 19 (1985), 22–26; D. Curran, *Traits of a Healthy Family* [1983]; N. Stinnett & J. DeFrain, *Secrets of Strong Families* [1985]; W.G. Dyer & P.R. Kunz, *10 Critical Keys for Highly Effective Mormon Families* [1994].

7. L.L. Bumpass & J.A. Sweet, "Cohabitation, marriage, and union stability: Preliminary findings from NSFH2," *NSFH Working Paper No. 65.* [1995].

8. Only one's spouse and parents ranked higher than friendship. (See M. Argyle & A. Furnham, "Sources of satisfaction and conflict in long-term relationships," *Journal of Marriage and the Family* 45 [1983], 481–493.)

CHAPTER 4

1. Spencer W. Kimball, *The Teachings of Spencer W. Kimball*, ed. Edward L. Kimball [1982], 301.

2 F. Philip Rice, *Intimate Relationships, Marriages, and Families*, 3rd ed. [1999], 123.

3. Ibid., 198-200.

4. The amount of pornography and its negative effects on marriages are becoming a scourge among even our own people. Church leaders are often confronted with numerous cases within their ecclesiastical units.

CHAPTER 5

1. O. Leslie Stone, "Making Your Marriage Successful," *Ensign,* May 1978, 56.

2. This is the primary reason you will need your bishop's signature and that of your stake president. The stake president presides over the Melchizedek Priesthood in your stake and holds the keys of that priesthood in your stake.

3. We emphasize here that this order does not supersede the authority of the First Presidency of the Church or the Quorum of Twelve Apostles (D&C 107:22–23). Fundamentalist groups are prone to misunderstand the authority associated with this order of the priesthood.

4. A woman does not "receive" the priesthood as men do in the other "orders" of the priesthood by the laying on of hands. A man and woman enter the patriarchal order together as husband and wife when they are sealed in a temple marriage ceremony.

5. We don't live the full patriarchal order at the present time. After marriage, your "kingdom" is small. But in time, your posterity will grow geometrically and your kingdom will be such that the offices of king and queen, priest and priestess, will become more meaningful.

6. "By the Holy Spirit of Promise, every [faithful] member of the Church may receive divine assurance, while mortal, that exaltation is assured" (see Joseph

Fielding Smith, *Doctrines of Salvation,* 2:94–95). It is important to note that if one spouse has broken his or her covenants, the following statement is pertinent: "If a man or woman who has been sealed in the temple for time and eternity should sin and lose the right to receive the exaltation in the celestial kingdom, he or she could not retard the progress of the injured companion who had been faithful. Everyone will be judged according to his works, and there would be no justice in condemning the innocent for the sins of the guilty" (Bruce R. McConkie, comp., *Doctrines of Salvation,* 2: 177).

7. Children who are not born in the covenant but who are later sealed to their parents are promised that they, too, as children, will inherit all of the blessings of the gospel as if their birth had been in the covenant in the first place.

8. As we learned in previous dispensations, being the "chosen seed" does not in any way guarantee spiritual safety or exaltation. Only faithful observance of gospel principles and obedience to covenants ensures eternal life. This is not meant to be an elitist doctrine.

9. Certain apostate groups have misunderstood the patriarchal order and have supposed it to be a higher authority than that of the President of the Church, or the First Presidency. There is no higher authority in the kingdom of God than the Lord's prophet and his counselors who preside as "three Presiding High Priests" over the Church and kingdom (D&C 107:22; see also D&C 124:45–46). The patriarchal order is an order of the Melchizedek Priesthood.

CHAPTER 6

1. Glenn L. Pace, *Why?* [address delivered at Ricks College devotional, 24 Sept.1991], 8.

2. In this situation, both individuals need to talk to their bishop and begin the repentance process. If they decide to proceed with their marriage, it would be a civil marriage performed by the bishop or another authority. A year later, after completing their repentance, they could be sealed as husband and wife in a temple ceremony.

3. "How Should We Teach Our Children About Sex?" *Time,* 24 May 1993, 61.

4. Brent A. Barlow, *Worth Waiting For* [1995], 14.

5. Brent A. Barlow, *Worth Waiting For* [1995], 14.

6. Elder Maxwell taught that "if we entertain temptations, soon they begin entertaining us!" (*Ensign,* "Overcome . . . Even As I Also Overcame," May 1987, 71).

7. "I do not know what I shall do next year; I always speak for the present. . . . You never heard me say that I was going to be true to my God; for I know too much of human weakness: but I pray God to preserve me from falling away—to preserve me in the truth. I depend not upon myself; for I know too much of . . . myself, to indulge in such remarks" (Brigham Young, *Journal of Discourses* 5:212-213).

8.   "The syphilis rate for teens age 15–19 has jumped 67% since 1985 "("The Dangers of Doing It," *Newsweek* Special Issue, June 1990, 57).

9.   For true stories of children raised by a single-parent, read David Popenoe's *Life Without Father*, or David Blankenhorn's *Fatherless America*.

     *Even if children are not completely abandoned by their father at birth, "one of the greatest problems for children living with a cohabiting couple is the high risk that the couple will break up. Fully three quarters of children born to cohabiting parents will see their parents split up before they reach age sixteen, whereas only about a third of children born to married parents face a similar fate. One reason is that marriage rates for cohabiting couples have been plummeting. In the last decade, the proportion of cohabiting mothers who go on to eventually marry the child's father declined from 57% to 44%. . . . One study found that children currently living with a mother and her unmarried partner had significantly more behavior problems and lower academic performance than children from intact families. . . . We do have abuse-prevalence studies that look at stepparent families (both married and unmarried) and mother's boyfriends (both cohabiting and dating). Both show far higher levels of child abuse than is found in intact families." (Popenoe, David and Barbara Dafoe Whitehead. "Should We Live Together? What Young Adults Need to Know About Cohabitation Before Marriage: A Comprehensive Review of Recent Research," Piscataway, NJ: National Marriage Project, Rutgers University (1999)).

10. "About 3% to 6% of Americans have sexual addiction" (Carnes, P.J. *Don't Call it Love: Recovery from Sexual Addiction* [1991], 42–44).

11. "Those who engage in premarital sex have a much stronger likelihood of being involved in extramarital affairs later. Immorality is indicative of a weakness, and in times of stress during marriage, those who have that weakness might find it easier to revert to old habits. Staying morally clean before marriage is good insurance against marital infidelity afterward" (Susan Pace, "How to Teach Youths the Reason for Chastity," *Church News*, 21 July 1990, 15).

CHAPTER 7

1.   Quote from Douglas E. Brinley.

CHAPTER 8

1.   J. Golden Kimball, in Claude Richards, *J. Golden Kimball: The Story of a Unique Personality* [1966], 99–100.

2.   James Dobson, *Love for a Lifetime* [1987], 59, 65.

3.   *Utah's Vital Statistics*, Technical Report No. 146, February 1992, and 1988

Annual Report, Bureau of Vital Records and Health Statistics, Utah Department of Health, Salt Lake City, Utah; as cited in B.A. Barlow, *Just for Newlyweds* [1992], 7.*

   *We use data from Utah because 75 percent, or one person in every 1.3 of the population are members of the Church (see *1997–1998 Church Almanac* [1998], 258).

4.   As cited in T.B. Holman, J.H. Larson, & R.F. Stahmann, "Preparing for an Eternal Marriage," in *Strengthening Our Families: An In-Depth Look at the Proclamation on the Family,* ed. D.C. Dollahite [2000], 39.

CHAPTER 9

1.   President Spencer W. Kimball as quoted by L. Tom Perry, "If Ye Are Prepared Ye Shall Not Fear," *Ensign,* Nov. 1995, 35.

2.   B. O'Neill, 1994, Financial counseling and planning research priorities 1995-2000: A practitioner's viewpoint. In R. Lytton (Ed.), *The Association for Financial Counseling and Planning Educational Proceedings,* (57–68). Blacksburg, Va.: Virginia Polytech Institute and State University.

3.   In a study conducted by Bae, Hanna, and Lindamood, it was reported that "40% of American households spent more than their take-home incomes and 25% of the sample spent at least 127% of their take-home income."(C. Jayathirtha & J.J. Fox, 1996, "Home ownership and the decision to over-spend" *Financial Counseling and Planning,* 97).

CHAPTER 10

1.   N. Eldon Tanner, "Constancy Amid Change," *Ensign,* Nov. 1979, 119–120.

2.   Faithful Latter-day Saints pay a tenth of their income to the Church. Others not of our faith typically contribute one percent of their gross income to church and charitable agencies combined.

CHAPTER 11

1.   Hugh B. Brown, *You and Your Marriage* [1979], 73–74.

2.   If you righteously decide that you will postpone children for a brief period of time, you will not want to use barrier forms of birth control such as condoms or diaphragms. They are unreliable and are somewhat difficult for newlyweds to negotiate.

3. Stephen E. Lamb and Douglas E. Brinley, *Between Husband & Wife: Gospel Perspectives on Marital Intimacy* [2000].

CHAPTER 12

1. President Gordon B. Hinckley, *Teachings of Gordon B. Hinckley* [1997], 329.

2. Some of these suggestions are from Victor Cline's *How to Make A Good Marriage Great* [1987], 81–83.

CHAPTER 13

1. Richard G. Scott, "The Power of Correct Principles," *Ensign*, May 1993, 34.

An excerpt from Douglas E. Brinley and Stephen E. Lamb's . . .

Between
HUSBAND
&
WIFE

Generally speaking, the quality of marital intimacy is related to the quality of the marriage relationship. Couples who struggle in their marriages tend to avoid physical contact, while happily married people find physical intimacy to be a natural expression of their feelings. Strengthening the love that exists between a couple will normally increase their desire for a healthy sexual relationship. Happily married couples find that physical touches—kisses, hugs, embraces, massages, sexual relations—provide enjoyment and therapy in the marriage.

The most effective way Latter-day Saints can improve their marriages, and thus their sexual intimacy in marriage, is to understand the true purpose and nature of marriage as outlined in Church doctrine. President Boyd K. Packer taught that "a knowledge of the principles and doctrines of the gospel will affect your behavior more than talking about behavior" (*Ensign*, May 1997:9). This chapter will briefly review the place and importance of marriage in the Plan of Salvation. When we understand these doctrines and principles, we will better understand the need to do our best as marriage partners. An important part of this effort includes the way we interact as husbands and wives in our physical relationship.

In 1995, President Gordon B. Hinckley introduced a proclamation concerning marriage and the family (*Ensign*, November 1995:105). In essence, this pronouncement outlined the principle that "marriage is ordained of God unto man," (D&C 49:15). This proclamation on the family reaffirmed the Church's position that marriage and family are important theological imperatives. Latter-day Saints are taught that marriage is the most important of all priesthood ordinances. Through temple marriage, a couple may be joined together not just for this life, but as partners for eternity.

Gospel doctrine reveals that in the premortal realm we were sons and daughters of God, brothers and sisters to each other. But for us to become husbands and fathers, wives and mothers, it was necessary for us to come to earth to obtain physical bodies. President Spencer W. Kimball explained: "It is the normal thing to marry. It was arranged by God in the beginning. . . . Every person should want to be married. There are some who might not be able to. But every person should want to be married because that is what God in heaven planned for us," (Kimball, *Teachings*, 291).

THE DOCTRINE OF MARRIAGE

Heavenly Father did not intend the husband-wife relationship to last only for this life. Adam and Eve were married by God before the Fall, and their actions in the garden did not negate their holy marriage. Although death does separate husband and wife briefly, it does not divorce them. After Adam and Eve died, they were reunited as companions in the spirit world. Elder Bruce R. McConkie explained:

> We have the power to perform a marriage, and we can do it so that the man and the woman become husband and wife here and now and—if they keep the covenant there and then made—they will remain husband and wife in the spirit world and will come up in glory and dominion with kingdoms and exaltation in the resurrection, being husband and wife and having eternal life. ("Celestial Marriage," 172.)

The resurrection restores our physical and spirit bodies to an immortal union, thus making it possible to continue as husband and wife eternally, for as resurrected beings, we cannot die again (Alma 11:45). If we have complied with the laws of God and faithfully observed our covenants during this life, we can be eligible for exaltation. Our temple sealing allows us and our posterity—adults sealed to their own spouses—to be part of an everlasting kingdom. If we live worthily, we will one day dwell together forever in the highest degree of the celestial glory (D&C 131:1–4).

Elder Robert D. Hales reminded us:

An eternal bond doesn't just happen as a result of sealing covenants we make in the temple. How we conduct ourselves in this life will determine what we will be in all the eternities to come. To receive the blessings of the sealing that our Heavenly Father has given to us, *we have to keep the commandments and conduct ourselves in such a way that our families will want to live with us in the eternities.* The family relationships we have here on this earth are important, but they are much more important for their effect on our families for generations in mortality and throughout all eternity. (*Ensign,* November 1996:65, emphasis added.)

We will only be companions in the next life if we like each other here! Therefore, we must cultivate love and respect for each other while in this life, so that we want to be together forever.

THE HEAVENLY PATTERN

As mortals, we pattern our lives after a heavenly model. "Our theology begins with heavenly parents," said Elder Dallin H. Oaks, "and our highest aspiration is to be like them," (*Ensign,* May 1995:87). We are their offspring, and our gender began at the time of our spirit birth. The proclamation on the family states that each of us is "a beloved spirit son or daughter of heavenly parents," and "gender is an essential characteristic of individual premortal, mortal, and eternal identity and purpose." President Gordon B. Hinckley said, "I know of no doctrine which states that we made a choice when we came to earth as to whether we wished to be male or female. That choice was made by our Father in Heaven in his infinite wisdom," (*Ensign,* November 1983:83).

Our Heavenly Father apparently passed through a mortal experience similar to our own. "It is the first principle of the Gospel," the Prophet Joseph Smith taught, "to know for a certainty the character of God, and to know that we may converse with him as one man converses with another, and that he was once a man like us; yea, that God himself, the Father of us all, dwelt on an earth," (Smith, *Teachings,* 345–46).

Brigham Young taught that "God the Father was once a man on another planet" who "passed the ordeals we are now passing through . . . and knows all that we know regarding the toils, sufferings, life and death of this mortality," (*Discourses,* 22). Thus, our Heavenly Father, like our earthly parents, knows of our joys and sorrows and how to succor us.

Church leaders have explained that "all men and women are in the similitude of the universal Father and Mother, and are literally the sons and daughters of Deity. . . . Man, as a spirit, was begotten and born of heavenly parents, and reared to maturity in the eternal mansions of the Father, prior to coming upon the earth in a temporal body to undergo an experience in mortality," (Clark, *Messages,* 203, 205).

These statements help us understand that exaltation always involves a male and female, a husband and wife, and that no one achieves such promised glory in isolation. Righteous unmarried singles will yet have the opportunity to marry. "No blessing, including that of eternal marriage and an eternal family, will be denied to any worthy individual. While it may take somewhat longer," said President Howard W. Hunter, "perhaps even beyond this mortal life for some to achieve this blessing, it will not be denied," (*Ensign*, June 1989:76).

We are presently moving through the mortal phase of the Plan of Salvation, acquiring information and knowledge, priesthood power and ordinances, and experiences that will prepare us for exaltation. In our mortal state, we learn the proper use of agency. We do this here on earth, where we are unable to see or remember our heavenly home, and where the full consequences of our choices are not always immediate. Thus, our mortal life is a time to try, to evaluate, and to repent, before the Final Judgment consigns us to an eternal destiny. In mortality, we taste the bitter and the sweet side by side and make conscious choices that will determine our destiny. "Behold, here is the agency of man," the Lord told Joseph Smith, "and here is the condemnation of man; because that which was from the beginning is plainly manifest unto them, and they receive not the light. And every man whose spirit receiveth not the light is under condemnation," (D&C 93:31–32). In mortality we experience the joy of righteous obedience and the exquisitely painful consequences of sin.

Following the resurrection, the possibility of being eternal companions is open to us through the sealing power of the Melchizedek Priesthood, (D&C 132:19-20). If we were to remain alone, without a marital companion, our progress would be eternally limited (D&C 131:4).

ETERNAL MARRIAGE AND INCREASE

Exalted beings continue the family unit by begetting spirit children. President Marion G. Romney gave this simple explanation to an acquaintance:

As to why we are here on earth, I reminded him of the self-evident fact that, as the offspring of God, we inherit the capability of reaching, in full maturity, the status of our heavenly parents just as we inherit from our mortal parents the capability to attain to their mortal status; and that since God has a body of flesh and bones, it was necessary and perfectly natural for us, his spirit offspring, to obtain such bodies in order that we might be like him; that coming to earth was the means provided for us to obtain these bodies. I further explained to him that this mortal probation provides us the opportunity to, while walking by faith, prove ourselves worthy to go on to perfection and exaltation in the likeness of our heavenly parents. (*Ensign,* May 1976:79.)

While mortal parents create mortal children, resurrected beings create spirit children. Elder Melvin J. Ballard explained the principle of eternal increase:

What do we mean by endless or eternal increase? We mean that through the righteousness and faithfulness of men and women who keep the commandments of God they will come forth with celestial bodies, fitted and prepared to enter into their great, high and eternal glory in the celestial kingdom of God, and unto them, through their preparation, there will come spirit children. I don't think that is very difficult to comprehend. The nature of the offspring is determined by the nature of the substance that flows in the veins of the being. When blood flows in the veins of the being, the offspring will be what blood produces, which is tangible flesh and bone; but when that which flows in the veins is spirit matter, a substance which is more refined and pure and glorious than blood, the offspring of such beings will be spirit children. (Ballard, "Three Degrees," 10.)

Joseph Smith also taught, "all will be raised by the power of God," in the resurrection, "having spirit in their bodies, and not blood," (*TPJS*, 199–200). Our sexual nature is not a temporary power limited to a brief period of mortality. If we receive exaltation, our resurrected bodies, like those of our heavenly parents, will be capable of procreation.

SATAN'S DAMNATION

Satan is damned forever from being a husband or a father. This is because spirits cannot reproduce or procreate. The Book of Mormon prophet Jacob explained that if there had been no Savior, then at death, we would become like Satan. "If the flesh should rise no more our spirits must become subject to that angel who fell from before the presence of the Eternal God, and became the devil, to rise no more. And our spirits must have become like unto him, and we become devils," (2 Nephi 9:8–9). If we were to remain spirits after death, we would lose our procreative powers, for spirits are unable to reproduce. Limited to a spirit body, we could not become parents ever again. And without the power of procreation, marriage would have no meaning, for in the Father's Plan, marriage and parenthood are linked together.

Satan lost the right to obtain a physical body because he chose not to sustain the Plan of Salvation. In addition to suffering the consequences, he also tried to remove agency from the Plan. He not only rebelled against the Father and the Son, but he sought to obtain their power (*see* Moses 4:1–4). He will never receive a physical body as we have. Consequently, he and his followers can never marry or become parents. "The adversary is jealous toward all who have the power to beget life," said Elder Boyd K. Packer. "He cannot beget life; he is impotent. He and those who followed him were cast out and forfeited the right to a mortal body," (*Ensign*, May 1992:66).

Jacob rejoiced in the "good news" of our deliverance: "O how great the goodness of our God, who prepareth a way for our escape from the grasp of this awful monster," (2 Nephi 9:9–10). The Savior's atonement and resurrection overcame the consequences of the Fall. "Is it any wonder, then," asked Elder Packer, "that in the Church marriage is so sacred and so important? Can you understand why your marriage, which releases these powers of creation for your use, should be the most carefully planned, the most solemnly considered step in your life? Ought we to consider it unusual that the Lord directed that temples be constructed for the purpose of performing marriage ceremonies?" (*Ensign*, July 1972:112).

THE CYCLE OF LIFE

Next to our discipleship, marriage is the most important of all commitments. "The most important step you have made or will make in your life is marriage," President Gordon B. Hinckley told a group of university graduates. "Its consequences are many, so important and so everlasting. No other decision will have such tremendous consequences for the future," (*Church News*, 1995:2). It is here in this life that we seek a companion, a sweetheart to whom we feel drawn and with whom we feel we can build an enduring relationship. Then, in marriage, we are commissioned to exercise our sexual powers to create physical bodies for the Father's spirit children. Perhaps in no more meaningful way do we approach the nobility and majesty of God and His work than through this endowment of procreation. God's work and His glory exist in the exaltation of His children, and we take part in that work as we nurture our children and raise them in righteousness (Moses 1:39).

Men learn from their wives how to serve effectively as husbands, while women learn from their husbands how to develop in their roles as wives. Parents learn how to be fathers and mothers from their children, and children are prepared for adulthood by their parents. Elder Packer said, "the ultimate purpose of all we teach is to unite parents and children in faith in the Lord Jesus Christ, that they are happy at home, sealed in an eternal marriage, linked to their generations, and assured of exaltation in the presence of our Heavenly Father," (*Ensign*, May 1995:8).

TEMPLES

We organize and seal families together in temples. A priesthood sealer, representing Heavenly Father, unites a couple in an "order of the priesthood [meaning the new and everlasting covenant of marriage]," (D&C 131:2). Elder Bruce R. McConkie described his own experience of receiving these sacred ordinances with his new bride:

> I went to the temple, and I took my wife with me, and we kneeled at the altar. There on that occasion we entered, the two of us, into an 'order of the priesthood.' When we did it, we had sealed upon us, on a conditional basis, every blessing that God promised Father Abraham—the blessings of exaltation and eternal increase. The name of that order of priesthood, which is patriarchal in nature, because Abraham was a natural patriarch to his posterity, is the New and Everlasting Covenant of marriage. (McConkie, Research Seminar, 50.)

Elder Packer explained the need for both male and female in the temple setting:

> No man receives the fulness of the priesthood without a woman at his side. For no man, the Prophet [Joseph Smith] said, can obtain the fulness of the priesthood outside the temple of the Lord (D&C 131:1–4). And she is there beside him in that sacred place. She shares in all that he receives. The man and the woman individually receive the ordinances encompassed in the endowment. But the man cannot ascend to the highest ordinances—the sealing ordinances—without her at his side. No man achieves the supernal exalting status of worthy fatherhood except as a gift from his wife. (*Ensign,* May 1998:73.)

APPLICATION

Courtship can help us to develop the kind of love that leads to marriage. When we marry in the temple, we enter the patriarchal order of marriage (D&C 131:1–4). We invite Heavenly Father's children to join our family unit and we devote ourselves to each other. Unfortunately, we make mistakes, but when we err, we apologize and do our best to make amends. Our potential for exaltation should be a motivating factor for us to do our best. "Except a man and his wife enter into an everlasting covenant and be married for eternity, while in this probation, by the power and authority of the Holy Priesthood," Joseph Smith taught, "they will cease to increase when they die; that is, they will not have any children after the resurrection," (*DHC* 5:391). A profound destiny awaits faithful couples who honor their covenants.